S0-ANN-690

arousing
the BUY
curious™

ADVANCE READING COPY. NOT FOR SALE.

arousing
the BUY
curious™

Real Estate Pillow Talk
for Patrons and
Professionals

By Becki Saltzman

OOMAU Media

Portland, Oregon

Arousing the Buy Curious: Real Estate Pillow Talk for Patrons and
Professionals

Oomau Media, Portland, Oregon 97239

© 2013
All rights reserved. Published 2013.

Cover design by Jim Parker and photography by Laura Domela
Editing, interior design, and production by Indigo Editing & Publications.

Printed in the United States of America.
21 20 19 18 17 16 15 14 13 12   1 2 3 4 5

ISBN: 978-0-9890935-0-7

Dedicated to the memory of my sparkly mom and all the nudniks who drove me crazy about writing the book already. You know who you are.

CONTENTS

PART 4: WORK IT!

Tiny Favor Requested by the Author

I ask you to read this foreword so you understand that, although this is my very first book, you don't have to take my word for it that it is worthwhile and marvelous and adequately helpful and entertaining. Take the word of this top international sexy beast of an impressive authority on books and publishing who has taken seconds out of a busy schedule to write this foreword. Read it before you buy and you'll know that you have spent your valuable money on far more stupid things. If this doesn't convince you, put the book down and walk away. This is especially effective for my needs if this is done after you click "confirm purchase" and delivery has been made. (But really, how else would you be able to actually set it down?)

Foreword

When Becki says this book is incredible and will make all your wildest dreams come true-ish, she means it. There are many sales books that are no longer called sales books because the word *sales* has such a stink on it. Why do you think most MBA programs no longer even *teach* sales? It is pushy, antiquated, and annoying—and this book embraces it with unabashed pride. Understanding that we're all buy curious is good for you and for the people you'll help.

You may laugh out loud while reading, but this book is no joke. It's wise and witty and will educate not only fellow practitioners in the real estate profession but also the millions of patrons (clients and customers) who work with them. It is based on the author's early education among the old Jewish master junk-and-auction men, a lot of years in sales, real-live research, and some made-up stuff.

This book is specifically about real estate, and since the American dream is to own a home (preferably with little or no down payment), it is not entirely crazy to think that any true-blooded 'merican would want to read it. Certainly anyone interested in real estate sales will find it incredibly helpful.

Enjoy this sordid, story-filled, revealing book of the wonderful world of real estate. It's the inside scoop. With Becki's background in psychology, there is a lot of focus on sexy science rather than on how many prospecting calls to make per day in order to apply for the gold medal sales star. It's about what to do with the successful prospecting calls once they become true prospects. It's about how to stop calling yourself a facilitator, customer service specialist, advocate, change agent, trusted advisor, etc. and to start grabbing your inner babushka and sell, baby, sell. Beyond that, if you're a buyer or seller, you'll learn how to be a good client and get the best out of your real estate salesperson. This is the first book that puts patrons in bed with the professionals, revealing all the goods to both parties. This is huge.

Oh, and Becki has assured me that any sarcasm seemingly aimed at other nonfiction business books is totally unintended. And knowing her, I know that is total bullshit.

Becki wrote this book before ever studying how nonfiction books are organized. I told her, "You know sales. You know humor. You know speaking. You know real estate. You know communication, behavior, and people. You do **not** know book publishing."

She said, "So fix it for me."

I said, "I have my own job to do, bitch."

She said, "Okay, then will you please write the foreword for this book?"

I said, "If you pay me."

She said, "I'll do you a huge [wink] favor."

I said, "Okay, I'll write the foreword."

I know there is no way in hell that Becki will ever make good on that promise, and I'm too close with her husband to even think about calling in what I think that favor is, but it was such an outrageous proposition that I simply had no choice but to write.

This is a great book and a very worthy read.

—*Pat Down, Bi Curious & Senior International*
Publishing Genius

ADVANCE READING COPY. NOT FOR SALE.

INTRODUCTION

I have been blessed to have sold a lot of real estate over the past twenty years—and I've had a blast getting to know wonderful and amazing people in the process. From the beginning of my career, I knew that my long-term success would rely on analyzing every individual success or failure I experienced. Reviewing my failures often kicked my ass and hurt my feelings. My successes made me feel great…and curious. I paid attention to what happened around me too. What worked for my peers led to *my* successes because I'm a thief when it comes to what works best. I am as grateful for all of my many mistakes as I am for all of my achievements. Okay, that's so not true, but it sounds right and a little less slutty than the all-out truth would. Eventually, my skin callused (and sagged), so these analyses have become exhilarating while other things have just become exhausting. I share my experiences and analyses here with you so you can take over the spotlight while I head for my Botox treatment.

My Baggage

I was bred for sales. When I was six, my parents dressed me as a boy and dragged me to what would be my first of hundreds of dusty industrial auctions so I could learn the art of selling from the Jewish masters. As a girl, I would have never been allowed to learn the crass and effective auctioning techniques that were often inspired by ball scratching and words deemed inappropriate for a little girl's ears. To my parents' initial chagrin, I was already using those words, and I had successfully hawked my baseball trading card collection to a formidable status. They finally accepted the fact that sales were in my blood and that it was time to have me learn the true art of sales from the make-it-or-break-it gurus so I could become a *great* salesperson.

The incredible education I received at the feet of these formally uneducated men would be hard to replicate, and yet I dismissed it for what I perceived to be a lack of sophistication. Years later, during my snobbish years while finishing my master's thesis in psychology on behavior prediction, I discovered, in the dusty halls of academia, empirical data that validated everything I'd learned in those dirty warehouses and sawmills.

As a retail buyer after grad school, I learned how it felt to be the customer. While the accents of the East Coast Garment District men—*garmentos*—were different from those of the West Coast liquidators of my youth, I felt as though I had walked into the same world all over again. Whether the product was knockoff designer dresses or oil-leaking forklifts, the methods of successful selling were the same. The techniques of successful buying didn't change either. No matter the industry, I learned, being a good customer is every bit as important as being an artful salesperson. At various points along the line, you will be both, and you gotta know how to ask the right questions.

As my career in real estate sales took off, I felt completely in my element. Well, not at those ridiculous training seminars that only regurgitated hokey sales scripts, but when I got to customize tactics with my own style, I was kicking down doors and taking names.

That's when my mom told me I had to write this book. Her cancer had progressed to the point that she couldn't do much, so she derived great pleasure from eavesdropping on my phone conversations with my clients. Her hmm moment might have been when I asked a client what orifice she needed to pull her head out of in order to accept the fat offer on her property that she clearly needed to sell. Or maybe it was when I told another client that he knew damn well that he should make an offer on the house because the thought of it clearly gave him morning wood that lasted long after the noon hour.

"Beuksties," my mom said to me. "The way you communicate is…not normal." She said that my academic training, personal research, and unique practical experience had paid off. She told me nice-girl things about myself that I would feel embarrassed to share with strangers. And she made me promise to focus my life on helping more people improve their lives…right now.

ADVANCE READING COPY. NOT FOR SALE.

Now, as promised, I share the lessons of my youth, the data from my studies, and the experiences of my sales career to help readers like you who have clearly gotten so far into this book that there is no denying that you have peeped at your fair share of real estate porn. Don't be a denyhard. Join the believolution and admit that we are all just a little buy curious.

Real Estate in You

If your aspirations of stardom have dimmed to the point that the dream of your name in lights will only be achieved when the officer shines his flashlight on your driver's license, you can still have a fun and lucrative acting career in the wonderful world of real estate.

If you're contemplating such an alternative show-biz career, this book is 100 percent guaranteed to make you at least twice the money that it cost you to buy it. If you're just dabbling in the industry for personal gain, this book could potentially save you tremendous amounts of time and money.

For Buy Curious Prospective Patrons

There is no other book, podcast, or seminar that will give you the *real* inside scoop on real estate. Not with naughty words, anyway. Nowhere else will you be made privy to the secrets, stories, and techniques that industry pros swear by more than they do a high-end foreign vehicle with fine Corinthian leather.

There are some technical differences between clients and customers. In most states a client has a contractual relationship with the pro and a customer does not. For the purposes of this book, we won't worry about that, but feel free to check with your pro so you know what to call yourself. Clients, customers, patrons... we're flexible, right? As a patron, you will find sharing a book with the professionals is as revealing as the most excellent wardrobe malfunction. Best of all, you'll know who to take home. This will be extremely lucrative for you. Otherwise, even in the best-case scenario of hiring the *wrong* real estate professional, you could pay tens of thousands of dollars extra and never know it. In the worst case, hiring the wrong real estate professional can cost you

ADVANCE READING COPY. NOT FOR SALE.

a painfully obvious sum of money. Therefore, this book is one of the best investments you can make today.

For Buy Curious Potential Professionals

I don't mean to bum you out, but you must know that to really succeed in this industry, you have to work hard and work a lot. You *could* do this job without being a tryhard and still have a good life, though. However, prospective patrons—especially those who are reading this—can easily figure out why your services might be a poor investment if you aren't working toward becoming out-standing in your chosen industry. Prospective clients who gave birth to you or are sleeping with you don't count—those biases often outweigh their concern for rock star real estate represen-tation. If you're lazy when vertical, you're no rock star—you're just a blogger with a Donald Trump complex—and you might be cheating your clients.

If you heed the advice in this book, you will do exceedingly well in real estate. Be careful to ease into your success in front of experienced agents as you rocket past them on your climb up the Billboard charts.

For Buy Curious Real Estate Rock Stars

If you're already fully addicted to this crazy career and the golden handcuffs are tightly locked around your wrists, this book might be a bit awkward because nowhere else are the secrets of the real estate universe revealed like this—to you *and* your clients. If you're hugely successful, you recognize some of the best techniques in this book. and you'd rather not have your clients know about them, get over it. Much of this information is specific to the real estate industry, but the higher truth is that most of this information, if squished and molded, is universal to all sales and all communi-cations. Laugh with me here.

True**STORIES**

I'd long since given up my dream to be an A-list ac-tress and embraced my role as a real estate sales actress. I was

ADVANCE READING COPY. NOT FOR SALE.

heading to a property for an appraisal so the sellers and I could finally close on this house that we'd had on the market since before we all needed Botox. I didn't want any more delays. The fewer distractions for the appraiser, the better, so we had wisely scheduled the appraisal to happen after the contractor finished some minor repairs and other work happening on the property would not be underway. Or so I thought.

The contractor had been avoiding my calls for weeks, and when I arrived at the property, the driveway and surrounding street were inundated with work trucks that basically shouted, "Massive work being done here!" Shit. One large van started to slow in front, and I realized the contractor whom we had been trying to schedule for weeks was prowling for a parking space.

It was at this exact moment that the psychotic neighbor appeared in the street growling, "Get off my goddamn property!" Never mind that not a single truck was parked anywhere near where a normal person (and I give a lot of leeway here) would ever dream his private property rights extended to. Worried the wimpy contractor would drive away from a situation that looked a bit scary, I chased him down and asked him to park up the street and wait for me.

Now it was time to deal with the insane neighbor. As I approached him, I tried to twist my face in an unhinged *je ne sais quoi* expression to match his. The red flame of his alcoholic cheeks was harder to match. I said, with indignation and facial contortions that seemed ugly enough to do the trick, "Are they parking on your goddamn property? They probably think they will be here all day, but they have another thing comin'. I will make sure they are off your goddamn property in one hour, or they will have hell to pay and me to contend with!"

He grunted in his hunched-over greed (a man *can* love his driveway), "Oh, yer good. Yer real good."

Although any praise is greatly appreciated, this time I stifled my laughter and maintained my crooked, conspiratorial grimace. I then ran down the street and told the contractor waiting in the van to follow me to the house so he could complete his fifteen-minute repair and be on his way.

ADVANCE READING COPY. NOT FOR SALE.

Just as the last of the Playboy mud flaps from the work trucks disappeared down the street, the appraiser arrived. Things were going swimmingly, with all of the last-minute repairs a distant memory to me and appropriately nowhere in the memory of the appraiser. The helpful neighbor certainly sealed the deal when he stumbled by to wink at me and slur to the appraiser, "You know, thish here home is not a shithole…and neither is she." The acting job paid off because when Realtors and appraisers laugh together, the appraisal generally comes in…at value.

For Virgins (Who, I Still Contend, Are Buy Curious)
If you fall in the categories of super classy, easily offended, or generally opposed to reading fuckery of any kind…yikes, this book is not rated PG-13!

Real-Live Truth about Learning
I learned a few secrets about memory when I observed the Jewish masters of auctioneering as a kid. I've tested them out in several industries and at various stages of my life only to find that they hold true in every situation. They served me well in upgrading my baseball cards, they never failed me in retail buying, they led to many successful real estate closings, and now I use them as an author. The three secrets are:

1. Motivation is not positively correlated with memory. This means that all the excellent motivational training that you've ever had will, for the most part, be forgotten. If you are a person who immediately implements the systems and strategies from motivation-based training, good for you. But you are not in crowded company.
2. Humor is positively correlated with memory. If you can laugh at a humorous and teachable story, you won't forget the teachable part. The more absurd, the better it sticks.
3. Provocation, when added to humor, seals the memory like superglue for the mind. Top memory athletes know this. They create humorous story recipes sprinkled with sexual spice in order to compete in memory feats at the highest levels. This has been the case for as long as humans have told stories.

ADVANCE READING COPY. NOT FOR SALE.

If you want to remember this stuff, please try to get over the fact that this book is not rated PG-13—most of you are older than twice that anyway. See? I'm not all naughty. I said please.

SECRETS for Clients

If your agent is new, buy an extra copy of this book as a gift.

In this book you will learn that tricks are good and disruption is effective—these facts are psychologically proven. Stories and humor provide the skull superglue that implants information like you wouldn't believe. I admit that this book is sometimes cringe worthy and some of the things I say would make a sailor blush but, while the words may be mine, the ideas are universal, so make them your own.

Before starting, figure out the accent you'll use to read this book and stick to it. My editor says nothing is worse than an inconsistent voice.

ADVANCE READING COPY. NOT FOR SALE.

PART 1

Are **YOU** a
Real Estate
Wantrepreneur

Are You a Real Estate Wantrepeneur?

So you think you can sell, huh? Let me guess—you've got all the telltale symptoms of agent lust:

- You love touring open houses.
- You think you're immune to agent ass.
- Your friends and family all tell you you'd be great.
- You want to help people find their special spot.
- You know you can rock this industry (and you just may be right!).

Since we all get by with a little bit of it, help is on the way. Here is an open-book test for those of you who are up in the darkest hours of the night pondering a new career in real estate. If you've already taken the plunge and passed your exams, these chapter cheats will help you decide whether you should proclaim to the world that real estate is your life. If you're deeply entrenched, you can look back with knowing reminiscence and nostalgia on those early questioning days.

SECRETSforClients

Clients, don't think I forgot you when I wrote this handy arousal section for wannabe agents. There's lots of valuable money-saving stuff here for you to consider too. I've even included your very own chapter that you don't have to share!

No matter how you're wording those soul-searching questions to yourself, if you've adopted real estate as your new lifestyle, you can be assured of one certainty:

things are about to change…and you'll be ready.

CHAPTER 1

WAIT, THERE'S STILL TIME TO RUN

If you are contemplating a career change, real estate is a viable option because it doesn't take much to call yourself a real estate professional. You might want to have a career title more than you want an actual career, and "real estate professional" can have a nice ring. After all, when the underwear model at the cocktail party asks what you do, you really don't want to answer with any of these:

- Stay-at-home dad or mom: These are respectable titles, yes, but they're perhaps not so appropriate when your kids are out of college and entering their first stint in rehab.
- Retired: This is also a perfectly acceptable title, but it can be so annoying when some nosy acquaintance asks you from *what*, exactly, you are retired.
- Trust fund check casher: This answer is generally not well received (although I wouldn't mind marrying you).

If you're worried the underwear model will respond to your real estate title with a question about interest rates, "tennis player and happy hour aficionado" can be a snappy alternative job title.

If you choose to stick with the real estate line, though, be careful—saying you're a real estate agent can result in having to...work. Don't let your guard down too much as you lunch with the ladies or golf with the guys (or gals). If you answer their questions about the status of the market, the next thing you know, you could be required to go on an actual listing appointment. Oy.

If you're beyond the need for a career title and just love looking at pretty houses:

1. Stop.
2. Drop.
3. Roll.

Real estate is not for you. It will be *way* easier to join a club or organization with rich people—people you can lure into friendship in order to surround yourself with hyperdecorated environs. As an instructional example, think of the friends you buddy up to every summer because they have pools. Granted, that's pretty easy because you only have to maintain a seasonal commitment—and perhaps bone the cabana boy in the off season to know when the pool will be ready and your calls should start up again. Failing the acquisition of rich friends, there are also tours of homes sponsored by various charities, if you're able to score a ticket before they sell out. That's a double whammy because your voyeurism can be cloaked as altruism.

SECRETSforClients

If you're buying or selling and you plan on representing yourself, you will meet some people who think that a real estate license is a good thing to have. Like the decision to get one more plastic surgery, this depends. There are codes and expectations that come with licensure. You can no longer offer the neighborhood granny a plate of bran muffins and a 1967 price for her precious bungalow. There are disclosure laws, ethics trainings, and fees. The continuing education alone can get in the way of Pilates classes. You might save money; you might lose it.

TrueSTORIES

I once had a friend, Myra, visiting from out of town, but I wasn't able to take off enough time to hang out and play with her,

ADVANCE READING COPY. NOT FOR SALE.

so I brought her along on a weekly brokers' tour of homes. Myra owned a very successful marketing company, but a tour of a particularly well-decorated and glorious home had her contemplating a career in real estate. By the time we pulled into the driveway of the next home, she was looking up real estate schools on her smartphone.

As we entered the second home, where the furniture was less than fabulous, she immediately closed out of her search app and thus ended her pursuit of a career in real estate. Myra hated the home because it wasn't breathtaking, and she said she could never sell homes that she didn't personally like. "That would be too pushy for my personality," she justified. In saying this, she was attempting to prove that she was not the type of salesperson who would sell her client just any home. Good for her ethical self, right? Wrong. If looking at pretty homes is what draws you to the real estate profession, be ready to live off of your divorce settlement.

Don't you love it when one of your clients asks if they can have their very dynamic friend call you to pick your brain about the real estate profession? "Oooohkay," I say because I'm always looking for another reason to flip myself off. Sometimes I tell them the truth: I would never suggest that someone I like go into real estate. This has less to do with discouraging competition and more to do with the fact that I might have to continue being friends with this person when she realizes what she's gotten herself into with my blessing.

TRIALS&Titillations™

For the next week, set your alarm to go off every half hour between 8:00 a.m. and 8:00 p.m. Reduce the time to fifteen minutes on Saturday and Sunday. Every time it goes off, jump in your car and go somewhere. In between, read inspirational quotes on your favorite social media sites and try to believe them. Honestly assess how true you find those quotes on the first day and then again on the last day of this exercise.

ADVANCE READING COPY. NOT FOR SALE.

The Truth

Know the truth before you have to face it:

- If you hate free nights and weekends, you should consider a career in real estate.
- If, at a party, you have the ability to maintain a lucid conversation about your work after the consumption of uncountable cocktails, you should consider a career in real estate.
- If you love being stopped at the grocery store and solicited for free advice about what you get paid for advising, you should consider a career in real estate.
- If you love selling and think you don't suck at sales, you should consider a career in real estate.
- If you don't mind your now-ex–best friend paying a commission to someone else, you should consider a career in real estate.
- If you love spending your vacations taking phone calls and checking emails, you should consider a career in real estate.

If the above statements of truth apply to you, repeat after me: "Oh no"—be sure to maintain your plastered-on fake smile—"you are infinitely more important than my dinner with Anthony Bourdain that I won six months ago at an auction in the Hamptons. You're right, the condo association president should have told us about the new bike storage policy. You didn't even budget for a new bike lock!"

True**STORIES**

Many years ago I was at my son's soccer game and dared to walk away from the gaggle of soccer moms to take a phone call. When I returned to the hen's coop, I was chastised by one of the multitasking moms who had momentarily peeled her eyes from the field to witness my transgression.

"It's not like you're a doctor or something. Why would you walk away to take a phone call and risk missing your son kick the ball or score a goal?"

ADVANCE READING COPY. NOT FOR SALE.

Now, she and I both knew that the biggest risk I was taking was missing an opportunity to see my son find the perfect four-leafed clover in the field—but she was being generous.

I apologized to the group of soccer moms for daring to risk missing seeing my son (and their sons) in a moment of glory, and I asked them all to give me some advice. I said, "If you were driving through your favorite neighborhood and at that exact moment you saw someone hammering a for-sale sign into a lawn, would you call your agent? What if you had been looking for the perfect property for two years and this was your absolute dream home? What if you knew that it was also the dream home of several of your friends and neighbors, and it had never before been on the market? What if your agent returned your call three hours later and, by then, your golf partner had an accepted offer on that home? Would it be okay for your agent to explain that she missed your call because she was watching her son trip over a (fucking) soccer ball?" I used my inside voice for the *fucking* part.

Just then, through divine intervention, my sister called. I looked at the moms with their chicken-beaked lips until the inquisitive bitch shouted, "Answer the phone!" I still owe my sister for that fine act of telepathy.

When you're in real estate, your life is not your own—unless you want it to be. Tom Hopkins, the sales guru, said that selling is the highest paid hard work…and the lowest paid easy work. If you go to dinner and then to the movies and then out to see (perform in?) some great midnight mud wrestling and then go home to some Viagra-enhanced sex, and you forget to check your voicemail, you might very well lose a sale. Never mind how hard this extracurricular work actually was—you probably aren't getting paid unless you can really wrestle. You might also lose some clients who will, in turn, tell several of their friends how audacious you were to have an evening on *their* time.

ADVANCE READING COPY. NOT FOR SALE.

CHAPTER 2

AND YOU ASK YOURSELF

If you've already gotten fired from many other jobs just for giving too much of yourself, you have decided that you've never really liked your life much anyway, and you already have all of the photographs of your kids labeled, copied and put in chronological order in the event that they are abducted, you might feel ready to take the plunge into a career in real estate—but you still have some additional questions to ask yourself. Just as with any other career, there will be theories to apply and lots of books to learn from (or to put on your shelf next to your diet books). Ultimately, none of the information will matter unless you internalize it and mix it into you-juice.

Ask yourself, *Am I the most open-minded person I know?* When it comes to training and coaching, I assure you that you're more open-minded than I was. I used to roar with laughter (and admittedly, sometimes I still smirk a bit) when one of my acquaintances would have trouble finding a job and take one of the many courses in how to be a life coach. Priceless.

Coachie, Coachie, Coo

Hiring One: A life coach will help you answer your call to distinction. If your life doesn't suck that much, but you want it to suck even less, a life coach is for you!

Being One: If your life does suck because you don't have a job, you can get an advanced, online degree in life coaching. This will cost you a bunch of money that unemployment doesn't cover. It will allow you to charge others to tell them to do things that, if you had a normal job, would make them *your* boss

You're going to have be open-minded in your new career in real estate—there are very few other industries that have so many hokey sales tactics. I was at a training one time when Mr. Pursuit of Most Excellence suggested that I ask a potential client, "What can I do to get you to buy this house today?" I knew there was no way in hell those words would ever come out of my mouth.

My skepticism toward training and life coaching comes from actual research I embarked upon in my academic life. I always wanted to be a doctor. In addition to the fact that I had an affinity for science and a natural intrigue with the human body, I even felt at home in the hospital environment. Blood? Love it. But when I had an opportunity to work with people with severe mental illness, I realized that I enjoyed the science of the mind even more than I did physical medicine. Aside from the fact that I was good at helping these people, I really enjoyed the quirks of their illnesses. I'll share with you the quest that changed the course of my life.

True**STORIES**

During my graduate training in psychology, I was invited to perform as a pseudopatient for a group of psychology grad students. I learned how even the best training could not teach a shy, academically strong but socially awkward wannabe therapist how to effectively interview my particular pseudopatient persona, that of a sexual masochist, much less begin to treat her. I took my role seriously—mine was a very well-studied persona—so most of these students had a hard time prying the details of my pseudolife out of me. So many had been taught the meat of good therapy but had not adapted it and practiced it enough for it to feel natural with their personalities.

As I watched the grad students struggling to use all of the theories, methodologies, and lessons they had been trained on, it was very clear that some of these students would never be great therapists. They were acting completely outside the parameters of their personality, so interviewing and treating patients would never come naturally. It was also clear that some of the students were going to be great therapists. I could see them instinctively

ADVANCE READING COPY. NOT FOR SALE.

incorporating their personalities into the lessons they had learned. They were able to successfully delve into my pseudosymptoms (I sure hope that they were all pseudosymptoms), and some of them even began to perform some actual therapy.

The successful students and future successful therapists were able to find the MEAT-YOU intersection. MEAT makes a cool acrostic (YOU means "you"):

Master
Every
Activating (or Asinine)
Theory

MEAT is definitely something that I embrace in every sense of the word (all puns intended). It is the stuff that you learn you must do, find out, or impart in order to treat, sell, and help. The key to successful MEAT is to make it your own (and don't give me your vegetarian bullshit). Therapists, life coaches, trainers, and even real estate sales professionals must know this information and be able to impart it in order to be helpful.

MEAT doesn't matter if you don't integrate it with YOU, though. You can know every theory and tactic inside and out, but they won't help you unless you can tap in to their knowledge and deliver their tactics while still acting from a place of authenticity. Finding authenticity is an overrated *and* completely imperative skill, and here's why.

My love of psychology led me to research if there was any scientifically significant type of nonmedicinal therapy that was measurably more effective than medicine in treating the most common mental illnesses. Meaning, does anything but pills really work? I found that, although some therapists using specific types of therapy have measurable effectiveness with some patients, the effectiveness is more related to the specific therapists and their patients than it is to the treatment modalities used. There is no treatment that works for all therapists for a specific set of mental illnesses. In other words, the MEAT is bogus without a great therapist.

ADVANCE READING COPY. NOT FOR SALE.

When I coupled this information with the fact that all the good therapists I knew were fucked up, I came to a startling conclusion that I was not fucked up enough to play on their court. That meant that in order to be a good therapist, I would have needed to either have a worse childhood or start creating the kind of drama that would result in the desired level of fucked-uppery to become an excellent therapist. While this was a seemingly naïve assessment of the importance of having a tragic childhood, it did have a grain of truth to it. I did not have enough life experience to incorporate the MEAT of therapy with the YOU to become an outstanding therapist. If only I could have seen myself as I am now, what a great therapist I could have been.

If you're looking to make a career-enhancing investment, you should know that most life coaches inspire only temporary happy finishes at best. The good news is that if you're hoping for a different spin on that temporary rush, there is never a shortage of training programs and coaches that focus on the real estate industry.

The quality of the trainer and the preparedness of the trainee are what will determine the effectiveness of their relationship. In addition to a commitment by both parties to achieve lasting results, there needs to be a real vibe connection. Trainers who work with large groups are expected to tailor their programs to a broad spectrum of trainees, but they can't customize it for every single person. For that reason, the recipient of the information must bear the burden of completing that vibe connection.

Take the MEAT and make it your own. If you don't, you might still get that temporary tingle, but the training won't work over the long run. Ever.

TRIALS&Titillations™

Go through your shelves and count how many motivational books, CDs (cassettes if you're an old pack rat), and DVDs you have purchased over the years. Set aside those that you have never read or listened to. Add to the pile the stuff you found worthless. Now put them all in a box and deliver it to Goodwill. Take the appropriate tax deduction.

ADVANCE READING COPY. NOT FOR SALE.

Cocktail (or Smoothie) Time

Now raise your glass if you've ever rolled your eyes at those corny sales pitches you've heard at conferences or read in books. Cynicism and Skepticism are my first and last names. I will admit that they often serve me well…but not always. Sometimes I feel that if I listen to the message of the sales pitch instead of exactly how the message is conveyed, I might learn something. But most of the time I feel that if I listen at all, I will throw up a little bit in my mouth. I need a vibe connection.

Some people have tremendous success with sales tactics I deem hokey. Mr. Rogers made a mint, and his trademark was a friggin' cardigan sweater. My trademark happens to be less family friendly. You might be appalled by some of what you read in this book, but I promise that the ideas my potty mouth spouts are valid. Let yourself laugh. Then go about tailoring the messages to your authentic self.

SECRETSForClients

If your real estate agent sounds robotic in her approach, she is not necessarily bad or untrustworthy. She might be trying on some of the latest, greatest sales techniques and she's just not smooth with them yet. Let her know she sounds a bit like C3PO.

How *Do* You Do That?

If you've decided not to run away from real estate, the truth is, you're going to have to go through enough training programs to leave your stomach in a constant state of upheaval. But there are a few easy steps to make it through. Trust me—I've been there.

1. Determine what you're trying to learn. Be specific as to the actual skills and tools you aim to master. As obvious as that sounds, many people spend a lot of time and money on training without a plan. If you plan to learn one thing and end up stacking up unexpected tools (or just being entertained), that's cool too, but it's best to have a goal.
2. Listen beyond the presenter's style to the actual content. I am not good at this step. A dorky saying or gesture can send my mind a-spinnin' and my eyes a-rollin'…oh well, you're better than this.

ADVANCE READING COPY. NOT FOR SALE.

If you can master those steps, you can then start to internalize the information to put your own twist on it.

3. Tweak the MEAT until it's a useful tool for your personality. Telling you to be your authentic self sounds a little Oprah-y and, while I do love myself some Oprah, there are people who spend their entire lives trying to find out who they are by attaching themselves to Oprahs and other gurus. Don't be oxymoronic. The people who know and embrace their authentic selves will be the ones who internalize the sales training and catapult to the top of the selling food chain. No life coach, therapist, or trainer will inspire you to greatness beyond the coaching-session/post-therapy/seminar-elation period unless you internalize the message and practice it in your own voice.

4. Internalize and practice these tools at their MEAT-YOU intersection so that, long after the training session is over, they are habit. Play out challenging sales scenarios or difficult calls you must make and practice them…out loud. You can use these tools for practice: old tape recorder, mirror (full-length mirrors generally work better than handheld ones for this type of exercise), video camera, webcam, someone with whom you have been sleeping for a long time (newer partners will lie to get you back in the sack).

I practice with all of the aforementioned tools and, even with lots of practice, my kind of authenticity can prove to be a challenge. Although I wish that I was always classy, I'm not. I'm often obnoxious, nasty, and inappropriate. That might sometimes affect the type of client who will work well with me. I try to move myself along the inappropriate gradient to land just slightly more inappropriate than my client. With one client, I might suggest that her husband drive by the house and see if the location gives him wood. With other clients, however, this tactic may not work so well. With them, I might have to be more specific, coming right out and calling it a boner. See? It's important to be your authentic self—but within that authenticity, you must tailor yourself to relate to your clients.

ADVANCE READING COPY. NOT FOR SALE.

How classy, cultured, religious, or refined you see yourself might affect how well you internalize the information in this book. You might think that some of the tactics I suggest as important are things you would never see yourself doing. Hell, you might already be highly successful and see yourself as having never embraced any of these pearls. If my tone and language are not for you, then pour yourself a drink, or two or three, and find the deeper meaning. I'm pretty shallow, so you don't have to dig very far.

ADVANCE READING COPY. NOT FOR SALE.

CHAPTER 3
HOOKING UP

After you have attended training sessions and found your authentic self, you still have time to reconsider becoming a real estate professional. After you agree to call yourself a Realtor or real estate sales agent or real estate broker (depending on your state and the labels that it likes to bestow), you still have time to reconsider actually *doing* the job. Heck, plenty of people get their license and never go farther than that. But beyond those people, plenty more will go as far as to buy business cards and hook up with a real estate company.

Many real estate companies will clamor for you when you have a brand-new license, and it's a good idea to limit the amount of flattery you internalize unless you're totally okay with living in a fantasy world. You might find an easier game of Fantasyland in posting a Photoshopped "you" on a dating site and keeping the hookups strictly virtual. Some real estate companies are choosy and require experience—or, at the very least, a supportive bra. Other companies offer a desk to any cyclops licensee with a pulse. Chances are, immediately after exuviating your real estate sales examination cap and gown, you can affiliate with a company that is right for you.

The ethos of the office in which I work has always been an important love-connection consideration. When, after a few years, I was looking to transfer from my small, investment-focused company to a higher-end residential-focused company, I had a bit of a track record that enticed some of the more selective companies to consider me. I can say this without appearing braggy because, frankly, it's not like applying to the Ivy League, for fuck's sake.

One company had tremendous market share and a very close family feel. It awarded top agents with group trips to Hawaii (as a group) and celebrated weekly sales successes. That company would have required me to swallow way too much bile while grabbing my pom-poms, turning my smirk into a smile, and pretending that the "friends" in the office would be my first choice to join me under a palm tree with spiked liquid charm. The second company was much more laid back, much more blue haired, and didn't have any support for the investment and small commercial property that was part of my portfolio. The third company had good market share, a varied demographic, and a commercial division. They also could not have cared less if I joined them or not. I did.

Where Matters

Do a little homework and you'll avoid the kind of stressful work environment that requires a medical marijuana card. The location of the office (if there is an office, and I suggest that there be one) is of key importance. Consider all of the following:

1. Geography
    A. Close to home (stop oversupporting OPEC)
    B. Close to your clients (they don't want to schlep)
    C. Near a bar (bump into clients when slipping out for an afternoon nip—good for alcoholic clients)
    D. Near a salon (bump into clients when sneaking an afternoon mani/pedi—bad for clients who are softball-playing womyn and men who aren't metrosexual or homosexual)
2. Office architecture
    A. Historic building (good for highly educated and highly nostalgic patrons)
    B. Strip mall (good for mall-walking, coupon-clipping, suburbanite clients)
    C. Large office complex (good for corporate types and cubicle dwellers)
    D. Small house (good for intimate clients and first-time buyers)
    E. Your house (good for intimate clients and the visually impaired)

ADVANCE READING COPY. NOT FOR SALE.

3. The Kool-Aid served (otherwise known as the office vibe)
   A. Inclusive Up with People–esque environment (good for these kinds of agents: fraternity men who still do their secret handshake, Bunco players, gang members, and severe pet lovers)
   B. Competitive (bad for salespeople who subsist on open-house food and dwindling divorce settlements)
   C. Training centric (good for agents with ample time, mental masturbators, and newbies)
   D. Community involved (bad for Republicans and vegans without trust funds)
   E. Old established (good for high-end proclivity, multigenerational natives, and social climbers)
   F. Multilevel marketing (good for early adopters, company believers, and readers of motivational books)

When I was just starting out in real estate, with my wrinkle-free face and dimple-free thighs, I didn't give much thought to where my office was located except that I knew I wanted to focus on selling real estate in an urban environment, so I selected an office in an urban location. I also chose a small company that focused primarily on small commercial and investment properties. I learned a lot.

I especially learned that when interviewing to market higher-end residential listings, I spent more time explaining why my company was not a liability than pointing out why I was an asset. That was a lot of unnecessary 'splainin'. Since I knew that I wanted to sell urban residential real estate, I should have considered starting with a company where that was an emphasis and a strength. As it turns out, I learned tricks of the business that I probably would never have learned otherwise, so now I don't regret it for a minute.

He/She Is My *Business* Partner

Beyond the urban environment, the other reason I found the small, investment-focused company appealing was the person who got me into the business in the first place. I started my real estate career with a fantastically brilliant friend and business partner. Having moved back to my native city, I had a shit-ton of friends,

ADVANCE READING COPY. NOT FOR SALE.

connections, and moxie. I had no clue about real estate. My partner, Gregg, was a non-native with non-local connections, brains and generosity to spare, and many years of real estate experience. I knew I could convince the friends and family in my sphere to work with us if the *us* involved Gregg's smarts and experience and my friendships and trust. With Gregg's guidance, I sold my first property the day after receiving my real estate license. The success of my first partnership probably involved more luck than I suggest you rely on, but I can tell you that I have had three partnerships and they have all been resounding successes.

As real estate professionals become busy, we often wish that we had something as simple as a day off once in a rare while. That's when you've likely begun to look lovingly toward a partnership. Partnerships with benefits mean:

1. You can take time off without freaking out.
2. You can have help solving problems.
3. You can sound less insane when talking to yourself in the office behind closed doors.
4. You can laugh *with* someone instead of just *at* someone.
5. You can blame someone else (with your inside and outside voices).
6. You can provide better service to your clients.
7. You can work with someone who has a vested interest in what comes *out* of your mouth instead of what goes in.
8. You can increase your client base.
9. You can pool resources.
10. You can fulfill the fantasies of more clients.

Warning: Tread very lightly.

 **SORTA**Facts™

Over 87% of real estate partnerships do not work.
— *Courtesy of Sortafact*

(Okay, I totally made up that statistic and, yes, I pulled it out of my nether region. It is based on what I call a Sortafact. Nether regions are where these omnipresent Sortafacts come from, and

ADVANCE READING COPY. NOT FOR SALE.

you don't have to look much beyond our landscape of political repartee to see how statistics like these are highly valued.)

If you meet a fellow real estate mom at your kids' lacrosse game and you happen to have been in the same sorority and you're both hoping to take a few spring breaks off to pitch a tent and camp, you have found more reasons *not* to hook up as real estate partners than you have found reasons to do so. I'm not just talking about the fact that you're both crazy enough to choose to play Homelessness in the Woods (what many call camping) and claim that this constitutes a vacation. What I'm talking about is the fact that if your kids are on the same lacrosse team and are, therefore, close to the same age, you will be fighting over who gets to leave for spring break. You will also not be expanding your selling sphere if you both hang with the same sorority babes.

Finding the right real estate partner starts with knowing if you're really partnership material. Stop by Consideration Station to evaluate if you're on the right track. Ask yourself:

1. Self, why do I really want a partner? If you're looking for someone to keep you company while touring properties, start a carpool, not a real estate partnership.
2. Shithead, what was that first step again? If companionship is what you're looking for, join a book club or a twelve-step program.

If you've considered your motives and still want a partnership, it's time to look at some details about your potential partners. There are ten main questions to ask yourself and your potential partner. Free-associate about them, as I have here, and you'll see red or green flags in relation to the partnership's potential:

1. What is your work ethic? Up at 5:00 a.m. every day for yoga and bright eyed at the 7:00 a.m. listing appointment, golfing all day because no one called anyway, calling old and prospective clients when office has emptied for happy hour, apologizing for being unavailable to a client so you can sneak in a one-hour Saturday personal training session, looking forward to Saturday and Sunday as weekends (yeah, right)

ADVANCE READING COPY. NOT FOR SALE.

2. What are your professional goals? Grow into a large team, keep it simple, take lots of vacations, plaster your name on the side of a bus or bench, own a company, become a public figure, find a spouse

3. What are your strengths? Business acumen, pushy prospecting, seductive selling skills, laws and contracts, finance fierceness, office management competence, rule-following addiction, rule-breaking tendencies, creativity

4. What are your weaknesses? Tired and burned out, poor, reality TV addiction, chronic BO

5. What outside commitments do you have? Children, married or civilly unioned less than three years, demanding imaginary friend, philanthropic commitments, second job, schedules, vacations, other projects, responsibilities

6. Who are in your spheres of influence? Celebrities, people in academia, professional athletes, starving artists, people with trust funds, rehabbers, porn stars, attorney Doctor Who impersonators, country-club bridge groups, ashram-bound spiritual seekers *Note: Looking for similar types of friends but from different sources can be lucrative.*

7. What are your life goals? Retire early and knit, retire early and travel, die while showing property

8. What are your past successes? Sexual harassment suit settled out of court, perfectly executed plan to befriend now-dead spinster aunt, sold business, poster gal for LPGA

9. What are your past failures? Poor first husband, broken spine before first round of NFL draft, first sign of lactose intolerance announced itself during opening aria

10. What is your approach to life? Hate baby seals except when worn with four-inch heels, love assault rifles and stockpiling food, hate nobody but feel sorry for mean people, love spirit and stench of Burning Man, cry when team loses Super Bowl, cry when watching Save the Children commercials *Note: Decisions regarding spending and earning money are fundamental factors to consider.*

Mix and match these traits with delicacy and skepticism. Just be sure to discuss all of them with your chosen partner. You two might answer some of these questions differently and some the

ADVANCE READING COPY. NOT FOR SALE.

same, but it is absolutely essential to talk candidly about these things and keep from getting excited for the wrong reasons. You already know where that can end.

My first two partners were both gay and of the penile persuasion. They did not have children's school schedules to contend with, but they loved fabulous vacations at nonpeak rates. Early on I lived vicariously through their sippy cup–free existence, and as my children got older, I copied their vacation itineraries. I loved my fellow breeder-chick third partner even though school vacation schedules pained my ass. In all three cases, our work ethics were ridiculous, and our strengths and weaknesses formed a gestalt with a sum that was greater than the parts. My real estate career has been a perfect ménage à trois of partnerships.

Many fellow agents have approached me to ask the secret of my success with partnerships. I have had many friends who have partnered with close friends with compatible personalities only to have the partnership gently and ineffectively exist beyond its shelf life. In other cases it turned into the War of the Roses. This is bad and can be dangerously transparent to clients. A good partnership, like a good marriage, is a wonderful thing—but I find it best not to make sexual compatibility with my partners a top priority (even though my partners were all really hot).

SECRETSforClients

Having a team represent you has good and bad aspects. In general the good aspects outweigh the bad. If you're a control freak and must have one particular agent interface with you exclusively, a team won't work. With an individual, you will get consistent representation every minute of every day. Heaven help you if he needs to take a day off…or a shower. Heaven help you if he doesn't.

Ménage à Trois (Or Quatre for the Truly Busy and/or Adventurous)
When I started my new company, for a while I was working solo. I clocked the kind of hours that most people say they work when they're totally exaggerating. I was completely exhausted but too cheap to consider hiring an assistant. I had enough experience

ADVANCE READING COPY. NOT FOR SALE.

from my previous career to know that finding the wrong assistant can be almost as disastrous as joining with the wrong partner. Even later in my career, after I had hit the jackpot with my second partner, the assistant question came up. I should have known that partnering with someone who would need a vacation would result in one of us having a ridiculous workload in the absence of the other. We needed an assistant.

Being an assistant to anyone can be a crazy-hard job. Supporting is a skill not everyone has. Be very careful not to hire an assistant who is looking to learn from you and eventually become a competitor. Likewise, be very selective in joining a team *as* an assistant. Know yourself and whether or not you're assistant material.

SORTAꝑacts™

89% of real estate assistant/broker business relationships last less than five years.

—Courtesy of Sortafact

Where Have All the Assistants Gone?

The assistant relationship is often the real estate business equivalent of a one-night stand with similarly lasting respect. Assistants love and leave all too frequently, and they have all sorts of excuses:

- Going on to the next assistant/broker relationship
- Leaving the real estate business
- Having gathered all the ideas learned, now trying to become a competitor
- Finding a rich partner at an open house
- Going to jail or being on probation or becoming addicted to prescription drugs

Assistant Nirvana

A good assistant is better than—and as rare as—a continuasm. Okay, not better than. Look for these traits:

ADVANCE READING COPY. NOT FOR SALE.

- Is smart
- Prefers not being the front-stage person
- Knows how to support and loves that role
- Understands how to smooth out weaknesses so the main stage actor can always deliver a peak performance
- Wants to be part of a team and is not looking at the position as a launching pad for his own stage performance
- Wants to be a member of the successful troop that might ultimately shine with someone else's name in lights

When you have a team with the right skills and desires, coming to work is fun, stable, and lucrative (or at least not too shitty).

Be sure to train your assistant on how to tell clients that you're not in the office. Don't let him say, "She's not in the office yet." Tell him to avoid the word *yet* at all costs, as it makes you seem like a slacker. Instead, the client should know that you're out of the office on appointments—but not specifically that those appointments are hair, gynecologist/proctologist, Pilates, or another patron.

SECRETSforClients

Be nice to assistants. The damage they can do is way worse than what a pissed-off restaurant server with a full bladder is capable of.

TrueSTORIES

In New York a previously faithful but finally frustrated assistant bludgeoned her employer, real estate agent to the stars, to death. She used a piece of exercise equipment, which tells me that she couldn't have been working too hard—who has time to exercise? She testified that one of the reasons she committed this horrific murder was that her boss had blown marijuana smoke in her face. How this assistant could have interpreted this appreciative bonus as something worth killing over is beyond me. This does illustrate, however, how important it is to hire the right assistant.

ADVANCE READING COPY. NOT FOR SALE.

TRIALS&Titillations™

Research the top real estate teams in your area. Call the assistants and ask them how the team is structured. Ask what works best. Ask what they would like to change. Later call the main managing broker and ask the same questions. Copy the business models that work. You can benefit from stealing good ideas.

How you set up your team depends a lot on the legalities of your state and the policies of your company. My belief is that the right type of assistant will work on a percentage basis. If we are all commission based, we all have the same incentive to make the business successful. This has been particularly true as the market has gotten tough — many salaried assistants were laid off as business tapered, but commission assistants just worked harder. Being an independent contractor and hiring independent contractors as members of your team requires certain behaviors to maintain that contractor status. Paying people gets tricky, and there are a lot of pitfalls in terms of incentives, taxes, employment status, accounting, blah, blah, blah. Learn and know that shit by contacting your accountant and attorney so you can set yourself up in the best way.

Then forget about it and go and sell. Nothing pisses me off more than having to revisit this type of minutiae instead of making sales. Okay, many things piss me off, so maybe that's not the worst, but it's up there with having to sort out a restaurant bill with a bunch of women who all want to use coupons and are not interested in paying any portion of *my* cocktail bill. Wait until you're no longer pregnant or have given up on AA before you come dine with me and request that we split the bill.

Maybe you just want to set up a manageable business where you can discerningly choose the clients with whom you work. That's totally cool, and I envy the sperm shooter you chose to enable you to tap that trust fund for life. Be careful, however. By reading this book, you may accidentally develop a bigger following than you're willing to deal with, so find someone else in your office to refer your overflow to. A referral fee can also buy happiness, but first you have to… Well, you'll learn the words of our dear, diminutive friend Woody Allen in the next chapter.

ADVANCE READING COPY. NOT FOR SALE.

CHAPTER 4

SHOW UP

A good friend of mine was writing a book on what it takes to have a successful marriage—to be dedicated to her soon-to-be-married brother. She called up all her friends whom she deemed as having successful marriages to see if they could add pearls of wisdom. Since my husband and I had been married for more than a nano-second, she decided we qualified.

I immediately said, "You get what you buy." Since so many of my friends had embarked on ultimately unsuccessful marriages as change agents, I felt sufficiently sanctimonious in my acceptance of all of my husband's traits that I honestly knew were there before I married him. Granted, they do drive me crazy, but that's why tequila was invented, right?

My husband fired off a reply that was certainly not a departure from his totally unromantic self (but I knew that when I "bought" him, so I don't seek romance). He said, "Show up." Don't tell him, but I did really love him (and still do) for this response. It is totally straightforward and yet subtly profound.

Woody Allen first said, "Eighty percent of success is showing up," and it applies as much in real estate as it does in marriage.

True**STORIES**

A very smart real estate broker friend came into my office looking particularly fashionable and rested after sleeping in and working out. I commented on her killer outfit and invigorated appearance. She complained that she'd bought this new outfit because she had to look good for a job interview that day. Her business was so bad that she needed to go out and get a nine-to-five job. I'm not trying to sound self-righteous, but was her fabulous self really strolling into the office over four hours after I had started the daily real estate grind?! I wanted to suggest that perhaps she already had a nine-to-five (at least) job and if she worked it like that, she may need only one such job.

Because she is a good friend, I actually said, "Perhaps you should get your ass into your current job at 8:00 a.m. and you'll find that you don't have to worry about earning cleavage-requiring tips." Curiously enough, that was the only advice she needed. She started treating her real estate career like a big-girl job and, sure enough, her career took off.

Even without a single client, there is so much you can do to fill your day and build your business.

Progress in Pajamas — Suggested Reading
If you follow the wisdom of these gurus, inner peace will fill your heart and golden handcuffs will be locked and loaded on your glorious wrists. Don't believe me? Ask them.

Deepak Chopra (sorry, *Doctor* Deepak Chopra)
Larry Kendall
Brian Buffini
Stephen Covey
Mike Ferry
Tom Hopkins
Tony Robbins
Guru du Jour

Where did all the women go? Nationally there are more female residential real estate professionals then there are male. Not so with commercial real estate. Or the industry of telling people how to sell real estate — so bossy, those men. Read and listen to these bossy masters, and don't forget to show up.

Saggy? So What!
You can be old and very successful in real estate. For those of you who possess a vagina, real estate is one of the few professions

ADVANCE READING COPY. NOT FOR SALE.

in which the necessary use of bifocals does not have a negative effect on your job success. For you men, bifocals often make you look less blind than distinguished. Unlike in a lot of professions, a penis that doesn't work so well is pretty benign in this industry. You will not age out of this profession—at least not before you die.

SORTAfacts™

- 83% of women with bifocals have considered a career in real estate.
- 43% of men with a Viagra prescription have considered a career in real estate.
- The National Association of Realtors (NAR) is considering congressional lobbying to have its "Showin' Up Old" pamphlets included in all AARP publications.

—Courtesy of Sortafact

I used to admire the matriarch of real estate in my fair city as she teetered precipitously on six-inch heels touring clients around in *their* car. Although people didn't doubt her ability to dig up the best homes and get them the best deals, they wisely determined that, after her eightieth birthday was ancient history, it was better if she did the wheeling and dealing from somewhere other than behind the actual wheel. She was in the office nearly every day schmoozing and prying and sharing the deals "in her back pocket," as she said. Those of us who were also in the office enjoyed being privy to the scoop on potential deals before they ever hit the official market.

TRIALS&Titillations™

Stand in your underwear in your home office. Say out loud, "I have a buyer looking for a very special property. He wants a two-bedroom condo with a view of a yarn store." Look on the internet for that perfect view. See how fast "yarn store view" pops up in your search…or in response to your echoing pleas.

ADVANCE READING COPY. NOT FOR SALE.

SECRETSforClients

Your agent with a virtual office might be the very best in all the land. This truly might be the wave of the future, and maybe all face-to-face collaboration will dissolve as the word *friend* continues to become less of a noun and more of a verb. Thankfully this is not yet the case. Some of the best deals are done in the still-valid antiquated office halls with the old-school O_2-to-CO_2 exchange. Ask your agent how he stays up on the latest inside scoop. This goes for buyers' agents looking for not-yet-listed homes as well as sellers' agents looking for not-yet-surfaced buyers.

TrueSTORIES

My friend in the office, Dylan, shared one of her favorite show-up stories. Her recent divorce had spurred her into this business. I'm not sure of the size of her divorce settlement and, although it would not be beneath me to ask, I actually only just now thought to do so.

She took a call from a guy who lived out of town but whom she had seen once at the country club. *(Note: Country clubs can be pretentious and delightful ways to meet prospective clients even at times when banks may require more than a leased Mercedes and a gold pinkie ring to provide a loan.)* He asked her to come to his condo under the auspices of her listing it. She hesitated and confirmed with her broker to make sure that the agent who historically handled his business did not need a concealed-weapon license. Because this was Dylan's first potential listing, she prepared everything she could think of: data on other condo units that had sold in his building and research on whether he preferred cleavage or short skirts (okay, I lied about that part).

When she showed up with all her paperwork and a low-cut blouse, he asked if she would like to see his view of the river. He had a glass of wine in his hand but she, being the consummate professional, declined the wine (because she hadn't read the chapter "Fluids"). He told her he didn't really want to sell his condo but just used that line to meet her. He wanted to spend the rest of his life with her, he said.

ADVANCE READING COPY. NOT FOR SALE.

Don't tell her, but I think this is a little creepy. But what do I know? Dylan married him. The point of this story is that showing up can also be an alternative to internet dating. Or maybe I do know something. It turned out that he was a bit of a manipulative control freak, and she is now happily married to someone else.

SORTAFacts™

91% of the time, showing up will result in a successful career; 27% of the time you'll snag yourself a future ex-spouse.
—*Courtesy of Sortafact*

Put On Some Clothes!
Another reason to get in the habit of showing up is to make sure you get dressed. There can be huge advantages to—and temptations of—spending the vast majority of your day working in your pajamas…commando. So much of real estate involves cooperating with other practitioners, and a lot of this can be maintained over the phone or email.

The virtual offices that are becoming increasingly popular are just not as good as physical offices for putting deals together. As much as people like to think that we, as real estate professionals, must be competitive with one another, we also have to play well with others. The sandbox is still the best place to do that. Many of my best deals were concocted and cooked in the hallways of my office. Someday these words might be anachronistic, but I still believe them to be true: there is no substitute for mouth-to-mouth communication.

Highly Suggested Pre-Showing-Up Agenda
Work is not a Phish concert, no matter what type of hippie properties you prefer to sell. Do these:

- Shower (please)
- Brush teeth (if still drunk, swish mouthwash)
- Shave (or heavily pluck, if applicable)
- Apply appropriate products (make sure deodorant is one of them, and let's be honest, salt crystals are no substitute)

ADVANCE READING COPY. NOT FOR SALE.

- Dress in client-appropriate attire (paying specific attention to making horizontal what shouldn't be vertical and vice versa)
- Take prescribed and necessary herbal mood enhancers

Woody Allen was right. Show up for work. Don't lie and say you're not feeling well. Don't lie and say you have a lot of personal things to do. Only you will know that you're fine, and with the right battery-powered Chinese imports, those personal things don't have to take very long. You don't want to start to question your own honesty. Potential clients will sense that you see yourself as a liar. The thing about being self-employed is that your boss will know your deepest, darkest secrets, and you don't want that boss to know you're a slacker. It will become the ultimate self-fulfilling prophecy.

SORTAFacts™

Cutting-edge research is about to be released by super-fancy institutions of higher education. This research will rock the world of perfectionists and people with mild to moderate cases of OCD. Here it is: success is 89% more positively correlated with quantity than quality. This translates loosely into a mantra for our future: Try More Shit and Success Is Bound to Stick.

—Courtesy of Sortafact

ADVANCE READING COPY. NOT FOR SALE.

CHAPTER 5

YOU CAN'T ALWAYS GET WHEN YOU WANT

When you call a hair stylist and ask her for an appointment, are you suspicious that she might suck if she has every time slot available? If you're like me, your roots might be very silvery and your layers horribly misaligned, but you will wait to get in with someone busier. It's not a risk worth taking. Hell hath no fury like a woman improperly shorn.

This applies in real estate too. You must use your schedule as a tool to appear busy and still accommodating. When a client asks you if you're available on a certain day, look at your schedule and offer a two-hour time slot. If he cannot work within that time slot and you really have more availability, ask him when he would ideally like to meet. Then tell him you will make some calls to tweak your schedule. He'll feel like a priority to someone who is busy enough to matter. This is easy and good.

This appearance of limited availability requires just the right balance. I have often said to a client who was demanding slightly more than her fair share of my time, "You might be my favorite client, but you are not my only client." If I see that I've hurt her feelings a little bit, I can always add, "But I sure wish they were all like you." Figure out ways to make your patrons feel special while still making them know that they are lucky to be able to work with you.

SECRETSforClients

If you have been a client of mine and you're reading this book, this does not apply to you because you really *were* my favorite—but don't tell anyone.

53

True**STORIES**

I had a particularly high-profile client, Shar, coming to town to look at property. As the apparent time frame approached, she was not committing to any specific date but was acting as if I would make myself available at the last minute on whatever date she came to town. Admittedly, Shar was used to people accommodating her. In order to make her see some value in my time and professionalism, I needed to make her see my status in my industry as equivalent to her stature in her field—I was not someone who would cater to her every bad behavior.

Of course, I had to strive for a balance because she was my client. I finally called her and said, "Okay, girlfriend, I want to make sure that I block out enough time to make the most of your trip." See? This says, *It's all about…you.* "You are very busy, and I want to be as efficient with your valuable time as possible." *I'm efficient…for you.* "My schedule is getting uglier by the minute with some equally busy clients who I want to schedule around your visit." *I'm a high-powered professional who works with important people…like you.* "I need to block out the time that you know for sure you will be here so you can be the priority in my schedule." *My priority is…you.* "There are some things that I really must show you, so let's get on the calendar by Tuesday at noon if at all possible." *I am taking charge here…for you.*

By giving a specific time and date, I'm giving her the opportunity to commit to me. I'm also on record with a specific warning of my expiration date. In this scenario, if Shar wanted to go beyond my expiration date, there is an implicit understanding that she might not get the freshest product—in this case, my full time and attention.

SORTA**Facts**™

Studies conducted at Reno's Saddle-n-Straddle Ranch found that entertainment specialists who were on the drop-in list earned 79% less than specialists requiring an appointment made

ADVANCE READING COPY. NOT FOR SALE.

in advance. This trend was reduced to 23% when bookings required more than a three-month advanced appointment.

—Courtesy of Sortafact

Excuses, Excuses

If you feel the need to tell your clients why you are unavailable but are having trouble coming up with good reasons, try one or two of these handy excuses:

- Reviewing offers on one of your listings
- Installing your art at MOMA
- Showing property to a celebrity buyer
- Treating a serious skin disorder
- Receiving a Nobel Peace Prize
- Rescuing the elderly from a natural disaster
- Appearing on the news as a real estate expert
- Hosting a client appreciation party featuring the real Elvis

But steer clear of these reasons to be unavailable:

- Attending a parole hearing
- Enjoying a children's choral recital at the school for the deaf
- Watching a college football game featuring schools for other states
- Nude scrapbooking with your partner (or any scrapbooking for that matter)
- Suffering a wardrobe malfunction
- Experiencing a relapse in your sex addiction (although this depends a lot on the client)
- Picking up your welfare check
- Nursing a hangover

Groucho Marx and Woody Allen summed up human nature well when they said they'd never join a club that would allow people like them to become members. With some people, you have to strike the right balance of them wanting you and you wanting them. Don't brush this off as the type of game playing that you

ADVANCE READING COPY. NOT FOR SALE.

hate in relationships. I think—no, I *know*—that a very delicate balancing act takes place, on some level, in every relationship.

As a salesperson, it is important to know this. Even alpha people like to be spanked once in a while, just as passive people like to feel empowered from time to time. Sometimes you're available, sometimes you can make yourself available, and sometimes you're booked solid. Be strategic and smart about when to spank and when to hand over a feather before hiding the key to the handcuffs. (What's this obsession with handcuffs?)

ADVANCE READING COPY. NOT FOR SALE.

CHAPTER 6

FOR CLIENTS ONLY

Patrons, in addition to the Secret for Clients sidebars you'll find throughout the book, this here chapter is all for you. If you buy this book for the ambitious real estate professionals in your life, please tell them to skip this chapter. It's not for them. And remember, greed is good.

You Just Can't Stay Out of This, Can You?

If you're a real estate professional or on your way to becoming one, this chapter is private and none of your fucking business. Are you still reading this, you misbehaving shit? You know I love you, but there are some things that must remain sacred.

Okay, I get it. There is no doubt that you are an overachiever and understand that the best way to help your clients is to know what they know about you. Read on, you little cheat.

Odd Bedfellows

There are a lot of books that will tell you *How to Buy Your Dream Home!!* Or *How to Invest in Real Estate with Someone Else's Money and Keep the Profits!!!* Or *Real Estate Heaven Is for Reals!!!!* Or the book Donald Trump should've written: *How to Sell Big House when Hung Like Field Mouse!!!!!* Obviously you will learn all that stuff here—and you'll also win the lottery and firm your thighs while you read.

There is a difference, however, between being told something by experts and being told what the experts are being told. "Your pillow talk is their pillow talk" is one of the most feared mantras in the world of sales. Putting patrons and professionals in the same bed will result in a massive authentication of the real estate industry. Make your own bed, or don't. Just be good in it.

SORTAFacts™
Studies show that agents who facilitate time sinks tend to be the agents who have a lot of extra time to sink. The time they sink could be yours.

—Courtesy of Sortafact

The Little Black Book That's Pretty Big

Even if you have no interest in real estate as a career, you are still not shielded from being tossed into a real estate perfect storm. Just as you're looking to make a move and think you may have found the ideal real estate professional in your little black book (aka, your cell phone), you can find yourself treading perilously on the plank between business and friendship.

See if you have experienced one of these scenarios. If you haven't yet, you might soon:

- You need to sell your house at the same time your dear friend announces, "I wanted to wait to tell you until I actually passed my real estate exam…and it only took three tries! I'm a real estate agent!!!!" *(Note: This is generally emailed or screeched just like that—with many exclamation points.)*
- You decide to buy a home and, with her ever-present sixth sense, your mom calls to tell you the serendipitous news that your previously unemployed brother has just accepted a job as a real estate agent with Righteous Realty.
- Your partner has left you for a Serbian bodybuilder and wants to split the proceeds of the sale of your home. As you're sharing a ninth cocktail with your best drinking buddy, he tells you, "I'm finally on my feeth and looking forward to getting…what was I shaying? I'm ready to change my life forever, and now I can help you. I got my real estate licensh!"
- Your six smart best friends are having a Real Estate License Getting Party. They've all invited you to the after-party.

ADVANCE READING COPY. NOT FOR SALE.

I cannot begin to count the number of friend-ships that have sunk in these perfect-storm scenarios. Anytime people are selling something that is so personal—like, you know, themselves—it's hard to extract emotions from the equation. Rejection is almost always taken personally.

SORTAfacts™

A large study by a major chemical company showed that that 94% of the time that people have to substantiate a claim made on social media in a face-to-face interaction, they pee in their underwear just a little bit.

—Courtesy of Sortafact

In some professions, selling yourself and the rejection that comes along with it are easier than in others—like when the rejection is due to a personal choice rather than a choice about the person: "I'm sorry, Trixie, but Mr. Pocketpool doesn't avoid your pole because he doesn't think you're a great dancer. It's just that he has always preferred when the curtains match the carpet."

In real estate, it's hard not to make rejection personal, but it is imperative that you know how to do this. The reason has less to do with your dwindling birthday party list and more to do with your wallet. You can keep the list long and the wallet fat if you use a few simple tricks, customized to various scenarios.

If your friend or family member is new to real estate and you give a shit about the relationship, follow these steps:

1. Call and tell her of your plans to buy or sell a home.
2. Convince her that her success is important to you (not like her phone call; never say a phone call is important to you).
3. Admit that her success has got to be tied to your success.
4. Establish the dipshit-to-dinero quotient. How much money you would sacrifice, if any, based on her general abilities and experience—or lack thereof.
5. Explain the good news that you want to include her in your interview process.

ADVANCE READING COPY. NOT FOR SALE.

6. Here's a little preinterview testy: Ask her what she charges. Then shut up and listen. The responses and what they mean could fill a whole book. If she tells you she works for free, know she is not just being nice—she is being a crappy negotiator. Say, "Really? Wow." And then breathe through your nose (*see* "STFU").

If you think it's best to proceed as if you were not informed of your friend or family member's new real estate status, don't be so quick to think you're out of the guilty quicksand. You might not care about this new real estate "professional" or about his success, but you might care what he says about you. You might care about the people who care about him. If you have a business in which those caring people are potential customers, this can create a Slip N' Slide of awkwardness.

Try this: "Marvin, thank you so much for renewing your son's membership in my Munchies with Meaning home delivery program. I heard he will be joining the real estate profession." Then pause and insert an option from the list below:

- Find a loud and distracting location and mumble your plans to buy or sell real estate.
- Make a supersubtle reference to your plans to buy or sell real estate. (Cross your fingers that he doesn't get it).
- All of the above.

If he doesn't respond with anything about his son's new real estate license status, thank the loud leaf blower you hired for the occasion. Later blame your friend/family member/customer for not saying anything when you told him you were looking for a real estate agent.

If he has good hearing, try one of these:

- Feign enthusiasm for the exciting news of his son getting his real estate license.
- Hide your snarky skepticism behind a supportive smile.

ADVANCE READING COPY. NOT FOR SALE.

- Make a reference to the market challenges. (Advanced: Insert a statistic from the *Wall Street Journal* or the *New York Times* to show just how seriously you take your real estate.)
- Agree that his son's background in scrapbooking with sharp scissors should really help him *cut it* in the tough market. (Okay, that's not fair since many scrapbookers are leaving lucrative professional careers for real estate—but I couldn't resist.)
- Plaster on the look of regret you learned in eighth-grade thespian camp.
- Say you wish you'd known about this exciting turn of events earlier.
- Shake your head solemnly and shut up.

Successfully avoiding the wrong representation can save you tremendous sums. Evading these disasters with aplomb can minimize the friends and business contacts you move from active to archived.

Yeah, You Can Do It

If you're like thousands of Americans, you may be thinking you can take care of your own real estate needs without hiring an agent. That would, after all, be easier to explain to Marvin than the fact that you don't want his son traipsing through your bedroom. Yes, you can stage your house to a glorious reveal. You can blast out to every real estate porn–addicted soul with an internet connection. You can price your house crisply and appropriately. You can sell your house for more or less than you thought. You can brag to all your friends how well you did and how happy you are. You can also say the same about your sex life…and sort of mean it.

Maybe you already have done all these things. And maybe you learned after the fact that you lost a shit-ton of money. Talk about a bummer. Reading on will fulfill your better-luck-next-time prophecy. But if you are someone for whom, even when the stakes are high, adequate is good enough, you can stop reading this chapter right here and satisfy your productivity goal by folding laundry.

ADVANCE READING COPY. NOT FOR SALE.

More, More, More

Still reading? Then welcome to the Greedy for Greatness Club. You've decided not to settle for the average job you might be able to do buying or selling a home and to rely on the expertise of a professional. The trick is making sure the person you hire is actually a professional.

People tend to believe recommendations that come from people like them. If your best friend recommends Sarah Jo as an agent, no matter how many negative reviews you read online, Sarah Jo will still stand out in your mind. Belief in a third party becomes a religious experience.

Referrals from your friends are good, but they are wrought with all kinds of biases. Just because Hank put up with someone else doesn't mean that agent will put out for you. Referrals should only be the starting point in your hunt to hire a pro. Even if your smartest, richest friend has referred her most favorite go-to agent, you need to interview the stud. You should also take the time to interview a couple other real estate pros to uncover which one will work best with you.

SORTAFacts™

Diversity experts agree that if your real estate professional suddenly appears in a burka, it's 63% more likely due to a bad hair day than to a spontaneous conversion.

— *Courtesy of Sortafact*

Identity Crisis

Before you even begin to interview potential real estate professionals, you can learn a tiny bit about their experience levels from their labels and designations. Different states have different laws governing real estate. Some licensees initially become agents, some immediately become brokers, and in some states an agent needs to advance based on state-determined criteria in order to become a broker. Each state differs in designations and requirements. The National Association of Realtors is an association that requires adherence to specific ethics and standards. A Realtor is a member of that association. A person can be licensed as a real

ADVANCE READING COPY. NOT FOR SALE.

estate professional with or without that association, though. I use the terms *agent, broker, and Realtor* interchangeably because I can't figure out a better way to do it for readers from every state. Good is good and sucky sucks regardless of the label bestowed.

Beyond those designations, real estate professionals have access to continuing education for more endorsements. More and more of these courses and endorsements are being invented all the time. Generally these are helpful to agents, but sometimes even great agents don't have time to sit and acquire extra endorsements. They might be too busy providing great representation and collecting referrals to collect badges. It's not all in a name.

The services that agents, brokers, and Realtors provide differ from state to state too. In some states, they can take care of the legal paperwork associated with property purchases. In many states, they must work with lawyers for that. Parents from a lawyer-y state like to advise their offspring in states that don't generally use lawyers that they are schmucks not to use one. In some states, escrow companies are commonly used.

Regardless of the state practices and norms, the methods of evaluating the best professional for you are the same no matter where you are: consider referrals but don't bet on them, interview several agents, and ask the tough questions.

Interview Tips

The real estate interviews with the best outcomes are two-way gigs. The goal is to look for a unique type of love connection with an agent. Start with assessing the interviewees' ability to sell themselves. The finesse they use to self-sell will provide a little peek into how well they will finesse the sale of your property. Does their boasting about their production make you feel like you were pelted with the trophies off the shelf of your klutzy third-grade child? Then they might try to obnoxiously slam your house down the throat of anyone with the nerve to ask a simple question about anything remotely related to real estate. Do they generously offer valuable insight as a way of showing and sharing their expertise? Are they comfortable and engaging with you? That is a likely indication of how they will interact with potential buyers for your home or sellers of your future home.

ADVANCE READING COPY. NOT FOR SALE.

If it was good for you, it is sort of good manners to ask if it was good for them. With some things, once you're satisfied you can get away with just pretending to care about the other party's needs, but I don't suggest faking it with your real estate relationship. Ask your interviewees if, even after the interview, they still want to work with you. If you're selling, ask them if they like your property. Ask why. Ask them what they don't like about your property. Ask them what they think are the unique strengths of your property. That's a trick question because not every house has unique traits, and that's okay. It's why we have "popular floor plans" and Home Depot. When they answer that they love the three spacious bedrooms with the closet organizers, feel free to do a little bitch test. Ask them why that's unique. The way they squirm and how they react will give you an indication of how they will respond to equally asshole-y questions that invariably fly at open houses. It's a good test o' finesse.

A fortune I once pulled from between the stale lips of my Chinese cookie said, "He who describes herself does not provide popular description." Although I was happy to see this particular fortune-cookie psychic being inclusive of transsexuals, I couldn't help but feel a bit taken aback by the insinuation that none of us are very self-aware. Maybe the psychic was just being critical of the self-assessment of gender benders, but I took the message to heart.

I tell you this to let you in on a little secret: the real estate industry is competitive, but the relationship that your real estate professional has with other agents is one of the most important factors in the outcome of your representation. Ask your interviewees how their top competitors would describe them. Ask them how a new agent would describe them. Ask them how they differ from other top agents. Ask them who they view as major competition and why. Put a smile of sincerity and curiosity on your face to reflect the sincere curiosity that you should have. Ask tough questions about their fellow industry folks that might cause a bit of discomfort. Look carefully for comfortable communication that reveals a constructive analysis of and healthy respect for other industry pros.

You might feel that an obvious cutthroat agent with a want-I-should-cut-you attitude is the right choice for sharp negotiations. You could, however, end up on the painful end of the negotiation

ADVANCE READING COPY. NOT FOR SALE.

shank. Successful negotiators do not claim to leave the carcasses of their opponents littered throughout the landfill. In real estate successful negotiators don't have opponents. Real estate is a business of facilitating negotiations. Successful negotiators will understand this and should reveal themselves as adept at answering tough questions. Sometimes that adeptness is revealed through silence and sometimes with thoughtful answers.

It is also important to see how client focused your potential pro might be. Asking him how he thinks he performs is no substitute for asking what his clients think. Ask how his satisfied clients would describe him. Ask how his dissatisfied clients would describe him. That last one is a tricky one because if he says he has never had an unsatisfied client, he needs to sell more property, stop being an obtuse fool, or eat more fortune cookies.

TrueSTORIES

A real estate broker friend, Russell, interviewed to represent a seller on a property that he really wanted to list. Not unlike a lot of real estate professionals talking amongst themselves, he referred to all of his listings as "great listings." But this one really did look uniquely great for Russell, who had game and a generous spirit and a slightly cracked moral compass. He'd be interviewing with a celebrity.

High-profile clients are often enough to make a listing particularly desirable to both brokers and buyers. In all honesty, though, this listing was a bit of a conundrum—high-profile, sexy client with a not-so-sexy house. But when the client is single and hot, this can still lead to a harmonic convergence…or so my friend hoped.

The interview process went well, and Russell was sure he would be selected to get the listing. He was equally certain that the celebrity status of the owner would be enough to entice a buyer to overpay for the three-bedroom, one-and-a-half bath model in the tract-home subdivision. He bravely and confidently presented his suggested price. He wanted it…bad.

When the seller thanked Russell for his belief in the true value of the home and his willingness to go the extra mile to get a price that was 45 percent more than the highest suggested price from

ADVANCE READING COPY. NOT FOR SALE.

any competing broker, my hopeful friend continued to present a confident front. His confidence teetered more than slightly when the seller explained that the house belonged to his newly divorced sister and she really needed to get every dollar out of the property. My friend's face wasn't the only thing to fall as he was awarded the listing and given the phone number for the rehab clinic from which the sister seller would soon be sprung in order to sign the rest of the listing paperwork.

Agents who suggest the highest prices for your house can make you feel proud, grateful, and understood. Just make sure they are not presenting the suggested price as a down payment for something else.

Get Curious

Just because you have to force yourself not to take the easy road and simply trust your friends' referrals doesn't mean your judgment totally sucks. Use it. Forget following your intuition. The only time intuition sheds light on a single fucking thing is after the fact. Please don't get me started.

A simpler and far more effective approach is to follow your curiosity. Be on the internal vibe-out for things that make you go, "Hmmm." This shifts the mind away from the need to avoid offending to the need to obtain information. Get curious, and then ask the questions that you're curious about.

Curiosity may have killed your fluffy cat that you love, love, loved, but the thing that killed your cat is the exact thing that will save your bacon.

TRIALS&Titillations™

(For Sellers): Ask your real estate professional if it's a good time to sell. Listen to her answer. Then ask her if it's a good time to buy.

(For Buyers): Ask your real estate professional if it's a good time to buy. Listen to his answer. Then ask him if it's a good time to sell.

ADVANCE READING COPY. NOT FOR SALE.

If you don't ask revealing questions of your barista or personal shopper, fine. If you don't ask revealing questions when you're looking for someone to represent you in the purchase or sale of what could be one of your largest financial assets, it could cost you more than the decision to buy your teenager discount condoms.

Squeak!

Once you're ready to hire, you get to sign a contract for representation. If you are a newly minted lawyer, you will be sure to read all your standard documents word for word. Read away — just be sure not to look up too quickly or you'll see the smirk on your agent's face before he has a chance to replace it with an impressed smile.

No matter the rock star status of your new real estate agent, you should be a squeaky wheel. Let your agent know what you will expect in terms of communication. I've always felt that I was pretty darn good at keeping in touch with my buyers and sellers. Your agent probably thinks she is too. When there is a lot of activity in the market, that's a fairly lame boast. It is, however, much more impressive when an agent communicates well even when there have been no showings of a seller's property or no new homes to show a buyer.

Every real estate professional likes her clients better when they don't bug her with calls asking about the status of their sale. But your goal isn't to be her favorite silent client. Real estate is an area where being too nice and complacent can cost you. Expect a weekly update from your agent no matter what the market is doing. When I knew that a client was going to call requesting an update — I'm not proud saying this — I tended to prioritize my attention on the squeaky wheel client. As much as I might like being blindfolded, I hate being blindsided.

With so many methods of communication to choose from these days, which is the best one? Email is a good way to memorialize status and keep a record of commitments, but nuance is lost. If you want to have a seriously strategic conversation, meet in person or use technology that will put your face screen-to-screen with your agent's. Your agent will have a solid grasp of your expectations,

ADVANCE READING COPY. NOT FOR SALE.

and you will get a clearer understanding of what it will take to successfully complete your sale.

Readers from various generations might argue differently, but e-unication is as different from in-person communication as talking about sex is from...having it. This might come as a surprise if you're young with a good imagination or if you're not a member of the Society for Creative Anachronism. Actually, maybe it will come as more of a surprise if you *are* a member of that wishful club.

SORTAFacts™

A major university study revealed that subjects shown photos of individuals dressed in either sports uniforms or anime costumes were able to pick out the virgins 99% of the time. Over the phone, the virgins were classified as "having game" 79% more often.

—Courtesy of Sortafact

The Whole Truth

Not too far back in the olden days of real estate representation, all real estate agents represented just sellers. If you enlisted an agent to assist you in your home search, he would kindly help you acquire that property but technically, and usually unbeknownst to you the buyer, his legal responsibility was to the seller. There was no discussion of whom he represented, and even if it felt like he had your back (and he might have), he was really representing the seller. He might never meet the seller, but on every property the agent showed, he was technically representing the seller. Buyers didn't know to care or ask about representation. It was a screwy situation. Laws differ state by state, but the vast majority of states now have disclosure requirements so buyers and sellers are clear on who officially represents whom. If this is not disclosed to you, it is not (and never was) a secret—all you have to do is ask.

There are good, smart real estate professionals who will represent you with fun and integrity. If that's what you're looking for, the information in this chapter will help you distinguish the

ADVANCE READING COPY. NOT FOR SALE.

agents you should consider from the agents you should not. Many people go into the profession of real estate because they love helping people. They will work to replace the image of the smarmy salesperson. You can trust them to be honest with you. This feels fantastic—a partnership made of rainbows. But betrayal can still happen, believe it or not. The hard part is when the honesty is challenged by the dreaded accidental error of omission.

If you're the type of person who likes to convince yourself that the homeless people you see are just waiting for the bus, this advice might stress you out a bit. If you're like me and think that the words *no problem* should be chased with skepticism pills or at least prune juice, you might benefit from working with a professional who is willing to discuss the real state of real estate—someone who has experience with and an awareness of the shit storms that can rage, and can help you smell them coming with enough warning to duck and cover.

If you're brave enough to ask your agent about worst-case scenarios, you will initially be paranoid. This leads to preparedness, however, which results in less reason for paranoia. Ask your agent to tell you what she would tell you about your property or property search if she had no concern for your feelings. Ask her what has gone wrong for her in the past. Ask her what she has learned from real estate disasters and what she would do differently. Take advantage of the mistakes she's experienced with her other clients so you can insert your disaster diaphragm accordingly.

This inside scoop is just the foreplay. In the chapters that follow, you will find some secrets laid out just for you, but the greater secrets lie buried in the advice to professionals. Use the lube provided in this chapter to smoothly slide the knowledge presented in future chapters into slammin' success.

ADVANCE READING COPY. NOT FOR SALE.

PART 2

PREACHING
the
Buy-ble!

Preaching the Buy-ble

Working with buyers is fun, active, rewarding, and exhausting. After I have spent years conducting thousands of formal and informal interviews, the results are in. People who say, "I'm a people person" love to work with buyers. This is quiet fun. You can sell a lot of real estate working with buyers, and your family and friends might never know it. There are no signs, ads, flyers, or social media opportunities to shout your successes working with buyers. That's okay because buyers are generally excited when they close on a house, and this excitement will rub off on you.

Working with buyers also seems like the easy entry point to real estate. You find the right property and, voilà, your job is done, right? Wrong. Your job is done after your commission check clears the bank, right? Wrong again (but you had a hint that wasn't right). What about once you have successfully fielded midnight calls from your pissed-off buyers after the first heavy rains oozed brownish liquid through the ceiling and onto the formerly finally-sleeping baby's soft forehead, turning her into a now screaming, inconsolable devil spawn? Okay, your job can be done now if you want… but not if you mind the buyers telling all their friends that you sold them a piece of shit.

Successfully working with buyers is like entering into a bunch of long-term relationships. You can't just seal the deal and then disappear once you've written a nice note. Right, buyers? You want someone who will be around and will continue to treat you with the same level of desire as before he handed you your keys.

SORTAfacts™

People who call with problems in the middle of the night are 78% more likely to have their calls screened throughout the day. They are also 83% more likely to inspire murderous thoughts in the recipient of that call.

—Courtesy of Sortafact

SECRETSꜰᴏʀClients

Please don't call or text your real estate professional in the middle of the night. If you intend to just leave a message, wait until morning. If you intend for your agent to answer, your last name had better be Windsor...or Winfrey.

Four Random Facts to Launch You into Buy-ble Study:
- Some experienced agents work only with buyers.
- Most experienced agents are more seller focused.
- Working with buyers is perceived to be easier than working with sellers. It's not necessarily.
- Buyer-agent compensation is sort of weird when you think about it. My crystal ball tells me it will change.

When you collapse at the end of a day of working with buyers, you might be too tired to get down with getting satisfied. However, when you've spent the day handing over keys to excited buyers, although you still might be too tired to experience satisfaction in any other way, you'll also feel so satisfied.

ADVANCE READING COPY. NOT FOR SALE.

CHAPTER 7

WHERE ARE THEY COMING FROM?

Understanding the past experiences of others is one of the most important tools in effective communication. I would also argue that this is the most important factor in world diplomacy, but I don't want to get too preachy.

True**STORIES**

Although I generally detest cute-kid stories, this one from early in my parenting adventure illustrates the importance of understanding what your client knows and has experienced.

I was attempting to tell my four-year-old son about pedophilia to teach him how to react to inappropriate touching. I told him that no one is allowed to touch his privates without his permission. This is a slippery slope because you want to strike the right balance so that he understands the naughty but will someday be comfortable with the nice. I said, "What would you do if someone touched your privates?" He immediately made a face like he was disgusted and indignantly announced, "I would say, 'Wash your hands!'"

Now, granted, we are a little germophobe-y in our family, but I thought this was ridiculous. I told this to one of my best friends, who freaked out because her son had answered the question in the exact same way. Who would've thunk?

In our parenting culture, all the books said to teach our children about the privacy of privates when they were four years old. Those books were parent bibles, and if you couldn't trust those books, who were you to call yourself a parent? The books, however, never said to think about the fact that to a four-year-old, touching privates means going to the bathroom and needing to wash off the pee afterward. We should have been told to adjust the delivery of the privates talk accordingly.

Later, of course, most parents hope their children adjust to new life experiences where touching privates is less often about using the toilet for traditional purposes—and that they still wash their hands.

Although I generally don't think it's necessary to ask your clients about their privates and related hygiene, it's not a bad idea if they're sharing your pen for signing contracts; more important, keep in mind where they're coming from. Clients don't necessarily have the same experiences with real estate as do professionals who deal with frequent industry changes.

True**STORIES**

I once listened to a very dynamic woman talk about her experiences growing up in generational poverty. In this case the term meant that her parents, grandparents, and great-grandparents were all migrant farmers. As a child she, too, was a crop picker, and when she was working, she could afford to eat and had a place to sleep. When she wasn't picking crops, she was hungry and homeless.

When her teacher sat her down and explained the importance of going to school, she was certain her teacher was conspiring to make her go without food and shelter. Therefore, she didn't trust or like her teacher. Her teacher didn't know what the girl knew or what she had experienced.

Also, coming from generational poverty made the girl believe that this life station was genetically hers to keep and pass on to her children (which she would feel compelled to start having at fifteen years old, like all her friends). She even felt that she had "poor person hair." It seemed to her that it was in her DNA, not that it had anything to do with the fact that she had to wash her hair in gas station bathrooms with the less-than-luxurious hair products from the dispenser on the wall. This was very different in her eyes than it would be to someone who was situationally poor.

ADVANCE READING COPY. NOT FOR SALE.

Your communication with your client should reflect an understanding of even more than your client's prior knowledge about real estate. Although there is tremendous focus on socioeconomic experiences affecting communication, very rarely are economic backgrounds assessed and considered separately from the sociological backgrounds. When someone appears financially able to buy property, we tend to check the qualified box in the affirmative. But if we stir in past economic experience, we'll have *all* the key ingredients in a successful communication caldron.

SORTAFacts™

4 out of 5 salespeople in Fortune 6000 companies have had their framed photograph hung in the break room after spending just six minutes per week understanding their clients' backgrounds.
— *Courtesy of Sortafact*

If you don't find out as much as you can about your clients and their life experiences as well as their likes and dislikes, you will never be able to totally and effectively communicate with them. You also might not ever earn a commission. They have every right to blame you for believing what they say, not what they mean.

When you have clients who are couples, in the process of learning about their background, you might learn that they haven't even taken the time to figure out each other. This is when you have to be extra careful to sell them something that will be easy to resell. When they learn just enough about each other to call you to list their house, they'll be in a hurry to split up the proceeds as they split up their relationship.

TrueSTORIES

One of my escrow officer friends, Kimberly, told me this story. A young, newly married couple sat cuddling and kissing as they signed their closing papers. One of the many common documents that must be signed along with the loan paperwork is the statement of identity. This has a list of every name by which each buyer has ever been officially referred, and it requires that patron

ADVANCE READING COPY. NOT FOR SALE.

to sign off on all those names. As Kimberly pushed the three-page document across the table for the wife to sign, the husband was clearly disturbed by the number of her aliases.

"Who are all those people?" he asked.

"Oh!" Brytnie Nelson Anderson Jones Stewart Michaels Wilson Cliff-Simpson cheerfully exclaimed. "Those are me. Didn't I tell you about my other husbands?"

That was the end of the kissy-kissy—and the commission.

Like spousal baggage, buyer baggage often can be subtly obtained. We have to pay attention to interactions and microexpressions. That's why it's always useful to weasel yourself an invitation to your buyers' current home. Find out what they like and don't like about it and secretly look around for the way they live—it's often better than reality TV because it's actually reality.

SORTAFacts™

Interrogations result in revelations for the interrogator 87% less often than for the interrogated.

—Courtesy of Sortafact

SECRETSfor**Clients**

Don't be insulted if your agent asks you a lot about yourself that doesn't seem related to real estate. Residential real estate is really personal—that's why it is the number-two cocktail party topic in this country. Remember, too, that real estate professionals live and breathe this topic, and sometimes they need a little distraction. Give them some good gossip on your personal life. Throw a few really juicy tidbits their way, and it will have the added bonus of keeping them entertained. Most important, a better understanding of you will help your agent help you make better decisions.

Start with curiosity about your client and then do something radical—come right out and ask what you're curious about. Try these questions for starters:

ADVANCE READING COPY. NOT FOR SALE.

- How do you feel about buying a home in this market?
- What are your thoughts about the market?
- What have your past real estate experiences been like?
- What is the most interesting story you have ever heard about someone's real estate experience?
- What can you tell me about your past experiences involving large purchases?
- What are your expectations?
- What are your hopes and dreams?
- What does your rap sheet look like?
- Do you like movies about gladiators? Turkish prisons?

Okay, you can skip the Turkish prison question if you really want to. Even if all you do is ask about your clients' specific feelings, likes, and dislikes about past real estate experiences or other types of sales, you have a cheat sheet to go by.

Take Note!

While you're taking mental notes about your clients' preferences, also watch for out-of-line expectations. Be extra aware when your clients gripe about past injustices at the hands of another real estate professional. Although most people experience an immediate tendency to agree with their clients in these situations, do so sparingly. If you don't listen carefully to whether such clients are massive kvetches with a ridiculous ax to grind, you might later be ground by that very ax. If they tell you about a negative experience they had with an agent in the past and you think the agent's behavior sounds completely acceptable, this could be a warning that your clients might need a little re-education...or you do.

They might innocently have unrealistic expectations. Test to see if you can align their expectations with how you work. Some of the best complaints about previous real estate experiences involve the unsatisfying meals that their agent provided or the substandard type of car that their agent drove. These complaints are far more ridiculous than the complaint I heard about an agent's hairy ass-crack making an appearance every time he bent over to open a lockbox. If you can't work within

ADVANCE READING COPY. NOT FOR SALE.

your clients' expected parameters, refer them to someone who is a better match...or buy a thong.

Don't work with clients when you have a nagging feeling that it won't work. They will be with you long enough to blame you for not meeting their unrealistic expectations. You, however, will not be with them long enough to change them. I have plenty of experience with trying to change a special someone...and it still hasn't entirely worked.

While we tend to rely on asking questions and expecting our clients to lay out their dirt, it's also a good skill to do a little of your own revealing.

ADVANCE READING COPY. NOT FOR SALE.

CHAPTER 8

Do Tell

It takes a certain prodding to find most people's really interesting juice. When clients make it easy to see that they're interesting, you should quickly add these people to your friendship repository. Finding what's interesting about your clients can make your job more interesting and, therefore, make you more successful. Sharing a little bit about who you are can help in that endeavor.

SORTAFacts™

Top bartenders suggest that downing more than five All the Ways on the rocks in a one- hour period can adversely affect your goal to be taken seriously. It can, however, make you a less-discerning sex partner.

—Courtesy of Sortafact

Always be strategic in choosing what you'll confess. A well-chosen confession will make clients feel comfortable with you and will make you relatable. When I was fresh out of college and on the interview circuit, I was often asked to reveal a weakness. The question was cliché, though it was sometimes cleverly cloaked in 1980s *Pack Your Own Parachute* interview-ese. No matter how the question was presented, the answer needed to be revealing and real but not a deterrent to nailing the interview and getting the job.

Some of the bad answers that my friends shared were positive things with a negative twist (see below). I used to say that when I was driving or even walking in a city, I had a poor sense of direction. That would be one of the bad things to say to a prospective buyer looking for a good real estate agent. Eventually I grew out of this weakness—my GPS helps.

There are all kinds of ways to answer the weakness question. Check the following options out. Are they good responses or bad ones? You be the judge:

- I'm such a people person that sometimes I bring my kneepads to interviews.
- Having risen from abject poverty to extreme success has not cured me of my need to dig through garbage cans.
- I don't like people, although I *love* animals and children.
- I don't like to talk about it.
- It might not be legal, but it works.
- I don't know, and I know that I would enjoy finding out.
- I like to bring canned asparagus to client potlucks.

We tend to reveal much more to friends than we would to clients, so when those two worlds collide, watch out. Friends who don't want to work with you *because* of your friendship probably feel this way because they don't think you're good. Face it, you might have told them so during that pole-dancing episode with the Red Bull and vodka. Don't hold that against them. Be willing to let those who know you best know you suck. There are plenty of people who don't know you that well.

Answering Client Questions

It's okay to share that you've made blunders, and it's okay to share that you don't know everything. Just be smart about it. I have witnessed some old pros answering the tricky question when a buyer asks if they think a house is overpriced. The agent might agree that the property might possibly be a tad overpriced. The old pro might also think that it will sell quickly anyway. The two factors can be mutually exclusive, and good agents should acknowledge this fact. One of my favorite agents often answers this question by pointing out that he agrees the house might be a bit pricey but also that he tends to think that so much is overpriced, he feels like an antique in the business. He also admits to hating it when he's wrong and the property sells quickly.

ADVANCE READING COPY. NOT FOR SALE.

Good properties often sell quickly in spite of being somewhat aggressively priced. Not always, but it certainly happens. There is a covert message that my friend enjoys and it is: I've been at this a long time and I know the ups and downs, but if the clients snooze, they might just lose.

SECRETS for Clients

Listen to agents willing to share their real estate stories. It will reveal that they have experience or that they are smart enough to take the time to study others with more experience. Over time, a good agent will learn that *overpriced* means nothing when people are willing to pay it. Seasoned experts will explain that many times a property sits idle on the market for months and then becomes the subject of a bidding war. This happens. Years in the business teach pros that properties sell below, at, and above the asking prices. Therefore, what does it mean for a property to be overpriced? Your agent should share personal examples so you understand that often the variable with price is time. We have all rapped our skulls over selling too low and buying too high. Trust the agent who shares personal examples of successes *and* screwups.

I have told the story many times about how my husband and I danced a real-estate-tycoon happy jig when we sold our house for $270,000, only to watch the same house sell again, not too long after we sold it, for over $800,000. What do I know? By revealing how my husband and I also did the happy jig when, in the past, we scored a big refinance at 8.5 percent interest, it can show how crazy we were then and how smart the buyers are now. This story provides the incentive to lock in and appreciate interest rates— even if they are higher than they were a week ago. The fact that prices often seem high in the moment but in hindsight can seem ridiculously affordable is best communicated through sharing your experience of learning that lesson the hard way.

Be sure to share how it can work in reverse as well. Your personal story of buying high and selling low will provide the honest and relatable impact necessary to make that point too.

ADVANCE READING COPY. NOT FOR SALE.

Your clients can then thank you for saving them from having to learn that same tough lesson.

This delicate dance with stupidity is best used when you have the expertise and trust to establish yourself as a market maven. If you don't have the experience yet, interview other agents who do have a successful track record, and share their experiences (without revealing names, of course). If you try to answer clients' questions without relatable personal stories, you could just look like a dumbshit, or a pushy dumbshit.

This is not to say that you shouldn't give pricing and market advice to your clients—just remember that there is no market Nostradamus (no matter who claims otherwise).

Storytelling Tips

When sharing stories, remember that people listen to information that fits with what they already believe. And when I say *people*, I don't just mean other people. I mean all people. Especially you… and a little bit me. The stronger our beliefs, the more the information and evidence we receive will be molded to fit our preexisting beliefs. We also discount information that doesn't fit with our preexisting beliefs.

Therefore, if clients believe that agents squish the market information and statistics to manipulate their clients, they will be out for blood anytime you disagree with their interpretation of the statistics. Sharing a story that confirms their preexisting beliefs about the market and *then* telling a story that you feel better represents the market is a much better way to convince them than outright refuting what they believe. Boldly telling clients that they're wrong will not work—they won't believe you and you'll be perceived to be on pushy-sales autopilot. Take the time to validate their beliefs, though, and you'll be positioned to educate them as the guiding expert that you are.

No One Is Immune

When I have been in the market to buy a home, I have not been much of a freaked-out buyer prone to buyer's remorse. I will reveal, however, that one of my real estate partners/best friends was a complete basket case when he was contemplating making an

ADVANCE READING COPY. NOT FOR SALE.

offer on a house in which he planned to live. He had bought and sold many homes and properties without incident, so his lack of assuredness came as a surprise to both of us.

This is why I know that I must always relate to my wacka-doodledooskie buyers—one day I will be one. I will wake up with buyer's remorse when I scored a great deal in a competitive bidding environment. Or when I don't get the house, I will re-gret not offering more when someone else paid more than I had the—what's the equivalent of balls for a woman?—guts to bid. I will mentally vilify the sellers by only relating to them in the context of an opponent.

Knowing that you are not immune to this potential onslaught of emotions is just what you need to remain relatable. Don't think you're so hot and emotionally stable, because someone, somewhere knows the real you. And all your clients—whether they've shown a propensity for craziness or not—are at risk for experiencing this gamut of emotions.

When you have new buyer clients, go through all the emotions you have seen your buyers experience. Point out how buyers like to vilify sellers, and don't join that war. Stories, stories, stories work better than preaching. The minute you are surprised at your buyers' emotions, you know you didn't prepare them appropriately and those emotions will get the best of all of you. The minute you tell your buyers that the sellers are being unreasonable assholes, you have let go of the steering wheel of facilitation and are careening toward the dreaded role of crash-test dummy.

In addition to stories about your own adventures in real es-tate share some stories about your friends' and family members' screwups. You might find that sharing others' mishaps is a good way to instill a sense of brilliance and self-satisfaction in your client. It could also get your client to open up and add one of her juicy stories to your collection.

True**STORIES**

I still laugh when I think of this story. One of my fabu-lous clients, Jamie, was under contract on a home that needed a lot of sexing up. She was a wonderful rehabber. We shared a

ADVANCE READING COPY. NOT FOR SALE.

vision for the type of home this one could become, so I sent her to a showroom to check out some cabinetry and other materials.

While at the showroom with her two-year-old, she had to use the restroom. When she attempted to flush the toilet and wash her hands, she realized she had inadvertently used the showroom model bathroom that never had any intention of being hooked up to plumbing. As her two-year-old attempted to open the door, revealing her whereabouts and her whatshedid, she plotted her exit. Jamie ended up quietly slithering over to the real bathroom, from which she exited as if nothing had happened. Then she headed across the showroom and immediately out the door.

Okay, this story may not directly relate to your clients' buying and selling questions, but it teaches the life skill of checking the plumbing in showrooms and vacant houses before…you know.

Sometimes I will tell you what you learn. Sometimes I won't.

SORTAFacts™

99% of buyers found that sellers chose their offer most often when the earnest money deposits were, in fact, money—as opposed to a deposit of a different sort (see above story).

—Courtesy of Sortafact

True**STORIES**

Tenants can crack me up. I was showing one of my duplex listings that was full of a bunch of delightful women-lovin' women. These tenants also loved to embarrass potential buyers away from buying and perhaps kicking them out. I often enjoy photos of women in various states of repose, so their posters didn't bother me. Of course, the tenants were banking on my octogenarian husband-and-wife clients not having the same taste as me. As I showed Ida and Sol the bedroom, my clients gasped in…erotic delight at the photos and accompanying goody-drawer apparatuses strewn about.

"Oh, these tenants must be spitfires," Ida and Sol said as they continued to thoroughly check out the investment opportunity.

ADVANCE READING COPY. NOT FOR SALE.

Although they were not quite inspired enough to make an offer, they assured me that they were indeed inspired. I, for once, didn't ask.

SORTAꜰacts™

Pill-poppin' octogenarians are out-sexing their placebo-induced septuagenarian counterparts 6 to 1. Chinese manufacturers are responding by increasing the font size of *low, medium,* and *high* on many toy imports.

—Courtesy of Sortafact

TrueSTORIES

My partner and I were conducting an inspection of an apartment building, and all the tenants had been appropriately notified. One of the units had one of those posters on the wall where you have to stare, blurry eyed, for a long time before a 3-D picture emerges. Remember those? Between the poster and me was a large, unmade, lumpy bed. As I leaned over, staring at the poster to try to see what secret dinosaur or animal lurked inside (and I was always horrible at seeing those), a bare ass rolled within inches of my face. It was tight and male and twenty-something, but still, it startled the hell out of me. I jumped back and might have screamed a little—but just a little. What would you have done? *(Note: I was not entirely alone, and I was already entirely married.)*

For many years I have been asking real estate professionals and regular folk to share their stories about real estate. I have seen or heard about enough private peccadilloes to make me feel boring and to give me good ideas. I share these few delightful tidbits to let you know that real estate adventures can be very funny, and it is perfectly okay not to take the profession or yourself too damn seriously. Sharing such stories with your clients can make the adventure a joy and a snappy delight.

ADVANCE READING COPY. NOT FOR SALE.

CHAPTER 9

VOYEURISM

One of the best things about real estate is the opportunity to hide behind the trench coat of your job requirements to satisfy your inner sneak-peep desires. Use your senses. If you sort of can't see, get laser surgery. If you still can't see, listen and smell. If you can't listen and smell, you're worse off than Helen Keller, so rely on pity. Garnering pity could be its own chapter, but it's not, so you'll have to wait for that lesson to be spelled out in your hand.

Walking into a house to preview it or show it to a client is as good as it gets when it comes to discovery. Real estate is the only industry I can think of in which you can legally enter the privacy of the very home of the people with whom you will be negotiating. Sometimes you even get to witness how they live without them even being there to assess you back. You can gawk with impunity. If you watched the TV show *House*, where the doctors routinely broke into patients' homes to unravel medical mysteries, you know how easy you have it. Even Dr. House knew that breaking in is easier than acquiring a search warrant. And a lockbox key is infinitely easier than that! Don't squander.

And be sure to pay attention in your role of voyeur. You'll need those details later.

SORTAfacts™

Probable cause is 93% harder to prove than an insatiable curiosity. An insatiable curiosity fulfills 53% of the requirements to obtain a lockbox key.

—Courtesy of Sortafact

True**STORIES**

I'll never forget the hapless salesperson, Kenny, who was smart enough to request he present his clients' offer in person to me *and* my sellers. Before getting to the dollars and cents of the deal, he artfully explained, with a requisite church-lady grin, that his buyers clearly saw the love that the sellers had given to the home. In fairness, they *had* given it love. He then dramatically pulled out a photo of an admittedly darling family with 2.5 children, matching white WWJD-emblazoned polo shirts, and a floppy-eared dog named Aslan. Upon noting these details, I was fearful of where this presentation might go, so I tried, to no avail, to gently steer the conversation back to the dollars and cents of the deal.

He continued, "That picture window was absolutely made for a huge Christmas tree, and these buyers envision singing many delightful carols around the piano right by that window."

At that point, a little bit of vomit came to my mouth, but as the facilitating professional I am, I swallowed hard and kept my face as pleasantly neutral as could be.

"They love that fact that all the families in the neighborhood belong to Holy Guacamole Church down the street," he said with deal-sealing satisfaction on his face.

I was baffled by how the hell Kenny had not noticed the lack of Christmas decorations in this home at Christmastime. Then the doorbell rang as the second agent arrived.

As Mr. Church Lady left, the sellers and I graciously greeted the second agent, Rita, and invited her to present her offer to us. Rita lovingly complimented them on how well they had maintained and updated the home. Check. She commented on a rowing trophy and ribbon that my clients' daughter had just won and mentioned that her buyers' daughter had just started rowing lessons. Sly. She clearly watched for a reaction from my sellers and saw that they were nice but ready to get on with the show-me-the money part of the deal. She reacted by focusing on the buyers' strong down payment, their qualification with the bank, her confidence in their love and understanding of the house, and the strength of their ability to close. All the while, she was spending her energy

ADVANCE READING COPY. NOT FOR SALE.

watching and reacting to the sellers. We listened, and my sellers smiled and nodded.

When Rita was done presenting, she asked, "Do you have any questions?" The sellers looked to me, and I asked some questions pertinent to the deal. The sellers then asked if the buyers' daughter had considered joining a particular rowing club. The deal had virtually been sealed.

During the post-presentation wrap-up, my sellers and I discussed the fact that the second offer was less financially enticing. But they were adamant that they had to sell to the second family, the one with the rowing offspring.

There were clearly some discrimination landmines to avoid, so I continued to talk with my clients. When the observant Rita proactively called back to increase her offer (she had correctly read those tea leaves), it was a done deal.

SORTAFacts™

People say opposites attract. For the most part, that is a lie. We just don't pay attention enough to know what alike looks like.

—Courtesy of Sortafact

Culture Shock

We all have ideas about how other cultures differ from ours. I've been asked, "Have you ever worked with a Chinese client? Have you ever worked with a client from the Middle East? Have you ever worked with someone from the South? New York?"

I love the way we so often seem to think we know what working with *that* kind of client means but we don't stop to think about what we should do to successfully make a deal happen. We'd rather bitch about the cultural differences—or, more accurately, the assumed cultural differences that we are untrained in or unwilling to deal with.

Cultural differences are not universal. Thinking they are creates a trap when you give more weight to cultural generalities than to personal characteristics. Being a great voyeur will prevent you from spewing deal-killing bile.

ADVANCE READING COPY. NOT FOR SALE.

SECRETSforClients

The best technique for touring homes with your agent is called Start Deep and Go Shallow. I learned it from the Kama Sutra and have found it especially helpful for buyers. At first, look beyond the personal effects in the home. Figure out if you can make the house your home. Once you decide to put the house on your mental short list, shift from looking past the shit to looking at the shit. Look closely *through* the owners' stuff and at the house. This will enhance your ability to work with your agent to negotiate appropriately.

TrueSTORIES

A friend, Fran, once complained to me that "ethnic" (her word) buyers, who did not want agent representation, had approached her about her listing. These buyers wanted to reduce the price of the home by reducing the portion of the commission that the listing agent would share with a cooperating broker, thereby paying themselves a commission. This is not legal in many states. It is also annoying to real estate professionals even though it's very enticing to some buyers.

The reason I point out the agent's reference to ethnicity is that it really was pertinent to Fran in this instance. Her perception of the offer was influenced by what she perceived those particular clients' ethnic norms to be. Her perception might have been completely ill founded, or it might have been spot on. The point is, she made an assumption based on their ethnicity. Period.

Let's face it—we all like a deal, and you really are a schmuck if you don't try for one, so it's hardly fair to criticize anyone or any ethnic group for trying to save a buck or two. How you as an agent respond, however, should be cloaked in a basic understanding of the person awaiting that response. Ethnicity and cultural background are two of the many aspects of people's characteristics, and you should, at the very least, be aware of them.

In this case, Fran was incensed at the nerve of these particular buyers, who kept writing what she perceived as a low offer and

ADVANCE READING COPY. NOT FOR SALE.

insisting she reduce her commission. She argued with them at length and bitched about their audacity to her sellers. The sellers were pissed too, of course. Why my friend thought that bringing the sellers to her pissed-off side was a good idea is beyond me. Sure, sharing the heat of your ire will cool *you* off but not the situation. We are not hired to fuel the fire—fanning those flames is rarely in the best interest of the client.

Telling these particular buyers that they could not do this was a complete waste of time. Instead, they needed to be told, "Thank you so much for asking about the commission. Commission is determined by a contract I have with sellers, so that won't be part of our negotiation, although I totally appreciate your asking. We are excited to receive an offer from you. Yes. Thank you." When buyers continue to discuss the commission—and the persistent ones will—it is best to keep a positive spin by telling them what they *can* do (submit an offer) rather than what they *can't* do (affect commission).

Smiles and nods are commonplace in our polite American culture. We use them throughout conversations to signify agreement or disagreement. In other cultures smiles and nods mean something entirely different. They can signify that the listener heard or did not hear, but there might be no indication of agreement or disagreement. A lack of gestures also has different meanings across cultures. People unfamiliar with these differences can leave a negotiation with the impression that it has gone far more favorably than, in fact, it has. A basic understanding of key cultural differences can help you avoid looking like a complete dipshit. Acknowledge the smiles and nods from across the table like the happy-bunny American that you are, but be aware that the nods might really be signifying, "That's all, folks."

SECRETSfor**Clients**

Don't write flowery letters to give to your agent to try to convince sellers to accept your offer. In addition to the fact that they are almost always annoying, much of what you want to share

ADVANCE READING COPY. NOT FOR SALE.

is information that can technically be discriminatory (e.g., family status, source of income, race, religion, disability). This varies state by state. Although those ass-kissing letters often provide great content for snarky bloggers, they backfire more often than not when it comes to buying property.

Volumes have been written on cross-cultural communication. If you're not too lazy, you should certainly buy some of those books. If the laziness kicks in after you buy a book or two, put them on your shelf for reading years later when globalization has made a mockery of the cultural differences referenced in those books. It's kind of like the old instructional manuals for being a good wife—iron *this*, motherfucker. In the meantime, here are some things to consider:

- Listening: Active listening is much different from hearing. Use your senses and listen to what people *mean* versus what they *say*.
- Appointments: Time has different values across cultures. Try to schedule an exact time for a watch repair in Italy and you'll see why wine is such an important aspect of Italian culture.
- Personal and environmental space: Consider the importance some people place on feng shui (the placement of stuff) and others on being close talkers (the placement of self).
- Touching: Placing your hand on some places of other people's bodies can be highly offensive…or tantalizing.
- Eye contact: This one can mean a lot of different things. The direct eye contact that we're taught as children could be culturally inappropriate with some clients—good news if you're on "the spectrum."

I have had several clients insist on the price adding up to eighteen, which represents *Chai,* or life. Other clients have been into astronomy, where numbers are vitally important. Some cultures are very uncomfortable with negotiation. While I have a soft spot in my heart for these people, I find them hardest to relate to. You have to prepare these clients for when the patron on the other end might have more fun in the wheeling-and-dealing souk

ADVANCE READING COPY. NOT FOR SALE.

environment, like I do. And, yes, I'm Jewish, but I know plenty of my peeps who prefer the expediency of putting a deal together over obtaining the absolute best price.

SORTAFacts™

Top negotiators understand that when their question is answered with a no and they don't like that answer, they can slightly tweak the question until they get the answer they want. However, a study concluded at an impressive think-tank has found results surprising to some religious fanatics and rapists: no matter what someone is wearing at a fraternity party, "No!" always means "No!"

—*Courtesy of Sortafact*

I confess that looking at pretty homes was never the real estate draw for me. Actually, I'm not really interested in that very much…at all. I much prefer adding up the clues to find out the juicy details of homeowners' lives. I can only imagine what a great shoe salesperson I would be if I could tour peoples' homes and closets, but no shoe salesperson ever gets that opportunity. Real estate professionals *do* get this chance. Don't squander.

TrueSTORIES

I once baffled my buyers by predicting exactly why a particular seller was looking to sell. All I did was walk around and see high design everywhere I looked. The closets were filled with neatly pressed men's threads, all adorned by notable designer labels. The other half of the closet had a sparse smattering of women's clothing. She had left the building. He had left the closet. 'Nuf said.

ADVANCE READING COPY. NOT FOR SALE.

CHAPTER 10

MOOBMENT OB DA PEOPLE

TRIALS&Titillations™

Pull out your sleeping bag and plan a slumber party in your parked car. Pop in your Bob Marley *Legend* CD and crank up the volume. Wake up and look around. If your car battery is not dead, ask yourself if you would otherwise be comfortable shuttling a client around in your car. If this makes no sense to you, refer to this chapter as: "What It Takes to Move People."

Always require a sit-down conversation with new clients. Always. If they're out of town, sit-n-Skype. Call it a buyer consultation if you want to sound official. It is a good way to discern the serious buyers from the ax murderers and friendless folks.

If they are too busy to have a meeting for such a serious transaction but still want to tour homes, then you must decide whether or not your prospective clients have *Taxicab Confession* potential—because you won't likely see a commission and you have to get *something* out of schlepping them around. Decide judiciously whether they are worth hearing their deepest secrets, seeing certain parts of their bodies, and hearing how those parts work. As much as I've been entertained by some of the confessions that have occurred in my car, there's no denying that the lack of commitment to an initial meeting usually leads to a lack of commitment in buying.

SORTAfacts™

Real estate professionals who fear requiring commitment end up with cheating partners and cheating clients 10 to 1 over those who do require commitment. They also tend to be poorer.

—Courtesy of Sortafact

Behavior Prediction

You know that adage "The best way to predict future behavior is to determine past behavior"? That is empirically proven to be true.

If you meet a married man who was schtuping the person who became his second wife while married to the first, and you think that the reason he is whisking you off to Tahiti is because you are the true love of his life, you might want to think again. No matter how unique he finds those cool Ping-Pong tricks you learned in Thailand and how much he loves you and only you forever for those tricks, you should consider his past behavior before accepting his marriage proposal. Just consider.

The same goes for working with a client who has hated, sued, and engaged in slanderous Facebook postings referencing every salesperson she has worked with. Either she has horrible taste in picking sales professionals or she's an asshole. If you're a masochist, she might just be the client for you.

A little empirical data tells us that salience and intention are the two factors that help predict people's behavior (*see* "Bit O' Science"). You should, therefore, always ask about your clients' intentions, and you should always delve into their past behavior. You will be amazed at your predicting skills. If you're curious, ask. If you are not curious, then don't complain about being surprised by their behavior.

SORTAFacts™

86% of all surprises are not surprises at all. The surprised party was just not paying attention.

—Courtesy of Sortafact

SECRETSFor**Clients**

If your agent does not insist on a buyer consultation, you could be gearing up for a hoedown at the Time-Wastin' Coral. If you're bored and voyeuristic, you might enjoy seeing a shit-ton

ADVANCE READING COPY. NOT FOR SALE.

of properties that bear no resemblance to something you would ever dream of owning. If you're not, find an agent who is smart enough to take the time to consult with you before he puts your ass in his car. Chances are, he is too busy to waste his time and too respectful to waste yours.

The Interrogation

One of the goals of a buyer consultation is to predict behavior as much as possible so you can successfully help your buyer.

First, schedule the buyer consultation to take place in your office. If the buyers want you to see their home, you can save that for the second date.

I love to ask several mundane questions and then throw a slightly inappropriate curveball to get to the real answer. Ask:

- What made you decide to contact me? (Be sure to ask this in a nice-smelling room or your facial expression can give the wrong impression.)
- Are you the type of person who likes to do a lot of research before making a purchase?
- How were your past buying/selling experiences?
- Did you have to make a lot of offers before you were able to land your loft in San Francisco?
- Were you happy with the salespeople you've worked with in the past?
- Are you familiar with how real estate works here/now?
- How long did you and your husband date before you knew you were pregnant? (I was just making sure you're paying attention.)
- Why did you move here? Where did you move from?
- Do you spend a lot of time looking at real estate porn (*see* "Porn")? (*Note: I have used this question a lot.*)

Why, why, why? What, what, what? How, how, how? Ask every question you can think of. Listen carefully and watch body language. I cannot emphasize too much how asking questions of your clients will not only inform you of their intentions but will also clarify their intentions for themselves. Really, it's a public service.

ADVANCE READING COPY. NOT FOR SALE.

After you ask, listen. Write stuff down. When you write while people talk, they think you're really listening to them. Get them to state their intentions out loud. Also, pay attention to your own body language. Recall that study where you learned to use active listening skills to draw the cute professor to your side of the room. Lean forward and look in the eyes of the speaker and slightly smile (beware of cultural differences and amblyopia). Nod while you write. This is the start of their association of the word *yes* with you. Deep.

SECRETSforClients

By now you know it's important to be asked the right questions in order for the real estate professional to fully understand you as a client. The rock star–level insight is that the right questions are vital for *you* to understand yourself as well. If an agent doesn't ask you the right questions, she's robbing you of the opportunity to make the best decisions for yourself. Don't be a robbery victim!

SORTAFacts™

Studies at fancy graduate schools prove that respondents orally answering questions are 84% more likely to report that their listener heard them when the listener is pretending to write notes than when the listener is staring into the respondent's eyes.
—*Courtesy of Sortafact*

Couples
When working with a couple, it is imperative to find out how they make decisions together. This gets difficult in the fundamentalist communities where polygamy is an accepted practice, so if you're targeting that market, you really have your work cut out for you. Even when you direct your questions to the timid husband, his answers might be influenced by the domineering wife. Try to help quieter people tell their stories. Then listen to the version from the one who won't shut up. If they each are empowered to write

ADVANCE READING COPY. NOT FOR SALE.

down their wants and needs, you can add the mousy husband's desires to those of his battle-ax wife, thereby getting a clearer picture of what the couple wants and how the buying process will likely proceed.

If they seem like a horrible couple, be extra careful that you sell them something that will be easy to resell in the near future. Try also to stay in touch with these bickering clients so that when the divorce is final, you are able to list and sell their home *and* sell each of them another property. Boom shakalaka.

True**STORIES**

A couple met my buff Realtor friend, Jessica for a buyer consultation meeting. Both were smart and had insisted on interviewing several agents, as they made very clear that they'd had a traumatic experience with their last agent. It was hard to determine who the dominant decision maker was because neither of them shut up long enough for the other to have a clear shot at the communication goal. They would have fit in well in my family.

As Jessica attempted to find out if they were reasonable in feeling traumatized by their previous agent, she asked a lot of questions. Their answers seemed to indicate that their previous agent had provided rock star representation, so my friend started to consider that this couple had unreasonable expectations. They tried to assure her that there was no way that they would have a similar problem working with her. Regardless, she was mentally planning her brush-off when she noticed that, as they kept chattering they also looked guilty and uncomfortable. She prodded further by asking, "What, specifically, about your previous agent really traumatized you?"

The nervous, chatty couple slyly glanced at each other and explained. They had been touring homes with their agent when they entered a great house with a huge waterbed in the center of the master bedroom. Something deep within their portly buyers' agent compelled her to swan dive into the center of the water bed—where she remained stuck…for several hours…until the seller came home to help the couple hoist her out of the bed.

ADVANCE READING COPY. NOT FOR SALE.

Buyer consultations can provide more than just the necessary tools to achieve great buyer representation. If you change the names to protect the innocent, they can also provide excellent stories to achieve cocktail party stardom.

List o' Desires

Many buyers come to their first consultation with a list of wants and needs. When it's in the form of a spreadsheet, ask the buyers what high-tech company they work for. You will then get an idea of how the inspection negotiations will go when you're at that point.

You need to do two things with the list:

1. Appreciate the list.
2. Question the list.

If your clients say (or the list says) that they must have a certain feature, ask them what-ifs: If all of the other aspects are perfect and that specific feature is missing, should you tell them about the property? If they say yes, then you know that the lack of the identified feature is not a nonstarter. If they indicate that you should not, under any circumstances, try to sell them something without that specific feature, tell them that you absolutely will not. But...follow that with permission for them to approach you with something that does not have that feature. You always want to give them the okay to contradict what they told you while also knowing that you will keep your promise to them. I say, "You can always call me about a property that costs $X over your stated price, but I will not initiate that conversation. Oh, and I will make fun of you for stepping outside your stated parameters, so just know that in advance."

When they say they want four bedrooms, ask them why. Why? is a way more important question than, what? Don't ask in a way that challenges what they want but rather in a way that defines *why* they want what they say they want. They might want to use one of those four bedrooms as an office, and the perfect three-bedroom-plus-a-den condo will never show up in your four-bedroom search.

ADVANCE READING COPY. NOT FOR SALE.

A private basement with an outside entrance can be very important to someone who likes black masks that cover the whole face and zip up the middle. Don't pretend you don't know what I'm talking about here, you *Fifty Shades of Grey* addict. Knowing this can be so much more interesting than falling for their suggestion that it's "for the kids."

Asking them the right questions about whether a family room off the kitchen is necessary or a bonus room upstairs would suffice can provide the difference between hearing about the latest in latex and handcuffs and *Beethoven for Babies*. You will better serve your clients by knowing them better, and you will better serve your curiosity by finding out what makes your clients compelling.

The better you sniff, the more you will find that the adage "Buyers are liars" should be changed to "Salespeople suck at getting to the truth." Too bad that doesn't rhyme.

SECRETSforClients

Agents who don't insist on buyer consultations generally don't find out that the adage "Buyers are liars" is not really true. Here's a very valuable secret that you must know: the way an agent conducts a buyer consultation is an indication of whether you will end up with what you really want and need versus what you initially think you will want and need. For some of you, there will be no distinction between the two. If that's the case, congratulations to you. You're a hyperevolved *Homo sapien, sapien, sapien a-go-go sapien*.

Can You Believe This Shit?

Don't forget that your new clients are going to be assessing their first impression of you too. Unless you spent high school truly embracing the Bob Marley lifestyle with all-too-frequent herbal therapies, you should have learned about the importance of first impressions. If you didn't learn this, you certainly know about "Exodus: Moobment ob da People" and how hard it is to get people moobin'…off the couch. It's no secret that getting buyers moobed is also hard and goes beyond the zoom-zoom in your car.

ADVANCE READING COPY. NOT FOR SALE.

First, clean your car, for god's sake. Second, map out your tour rather than relying on your GPS alone. You don't want to be driving the long, circuitous route through the ugly neighborhoods that your GPS bitch will lead you on. There are numerous stories of people following their GPS bosses to their ultimate doom. One guy in Switzerland followed his up a steep mountain and had to be retrieved by helicopter. Many others have followed their sneaky GPS voices into large bodies of water…and drowned. These stories are often not even urban legend. I know, I read about this on the internet, itself.

I have never been that into cars. I remember when, as a teenager, my friend bragged to me about a certain car that she was getting (or maybe it was a car that her father was getting) and I had to ask her, "Is that fancy?" She was incredibly disappointed that her bragging had fallen on deaf ears. When I first got into real estate, my husband told me to get a nice car, and I accused him of being a snob. Later, after hearing clients comment on other agents' cars, I realized that clients relate to the image of your car. My SUV with a ski rack on top was great for my outdoorsy clients, but it did take some 'splaining to my greener clients. I would borrow my husband's Prius for touring my greenies—well, at least I did when my ass could forgive the lack of a seat warmer.

I just read a Yelp comment with advice for real estate agents. Aside from cleaning your car, it also suggested that you wear a bra. Now, I can see how an agent might be able to get away without one if she's meeting with a certain type of super-sensible-shoe-wearing client… Well, no, the more I think about it, not really. If you have boobs, wear a bra, please.

Know-It-Alls

Your clients will also be summing up how much you know. You should do that too. Find out what your clients know. If they know more than you (and they might), that's okay. But it's not okay for you *not* to know that, because you will invariably look like an idiot. You can fill in the gaps between what you should know and what they know. Don't be didactic. No one likes a preacher. Okay, some do, but you'll be too busy working on Sundays to really know those people.

ADVANCE READING COPY. NOT FOR SALE.

Explain how you work. Don't expect someone from outside your industry to truly understand its idiosyncrasies. If you only work with people who sign a contract to work with you, tell them that. If you want people who are loyal to you, insist on that. Make them feel that you have as much skin in the game as they do, and tell them why you require what you require. For each stipulation you have, there should be a benefit to the client. Clients will be convinced to adhere to the requirement when they understand how it helps them too—not just you. Most people do not want to commit to giving more than they'll get. They generally like themselves more than they like you…or they're in therapy.

SECRETSforClients

As a prospective client at a buyer consultation meeting, the questions *you* ask can have a huge impact on your real estate future. Ask:

- Are you full time? (You'll find out whether or not you will miss out on your dream property while your agent is restocking the bag-o-snacks rack at the local convenience store.)
- How do you find out about properties not listed on the internet? (You'll learn if the agent works from a virtual office and if you want that.)
- Do most agents suck? (Finding out how they feel about other agents can give you insight into whether any offers that you make can be positively or negatively affected by agent relationships.)
- What's your incentive to negotiate the best price for me? (You'll find out how well they avoid getting defensive.)

Then listen. How agents respond to your tough questions in a buyer consultation meeting will be a great indicator of what kind of representation you can expect.

Buyer consultations should be moving experiences for everyone involved. If you start off on the right beat, you're likely to feel the jam through the rest of the process too.

ADVANCE READING COPY. NOT FOR SALE.

CHAPTER 11

PORN

In the precomputerized days of real estate, people were required to physically get out of their chairs. It was exhausting enough for agents to run to the phone to answer it all the time, let alone to pick up clients and take them to all the houses they wanted to see. I'm weary just thinking about it. People would talk to their friends and compare notes on how many houses they had to see before deciding to buy. It almost became a bragging right to claim to have rejected a large number of homes before deciding to buy a particular house. When I was pregnant, I would show houses all morning and then pull off to the side of the road to take a nap in my car before picking up the next customers to tour them around until our stomachs were begging for dinner.

Now, due to the proliferation of real estate websites and applications, our clients can see dozens or hundreds or even thousands of homes, inside and out, all without getting dressed—just like porn. For years, real estate professionals feared that this would lead to our extinction. Little did we know that the proliferation of websites for real estate professionals would allow those same clients to find and choose agents and brokers while commando. While this may seem to say that you can relax, beware. You could easily become obsolete if your clients know real estate porn better than you do.

SORTAFacts™

Recent studies have placed real estate porn only 32% behind sexual porn as causes of marital discontent.

—*Courtesy of Sortafact*

Numbers Game

In the days before real estate porn, clients would often stifle their enthusiasm for a particularly good home prospect by indicating that they felt they might not have seen enough homes. When I was fresh in the business, I would immediately try to fix the problem. Fix, fix, fix—that's what we do, right? In the event that I knew that we had seen fewer properties than my average client required, I would masochistically suggest we go out and see more property.

But what if the house that we were in was the *one*? By responding to the feeling instead of prying deeper into where that feeling was coming from, I was giving them permission to cater to their buyer fear, and I was contributing to my agent ass with too much car time. I was also jeopardizing a great love connection between my clients and their prospective home.

SECRETSforClients

It's not a bad idea to embrace real estate porn. Real estate is a huge part of most financial portfolios, and you likely want to feature it in yours too, so you should have a clue about what's out there. It's also good cocktail conversation. Be careful trusting those sites too much, though, as many provide inaccurate information. All too often the details—price, size, school district—are outright wrong. Don't fall for these tricks any more than you would believe that every porn actor is a porn star. Real estate porn can skew your view on reality. Just like regular porn, too much of any good thing can take over your life.

And don't think watching real estate porn makes you an agent. There is so much more that a great professional does for you, so you don't need to be too proud if you find your own property. Go ahead and pat yourself on the back, but don't kid yourself that the real work has even started.

SORTAFacts™

Agent ass of the car-seat kind has been replaced by agent ass of the office-seat kind, which enjoys a 76% correlation

ADVANCE READING COPY. NOT FOR SALE.

with the preponderance of online real estate porn.

— Courtesy of Sortafact

It's good to ask clients how many properties they think they should see before committing to the right home. Once they start to put an actual number on the process, together you can illuminate how arbitrary and worthless those numbers are when you have found a potential match.

Sharing past experiences can be helpful. Talk about the tiring old days when the only way buyers could see property was to spend a bazillion hours physically touring properties. This works best when rocking in a quilt-covered chair with a corn pipe between your teeth. Stand briskly as you contrast that with today's more efficient, smarter culture and clients' ability to control so much more about their search. Explain how it's easier to see more houses while physically visiting fewer now that we live in a share-the-knowledge culture. If you are new to the business, ask some of the more seasoned veterans to share their stories so you can let your clients know how much better they have it today. Get your patrons excited about the way it is, not nostalgic for the oh-so-primitive past.

Also on the subject of numbers, it used to be super important to pay attention to primacy and recency (*see* "Bit O' Science"), strategically showing the best house first. That was the clients' first exposure to the house. That's still a good tactic to keep in mind, but now with the advent of real estate porn, clients can be intimately familiar with a property long before the first physical date. And it's easy to see the lustful signs in your clients' eyes after showing very few properties. Unless you're really discrete, try to stay focused on the eyes.

In the event that your clients are attacked with the feeling of making a hasty decision, you can again ask how many properties they would have to see before feeling comfortable proceeding with the right one. Then you can casually toss out the fact that thankfully this number has been long surpassed by the sheer amount of time spent hovering and clicking around on real estate porn.

ADVANCE READING COPY. NOT FOR SALE.

True**STORIES**

One of my best friends and my business partner at one time, Ned, recently found himself acquiring a legitimate internet porn company (how *does* that happen?). You can imagine his gyrations as he proudly (and probably a little sheepishly) told his parents of his acquisition. His plan was to make this a short-term endeavor, a turn-around situation while strictly working from behind the desk...at a computer...crunching numbers and identifying business development opportunities. Is there no way to say this without sexual implication? Jeez, people.

Ned is also an avid political junkie who spends a lot of spare time reading political blogs. Every time he was sneaking in some of his *Huffington Post* political porn and another employee walked by his desk, he would have to quickly change his screen to traditional porn. They couldn't have the boss looking at inappropriate sites during office hours.

What does this have to do with real estate? Nothing except I love this story from my ex–real estate partner, and it helps remind me to stay on task.

TRIALS&Ti**tillations**™

Look up your own house on as many real estate sites as possible. Marvel at the invasion of privacy. Then invade the privacy of three people with whom you've slept by looking up information on their houses. Realize how productive you would be if you didn't waste time on this kind of porn. Repeat every three months.

The job of a real estate salesperson has changed and will continue to change. All the books on vetting and hiring a good real estate agent used to say that one of the key duties of an agent was to find the house for the buyer. Actually, most of them still say that. *Home Buying for Dummies* advises that you ask the agent's references if the agent was the one who found the home. *Cool Careers for Dummies*, however, says that online house hunting will

ADVANCE READING COPY. NOT FOR SALE.

eliminate much of the work that we real estate agents do. I would argue that online house hunting has eliminated the amount of time that our buyers spend on traditional porn.

Although I have nothing against porn—at all—it's nice to diversify, and looking at real estate can be an interesting diversion. It is also green; the amount of gas we used to burn and the time we used to spend driving our clients around can now be spent on other productive ways to better represent our clients…and also on porn, if we so choose.

ADVANCE READING COPY. NOT FOR SALE.

CHAPTER 12

LET THEM DO THE UNDRESSING

The almost sexiest people look better in skimpy clothes than they do naked. Note that I said the *almost* sexiest people because, face it, some people do look good naked. But most look better scantily clad. This has to do with the element of discovery. Allow your clients to fantasize. You owe them that.

Real Estate Strip Tease

You're standing in the kitchen of a home that you absolutely believe would work well for your buyers. All throughout the tour of the home, you've looked for stars in their eyes and you *sort of* saw them. When you got to the kitchen, an important room for these particular buyers, you saw the stars extinguish. All of this assumes you left enough time to actually watch your clients experience the house. Otherwise you have missed the ocular astrological signs that help you sell. If you have spent the entire time pointing out the wonderful, exotic African Owajameen hardwoods and the Brazilian rainforest heated marble bathroom floors and the updated, air-tight windows, you have stolen from your client.

Things That You Feel Need to Be Pointed Out…But Don't
- Anything that the patrons can obviously see

Oh sure, you think you're informing your clients and establishing yourself as an authority with a running diatribe. You worked so hard to acquire the knowledge that allows very few other professionals to distinguish between African Owajameen wood and the unique wood found only in the trees that grow adjacent to the pyramids in Egypt. How can you not share your brilliance? You must be more subtly didactic or you'll not only steal your clients' sense of discovery but you'll also miss key buyer-desire clues. You will look like an ass.

Back to that kitchen scenario. In this scene it is actually a good kitchen in a great house, but it could do with, quite frankly, more than just a lipstick-level makeover. Its needs are obvious to you, and you know the ultimate reveal could make this kitchen a winner and this home worthy of an offer. See if this can become obvious to your buyer without your obvious help.

TRIALS&Titillations™

Rest your hand gingerly on the wall that annoyingly divides this galley kitchen from the dining room, preventing an open *Iron Chef*–worthy culinary arena. Run your hand up and down the wall while saying, "What could be done to open up this kitchen?" If your clients are particularly dense, rub that wall harder… Okay, I'm back. Where was I?

I love the moment when the clients come up with the brilliant idea of removing a wall, thereby opening up the kitchen. I like to praise them for their insightfulness by suggesting that a good contractor might provide an estimate of the cost of wall removal. Would they be interested in arranging that to take place during their inspection period? Because the inspection period logically only follows an accepted offer, there is another subtle message here. Sly.

SORTAFacts™

Many very important and empirical studies have proven that 82% of people getting in the mood for some lovin' prefer to remove at least some of their partner's clothing themselves.

—Courtesy of Sortafact

ADVANCE READING COPY. NOT FOR SALE.

SECRETS for Clients

A good test of your agent's sincerity is whether he immediately tries to overcome your every objection. Lob a couple slow-pitch, easy objections to see if your agent swings the solution bat. If he is too eager with that bat, it might mean he thinks you're stupid. It might mean he wants the sale a little too much. Depending on how obviously lame the objection is, it might mean that he can't take a joke.

True STORIES

I was holding an open house when a sixty-something, skeptical, elegant couple came in the house. Their faces alone said, "We know way more than you, and we're way richer than you, and we really don't need your help." Having worn that mask myself, I liked them immediately.

I greeted them more formally and less eagerly than I would just anybody and allowed them to enter on their own terms. Just minutes later, they let down a wee bit of their shield and started to give the home a serious chance. I could see that their demographic was a perfect match for this home. Yeah, yeah, we're not supposed to pigeonhole demographical information like this, but sometimes it's just too obvious. I began to get my hopes up.

Right then, a broker friend, Ethyl, came into the open house to say hi and see the home. This broker friend has a graduate degree from Overcoming Every Objection University. When this couple resurfaced in the main room where I was casually yet strategically perched, my helpful broker friend was ready to pounce.

Clearly, these two people were size-of-dining-room queens (you know, size queens—liking them sizable) because they were discussing this very fact among themselves. Immediately, my friend put her graduate degree to work. She told them how they could do this or that and then proceeded to lay out a remodel of every common room to accommodate what she perceived as their objection.

ADVANCE READING COPY. NOT FOR SALE.

I wanted to punch her in the vulva. Instead, I just took her aside and said that I would kill her in cold blood if she didn't leave immediately and wait for me for a post–open house cocktail. There, I would proceed to rescind any invitation to any of my open houses, in perpetuity.

Once Ethyl had personally removed all of the potential objections from the potential buyers' minds, their work was over. They were no longer engaging in the process, so they left. They had been the perfect kind of buyers for this home, and I had observed signals indicating that they were seriously shopping for a house and definitely shopping for a broker. My friend's graduate degree in overcoming objections fucked it up for me on both counts. I shouldn't be too hard on her, though—it took me years to become a dropout from the same school o' thought.

Many studies have shown that when people discover important information on their own, in the presence of someone else, that someone else is perceived to be a beneficent benefactor. Salespeople who do this are assisting their clients in strengthening their bias of superior intellect. We all have a bit of a superiority complex, and people like other people who enhance that sense of self-worth. A trusted advisor is actually better at facilitating self-advising than giving overt advice. *Let them discover.* It will lead to better advice and a higher perceived level of trust.

Correcting Clients

When we correct our patrons' misperceptions or overtly question their opinions, we do so at our own peril. There are, however, times when we must correct misinformation. How do we do it without looking pushy? Here are some fun and snappy ways to correct:

- Respect and correct: Respond to a customer's ridiculous comment as if it is reasonable. Create a call to action that simultaneously respects and corrects the douchebaggery.

  A Little Cheat: A man walks into an open house and shouts, "I would never pay this much for this house!" You respond, with the most caring and serious face you can muster, "What

ADVANCE READING COPY. NOT FOR SALE.

time can you meet so you can write up a backup offer for what *you* think it's worth?"

• Confirm and correct: React to a strong, challenging statement by agreeing in an even more severe way. This move along the continuum is often enough to point out the dipshittery of the statement.

  A Little Cheat: A lady walks into an open house and asks, "Are the sellers flexible?" You respond, "Yes!" (Wait for it...) "They will even take more than the asking price."

• Agree and deflect: Many accusations are true in the specific but contradicted in the general. An unexpected agreement is often enough to negate the accusation. Follow it with a humorous truth and you'll add another member to your fan club.

  A Little Cheat: Your buyer asks, "You're commission based, so you have no incentive for getting me the best price on this house." You say, "Right you are." (Wait for it...) "And if I save you money, you will tell all your nice friends to hire me as their broker, and I will make much, much more in commission!"

• STFU (There's a whole chapter on this. *See* "STFU."): It is best not to feel the need to answer nonquestions. A pleasant smile can often be enough.

  A Little Cheat: An asshole walks into your open house and says, "Wow, these people sure have horrible taste." You tighten your butt cheeks and say, "."

TRIALS&Titillations™

Try applying those tactics to these fun fill-in-the-blanks. (Hint, there are many right answers, but some are righter than others):

1. Scenario: A man walks into your open house and asks, "Why would I pay to have these low-end appliances in this expensive house?"

Answer:

ADVANCE READING COPY. NOT FOR SALE.

2. Scenario: A woman lumbers up fifty stairs and through the front door of an open house and asks, panting, "Who would ever live in this house?"

Answer:

3. Scenario: A client comes into a buyer consultation with his real estate "expert" friend, and the friend says, "It's pretty obvious that you guys are totally just into it for the commission."

Answer:
(Hint: It doesn't start with flipping him off.)

4. Scenario: A woman walks into your listing and proclaims, "Wow, this is really overpriced!"

Answer:
(Hint: It involves breathing through your nose.)

Not every objection needs to be met with point-counterpoint precision. If you can avoid overcoming your clients' objections, you will be perceived as a co-conspirator in the home-buying process and they will feel righteous and smart. I cannot tell you the number of times that a patron has brilliantly overcome her own objection and then followed up her *eureka!* moment with the proclamation that she has really been considering going into real estate. You do that, kumquat.

ADVANCE READING COPY. NOT FOR SALE.

CHAPTER 13

Discovery

Clients' words can be juicier clues to what lies beneath than panty lines are. Hear what people say and listen for what they mean. This can be difficult when you're trying to impress and simultaneously assist. Stand up and speak only after you have sat down and listened.

The secret is a simple matter of reordering your priorities—them first, you second. A little tip is to start with curiosity. When it's your turn to speak, make the first thing out of your mouth a question. When I'm really caffeinated, this is hard for me to do, so after I ask the question, I trick myself into thinking I have something in my teeth so I keep my mouth shut. Clients usually allow a little snapshot of an answer to pop out, and then the pause allows their meaning to develop as if they were shaking a Polaroid picture.

Oh, the Places You'll Go

Everyone has a public life, a private life, and a secret life. Because my intense curiosity could almost be classified as a disability, it is not a challenge for me to attempt to peel back the layers of people's lives. As a result, my job—and life—are much more interesting.

This tactic requires finesse, though. When I'm not on my game, a lack of delicacy can result in resistance against my peeling ways. This is when I let my clients discover a little about me too. Sharing your stories about how personal knowledge has led to great buyer representation can provide them with the proper permission to share. Let your clients know that you understand how personal questions can seem. Follow that up with an explanation that their purchase is not only financially significant but also personally significant on every level.

Unless there are hugely strategic windows, to inhibitionists, a home is usually the one place where their public, private, and secret lives can all thrive. Therefore, you can provide the best representation only when you can understand your clients on a deep level. Lucky for you, these are far more interesting than anything salespeople of most other products get to learn about.

True**STORIES**

An agent I know, Harriet, was representing a couple who wanted to buy a home and said they were very noise sensitive. She set up a tour of homes on quiet streets, and the three of them set out. To Harriet's surprise, the couple frequently pointed out homes they liked when they were traversing busy streets on their way to the next quiet neighborhood. Confused, Harriet kept responding that they wouldn't like those homes because of the busy streets.

After viewing more than twenty homes with quiet residential outlooks, the couple revealed that they really needed the master bedroom to be in the rear of the house and they preferred their property to back up to green space. They had never said anything about needing anything other than a quiet street, a certain number of bedrooms, and modern vintage within a wide price range. Every house Harriet had shown them met the exact criteria of what they had initially stated. However, what they had initially stated did not cover the criteria of what they specifically needed.

Harriet set up more home tours. As they walked through what she had considered the least likely candidate because the hum of the freeway in no way sounded like tranquil ocean waves crashing, the couple's eyes lit up. They were beyond excited to find a complete film studio in the master bedroom at the back of the house. The black-out shades probably cost more than the down payment. "This is perfect," they said with barely containable excitement. "We'll take it furnished."

A year or so later, the real estate office got a bonus in the form of some special home movies when a broker happened to recognize the master bedroom as he "accidentally" opened a particular website.

ADVANCE READING COPY. NOT FOR SALE.

Even though it seems obvious why people would want to live in a quiet environment, many people clearly don't care about this feature. Therefore, it is entirely reasonable to ask enough questions to get to the root of the desire. Although this story had a happy ending, you can be a lot more efficient if you work hard to effectively discover. You'll also learn so much more about the world in the process.

SORTAfacts™

Survey conductors at a large religious institution were shocked to find that breathless chants of "God, God, God" were less likely to be inspired by words between the pages than by the whispers between the sheets.

—Courtesy of Sortafact

SECRETSforClients

The more you share your true real estate motivations, the better a great agent can represent you. If you are too suspicious to be honest, ask enough probing questions to know if your suspicions are warranted. If you are always suspicious and have had horrible real estate (and other) relationships, you might benefit from grabbing a mirror to investigate the root of your suspicions.

TrueSTORIES

My partner and I were referred to a patron who was interviewing agents to list his condominium at the beach. We were not in the beach community business, but this client was having trouble finding someone he felt comfortable working with. He was auto-mechanic masculine and dressed in the worst kind of straight-man attire—surprising considering he was moving out of town to be with his boyfriend.

My partner and I asked him why he was disappointed in his real estate agent selection process thus far, and he told us the agents had all been more interested in and sensitive to their own needs than to his needs. Since I had never had a male client so in

ADVANCE READING COPY. NOT FOR SALE.

tune with needs and sensitivity, I knew to listen to what he meant more than what he said. I admit that my skills at doing this are not always top-notch and certainly diminish with cocktail consumption, but this time I was genuinely interested.

By asking probing questions with the proper concern for his perplexingly fragile demeanor, we learned that this condo had been a transition home. Thankfully we didn't jump to the most likely conclusion that he had only been there a short time and that there was less emotional baggage to pack for a move. This transition was clearly of a different nature: he had purchased the home as a she and was selling the home as a he.

He was comfortable with us because we were respectfully curious about him. This gave him permission to share so we could provide the best service—in this case a perfect referral to our transitioning agent friend, Sam, at the coast who was as outstanding then as a broker as she is now as a brokeress.

Words Matter

Litigators know that when questioning witnesses on the stand, they should never ask a question they don't already have an answer to. Of course, this presupposes that a lot of questions have been asked before the witness ever steps up to the stand. Good litigators know just how to manipulate their words to create the right drama and extract the right memories necessary to win their case. Discovery comes first, then success.

In online dating profiles, you might be tempted to pay attention just to the words in ALL CAPS, but the truly important details might be glaringly obvious in the text that blends in. Did you really expect your relationship to last beyond green card acquisition when you read Gergana's profile on the Rent-A-Bride site?

Witnesses show up at the courthouse for questioning *after* the discovery. Just as you would—I hope—at least check with the message board monitor before meeting your very own special bride for the first time on the courthouse steps. You must discover your clients' true stories before you can hope to lead them toward happily ever after.

ADVANCE READING COPY. NOT FOR SALE.

Test

Here's a little test just for you. Pretend you've just listed a delightful home that is three blocks to/from the school, and you're hosting an open house. A man walks in and asks, "Is this house close to a school?" What do you say?

Don't cheat. You were really supposed to ask yourself, so now confess, what did you say?

Hint: The home is three blocks *to* the school for some and three blocks *from* the school for others.

Answer: First, what did you see and hear? Size up the questioner, but don't rely too much on what you see because Momma always said that looks can be deceiving. He might look like a young breeder but…I hope you listened. Did he say "…*a* school" or "…*the* school"? That might give you clue as to whether he sort of knows the neighborhood. Maybe.

Now ask: "Is it important to you to be close to a school?" If his answer is yes, then the school is *only* three blocks away. If the answer is no, then it is three blocks away. If his answer is an emphatic no, then first don a dismissive expression and only then answer that the school is three (loooong) blocks away.

COT, SOT, and TBK

Let's step out of the real estate world for a minute to examine the kinds of questions we as consumers ask and the answers we look for. Think about a recent experience in a good restaurant. If it's the kind of place where the servers shove those canned pitches for gargantuan onion rings or frosty strawberry lemonade before I have the chance to ask what they truly recommend, it doesn't even qualify. I mean a *good* restaurant. Now, see if this sounds familiar.

I usually start by perusing the menu and mentally picking out the items that might be contenders for the trip down my gullet. At this point I ask the server what she recommends. It is through this process that I find out how good a salesperson she is. She will invariably fall into one of three categories of salespeople: COT, SOT, or TBK.

ADVANCE READING COPY. NOT FOR SALE.

If she says that everything on the menu is delicious, I have no further use for her beyond transporting my food from the kitchen. She either underwent a tastebudectomy or she is a liar. For the sake of a better label, let's call the salespeople in this category conveyors with opposable thumbs, or COT.

The second category of server will respond with a more discerning response such as, "I really like the scallops and the pork loin." She might even go on with some information about why she likes those particular items, which might show a comforting level of knowledge about the menu. I will trust this server a little bit, so let's call this category SOT: sort of trustworthy.

The two major problems with SOTs are that they might not relate at all to me and they might make me feel bad. She never took the time to discover (there's that word) what I'm about. Therefore, she never found out that I might be allergic to sea animals without faces and that I have a bleeding heart for land animals that are often killed while enjoying a delicious apple (or that I might keep kosher, which would actually rule out both choices in this scenario). Those items might not have made my initial mental cut for the gullet trip. Now, that server is banking on the possibility that I might consider her recommended foods, but that's a risk because if I don't, I'll feel slightly uncomfortable for not taking her suggestion after specifically asking for recommendations.

The category that will invariably result in my undying appreciation and thick-assed tip is called the best kind, or TBK. This type of server will be extremely knowledgeable about the menu, the restaurant, and the food scene in general. But knowledge alone is not enough—any of the other servers in this scenario could possess the same knowledge. When I've solicited a server recommendation, however, a TBK server knows the value of establishing a relationship, and I'm a sucker for this type of one-night stand.

A TBK server will always preface her answer with a question. "Mmmm," she'll think aloud. "A number of special, fresh, and incredible options tonight," she'll say with concentrating, narrowing eyes while giving my deep and important question the thought that it so deserves. Then, realizing I'm still there, she'll ask, "Oh, there are some very wonderful things on the menu today because the

ADVANCE READING COPY. NOT FOR SALE.

chef just got back from the James Beard event in New York. Before I direct you, are there any items that look particularly intriguing?"

I will then confess my attraction to a few items on the menu. "I'm really intrigued by the steak tartar and swordfish, but I do love a hamburger."

She will respond with the deep knowledge to truthfully explain the pros and cons of my choices. "Although there is one place in Tulsa serving steak tartar that people have literally died over, it has been said that our steak tartar is the second best in the country and you'll still leave tonight's experience alive. Our beef is from a sexy, local rancher who suckles his cows with a bottle spiked with single malt scotch, after which they are free to stumble around where the buffalo roam and the deer and the antelope play. This makes for an unsurpassed, raw experience that your mouth will never forget. The swordfish was line-caught today by a velvet-gloved fisherwoman who is world renowned for attracting only the most delicious ocean-dwelling creatures with house-building tools as snouts. I can't say more because, if you choose any of these dishes, I still need to carry your plate from the kitchen without devouring everything on it before arriving at your table. I don't usually eat the hamburger because it's always on the menu and customers sometimes rush to the restroom to splash themselves with cold water after experiencing the most intense palatory orgasm of their lives."

Wow. I will be smitten enough to place my gastronomical future in her hands.

SORTAFacts™

Women over ninety-seven years of age experience orgasms of the palate 99.9% more often than they experience traditional orgasms. This is also true for men over eighty-seven.
— *Courtesy of Sortafact*

This TBK server used several successful sales tactics. Discovery is certainly one of them. In this delicious example, a simple question to find out what was most intriguing to me was discovery

ADVANCE READING COPY. NOT FOR SALE.

enough because of her overall finesse. Relationship building is another tactic. She becomes a friend and confidant by letting me know how smart I am for choosing dishes that are special and well received. In the end, I still need to own my decision, so giving permission is the most nuanced of the tactics. The obvious way our TBK gives me, the diner, permission to make my own decision is by allowing me to express what I already decided. However, she does not simply echo my choices. By strategically admitting that the hamburger would not be this TBK's choicest choice but by still giving me permission to experience an outrageous orgasm of the palate that others have enjoyed, I see her honesty. Whatever I decide, it's my decision, but I can rest assured that it will be a good one because my new trusted friend and advisor told me so.

Just curious, what would you choose for dinner?

When you don't have commission on the brain, you can strive to be a TBK. A focus on discovery, an offer of choices that reflect that you have really discovered, and giving permission for your clients to decide will result in your clients thanking you with the very commission you forgot about.

ADVANCE READING COPY. NOT FOR SALE.

CHAPTER 14

FEAR NOT

Even after you and your buyers are solid dance partners in the house-buying tango, they will still have doubts. If they are fearful of not being made aware of happenin' property prospects, they might be constantly wondering if they have the wrong dance partner in you.

I always try to grease the skids in the beginning of buyer relationships. I first detail how I will stay on top of all listed properties meeting their criteria and will be delving for properties that are not yet officially listed. I then go on to explain that, right this very second, there could be two agents discussing the fact that their friends just had quadruplets and their two-bedroom townhouse is being overrun by baby swings and Diaper Genies. These agents could consummate a sale and we would not be privy until after it closes. I lay it out for them that there is never a way for a Realtor to know every single discussion or transaction that is taking place. It is important for your buyers to understand the futility of worrying about this.

However, let them know that you are certainly on top of things. Throughout the process, you should assure your buyers of your diligence by actually *being* diligent and presenting both listed and not-yet-listed homes. If a period of time passes when you don't hear about not-yet-listed homes that meet your patrons' criteria, tell them of a cool one that might not exactly meet their needs and ask them if it would be a love connection for anyone they know. A sale like this with a different buyer is not an entirely unrealistic side goal.

TRIALS&Titillations™

Ask your fellow real estaters about their secret listings not yet on the market. Then take one of your real estate–addicted friends to happy hour and find a way to weave your knowledge of the secret listing into the conversation. His love of real estate will help spread the word for you even if you have to apologize for not remembering that he is an AA sponsor.

Signs of Attraction

You must keep your eyeballs on your buyers to look for signs of attraction. Some are just too obvious to miss, and some are downright awkward. This can be a problem for beach and resort clients; if a Speedo is involved, bring them a towel so the signs of attraction don't become embarrassing for everyone.

Paying attention to your buyers' eyes and body movements will give you huge insight. It's amazing how much time I've wasted fantasizing about being able to read minds when there are human crystal balls before me. If you see body and microexpressions indicating the equivalent of a boner for a home, pay attention because this client probably is somewhat interested in the house…or the glamour shot on the wall…or you.

Fear of Losing the Property

In order to decipher whether the feelings are directed toward the house or not, you can begin looking for signs of another common buyer emotion: the fear of losing the property because another buyer pounced first.

TrueSTORIES

A potential buyer called a large real estate office in a panic. He had called his agent eight times but had not heard back, and he was ready to write an offer. The receptionist expressed her surprise, as this top agent was always very responsive and an excellent communicator.

ADVANCE READING COPY. NOT FOR SALE.

She asked, "How long has it been since you left a message?" The buyer responded that more than five minutes had passed since the most recent message.

The receptionist asked, "When did you leave the first message?"

The client indignantly responded, "Over eight minutes ago!"

Just then the buyer got a call on the other line. "Oh," he said. "I have to hang up. Here she is finally calling me. I hope I didn't lose the house."

Granted, this exchange happened during a market that was extremely brisk, but even in those fast-paced times, this guy's fear was freaking ridiculous. I'm sure that during those long eight minutes, that buyer did more damage to his excellent agent's reputation than he influenced his chances of getting the house.

Feel free to tell this story to your clients. It's great for setting expectations so they won't criticize you for silencing your phone when you're sliding down into the stirrups for your PAPpy.

SECRETSfor**Clients**

Understand that even the best agent has to get a pap smear from time to time. Ideally this should be an annual event, so if you don't make your home search last forever, you'll only have to deal with this once. You should, however, never have to wait hours and hours for a return phone call, text, or email. Discuss your expectations in advance. If you call to set up a time to interview your prospective agent and he takes forever to return your call, that might be a sign that you will find yourself stressing when you want to take action and he is still unresponsive.

Not to belittle scaredy-cat buyers too much, but there are some other phobias out there that might be greater than those pesky buyer fears:

- Drowning
- Realizing that you're naked in a business meeting
- Kissing a girl and liking it...a lot

ADVANCE READING COPY. NOT FOR SALE.

- Having to pee, and then doing it
- Getting a boner during a massage (and a happy ending is not part of the deal)
- Realizing your internet search history was not really deleted
- Leaving the car seat with the baby in it (one of my clients actually did this in a vacant house)
- Forgetting to *live* your life

Buyers' fear of losing property might start to surface when they ask about the sellers' motivation or other buyers' interest in the property. Because I'm not a lover of delayed gratification, when visitors at an open house ask these types of questions, I jump to it with a huge, friendly, and co-conspiratorial smile on my face. "Do you want to buy it?"

There are many books on sales in general, and real estate sales specifically, that claim that a salesperson should never ask questions that can be answered with yes or no. WTF? I find that people are conditioned to answer questions—the more direct the question, the more direct the answer. When I want to know something, I often find that a crazy way to obtain the answer is....drumroll please...to ask.

The truth is, you need the answer to this question more than they need direct answers to their questions. If the buyers are your clients, know that by asking about the sellers' motivation and other buyers' interest, they are showing fear of losing the property. Work with them to sort out whether or not they want to make an offer.

Very rarely are salespeople able to extract a solid "Yes, I'd like to buy it" or "No, I'm not interested." Often clients give subtle yes clues that you can and should cultivate into a sale. That's your job.

Fear of Being an Idiot

The way you talk to your buyers can make a big difference in how they perceive the potential sale and whether or not their fear thermometer will rise.

Tom Hopkins is one of the top real estate gurus. Although I can think of a lot scarier words, he says that the scariest words for buyers are: *commission, objection, deal, appointment, offer,* and

ADVANCE READING COPY. NOT FOR SALE.

down payment. I generally like to add *anal probe* to that list. Tom suggests that a prepayment penalty be called a prepayment privilege. Okaaaaay.

I admit that during a recent tough time in the market, I kept hearing people replace the word *appointment* with *pop-by*, and I kept thinking that they were saying pot-buy. I thought, *Hmm, that's an interesting way to relieve the stress and help your clients with a down paym— I mean, initial investment.* I'm a constant preacher and firm believer in paying explicit attention to the words we say as long as the words we substitute aren't douchebaggy and fake.

Many Realtors avoid calling themselves salespeople, but I'll let you in on a little secret: that's what you are! If you are facilitating, advising, coaching, and helping people achieve what's in their best interests and desires, you're a *good* salesperson.

There are many fun ways to create the proper imagery for buyers, giving them the sense of what it would be like to own and live in the home. This is the first of several times when you might have to take reality and add a dose of MSG to enhance your buyers' lifestyle imagery and move it away from the current sellers'. The sellers' house-vibe might repel the buyer. This is especially true when there has not been great staging and there are a lot of personal photos to mentally reconcile. Keep the buyer from identifying too much with the sellers in their current get-me-the-hell-out state. With resale, the buyer has to identify with the sellers as they were when they bought the home, not the sellers as they are when they are planning to move. It's different, though, when it comes to a new product being sold by a seller who is not an end user, as in new construction.

SECRETS for Clients

Sometimes the best deals are the worst furnished homes. Contending with a nasty odor can narrow the buyer field, meaning you have less competition and the sellers may lower their price. Just be sure that the nasty odor is removable—and don't move in and get used to it. That, you *should* fear.

ADVANCE READING COPY. NOT FOR SALE.

Fear of Paying Too Much

Moving from the fear of losing the property to the fear of paying too much for a property is all a part of the buying process. This is when you try to bracket the price for the buyers—a fancy way of describing playing the bases and schmuck pricing.

When figuring out the best strategy for offering and negotiating price, I often ask, "At what price would you consider this a home run? A base hit?" This may seem like a strange analogy coming from a woman who has never played softball without toenail polish and mascara. But I've played plenty of softball in my day, and my father-in-law was a professional baseball player while my brother and dad were semipros. Despite all that, I couldn't throw a ball straight from first to third if my life depended upon it. Still, we all know what constitutes a base hit and a home run. We have all played the bases in one form or another.

SORTAfacts™

7 out of 8 people dislike feeling like a schmuck. When consumers sense that they have paid too much for something, they experience this feeling nearly 91% of the time. This is suboptimal.
—*Courtesy of Sortafact*

Price Bracketing—Do This!

This baseball analogy is just a simple way to price bracket. There is always a price at or below which a purchase totally makes sense. There should also be a price at or above which a purchase does not make sense at all. I call this the Schmuck Price (*schmuck* means "putz" for those Yiddishly deficient).

Another way to price bracket is to ask your potential buyers to tell you at what point they would kick themselves if they heard someone else successfully obtained the property at or below that purchase price. Of course, people sometimes behave in ways that don't make sense, especially when it comes to money.

This price bracketing can help them swing test emotions before stepping up to the plate and perhaps striking out. It is best to remind them that to play, they have to be willing to lose. After all, one buyer's definition of *overpriced* could be a bargain to the next.

ADVANCE READING COPY. NOT FOR SALE.

I once called another agent to ask him if his clients who had just purchased a property would be willing to immediately sell that property. He quickly told me that they would not be interested. I think the word he used was *no.* I assured him that the answer was actually yes. He immediately got defensive, as people often do when they're surprised by a disruptive technique (*see* "The Art of Offering a Blowjob"). No matter what his response, the answer wasn't really yes or no but rather, what price? And yes, the sellers set a ridiculously high price. And no, the buyers had no intention of paying that price. And yes, we negotiated a successful transaction…six months later.

Playing the Field

If it's early in the process and your buyers-in-love haven't played enough bases, pull together some data to help with pricing decisions. If they have seen enough homes to truly understand prices, remind them of that along the way so they feel confident. As you tour homes together, engage your buyers on what proper prices should be to help minimize the symptoms of the fear of paying too much.

Create a game with your client. If your buyers have seen enough properties with you, they can begin to get the groove of pricing. It's fun and effective to withhold the flyer or the listing printout until after touring each home and have them guess the price. When touring homes that are clearly not contenders and, therefore, there is less emotion involved, ask them how they would price the home. Their knowledge of the market will be highlighted when they see that they know enough about what is available that they can actually price the homes similarly to a pro. They will be less fearful of not knowing the market and, as a result, when they do find a home that could be a love connection, they are prepared, not scared.

SORTAFacts™

People who try things tend to succeed 98% more often than people who don't.

—Courtesy of Sortafact

ADVANCE READING COPY. NOT FOR SALE.

Contract Deflowering

If the market is so crazy that it requires you to run from the first viewing of a house and jump on the hood of your car while pulling out your laptop to find unsecured Wi-Fi and immediately write the offer, it can be helpful to write a sample contract for your buyers to review in advance and sleep on.

If they find a house that they like but they clearly do not want to be rushed, this practice contract can allow them to take a step toward purchase, learn the latest contract forms, and not feel forced to commit when they're not quite ready. In a robustly speedy market, this practice is often the only way to ever experience contract writing without intense pressure. Go over it in detail and show your clients where they would sign. Engineers can go home with the contract and engage in the type of behavior that turns them on — creating their spreadsheets. It is best to try this on a house that the buyers would probably purchase if they were not feeling undue pressure, as many times this exercise can result in an excited buyer deciding to proceed with actually presenting the offer after further mental masturbation.

If, after sleeping on the contract and their decision to present an offer, your buyers decide to proceed, you have saved a lot of valuable time — they can sign the contract you wisely set up for practice and email it back to you for presentation to the seller right away. If they do not proceed, y'all will have covered much of the information that will come up when you write the real contract later.

SECRETSforClients

In a robust market, there will be huge incentives for new agents to join the ranks of real estate professionals. The first target for those newbies will be buyers, as it's considered somewhat easier for new agents to represent buyers. When real estate is rockin' and it seems like every friend and family member has jumped into real estate and they're doing great, know that the bucks that they find easy to make might not be the ones that ultimately end up in your bank account. Know that the right agent for you might not be determined by how many houses they have sold in the

ADVANCE READING COPY. NOT FOR SALE.

boom-boom years. Selecting the right buyers' agent will be more difficult and even more critical in robust market conditions when a busy agent might or might not be a good one.

After writing a contract with first-time buyers, warn them that they will be up all night worrying that their offer will not be accepted. Nervous, sweaty angst might just as well be from thinking about what will happen if their offer *is* accepted (*see* "Greasing the Skids"). The longer you're selling real estate, the more weird reactions you'll see from your buyers. To the extent that you can warn them of the many ways that they might feel and the many things that they might experience, the more comfortable they will be when they confront those feelings and situations.

Even the most seasoned buyers suffer from nerves in a rapid-fire market. These types of market conditions amp up skepticism even more than the line "Trust me" coming from a tool at a fraternity party. Your clients might have to miss out on a couple opportunities before they realize what skinny inventory does to your ability to control the process. One of my least favorite compliments was, "Thanks for helping me win that bidding war in 2007." Gulp.

Give Them Permission to Buy

There are times when your buyers might want the home so badly that they are willing to pay more than you think they should. Remember 2006, when buyers felt like they were missing out if they didn't buy regardless of price and they were able to because the only requirement for buying a home was a pulse (for financing) and an intense competitive spirit? Even though you think the price may be too high, remember that sometimes there are good and extenuating circumstances—special school or neighborhood considerations or unique home features, for example—in which a buyer must be aggressive in obtaining a home. These special needs can trump a good-deal price. It is a home, for god's sake. At the same time, it's never safe to let them buy at a price that you feel is way above market without any discussion. When they later call you to list the house, you can't be going over the property's issues for the first time.

ADVANCE READING COPY. NOT FOR SALE.

If your buyers are concerned about the investment aspect of the home, be honest about the short-term versus the long-term prospects without making them feel like dumbshits. They might not care much about the investment aspect now, though, so if they don't ask, address it gingerly and then move on. This is another one of those times when you want to spend more time asking than telling.

Still, you might be wrong—it might be a killer deal. And it's ultimately their decision whether or not to buy. I cannot tell you how many times I have told the story about selling a house of my own for a ridiculously high price only to have it sell a few years later, without too many improvements made, for several times more than I had ever dreamed possible (*see* "Do Tell").

Sometimes the buyers will just know, at least on some level, that they are ready to buy. I hate to be bossy, but here you must simply pay attention and stop selling. If they need one final shove, you can say, "How much more perfect does this place have to be for you to make up your mentally masturbating mind to buy it?" Or you can nod knowingly. Or just shut up. Admit that even with all your expertise, charm, and grace, you are still often guilty of underestimating the market because…you will be. Give them permission.

ADVANCE READING COPY. NOT FOR SALE.

CHAPTER 15

MULTIPLE O'S

Not all multiple O's take as much finesse as multiple offer scenarios. They can be tricky bastards whether you're representing the buyers or the sellers.

For those of you who worked in the glory days of real estate, when making money was as easy as falling out of a tree, you know the blissful chaos of bidding wars. Market surges like this have happened before and, if you're in this business long enough, will happen again—so be prepared.

Unless you're into both sadism and masochism, it is not fun to be the agent representing buyers who lose the bidding war. You can plead until you're hoarse, urging your buyers to bid high and bid fast for a property they really want. Some suspicious buyers act like you're trying to sell them something as desirable as your old Nokia phone or your used Crocs (even when you'd never be caught dead in Crocs in the first place). They have to see you working at your competent best and still lose a bidding war before they can be convinced to play to win. Just telling them what to do is not enough. Sometimes they need to experience being on the losing end of a multiple O ordeal in order to see the wisdom of your direction.

Losers Are Winners Too

When you're participating in a war, there is always a chance that you might lose. But who sets the definitions of *winning* and *losing*? Americans are great at creating enough ambiguity in our wars that the definition of *winning* can match whatever the outcome. When the brave troops pushed over that statue of Saddam

"Sudsy" Hussein, we felt victorious. By the time we found Sudsy in that hole, we couldn't even remember if we were looking for WMDs or BLTs (Google Ali G). This is brilliant, and it allows us to continue to feel like winners.

Remember this when you're taking your buyers' offer to the bidding war. Remember this when your buyers want you to present an offer that you highly doubt will be accepted. You create the scenario where you and your buyers come out as winners. This should not be tied, in any way, to whether your buyers come out with the offer that is ultimately accepted any more than America winning a war has to do with converting another country to baseball, apple pie, and mall hair.

SECRETSforClients

If you suggest a price and your agent tells you unequivocally that the price you're suggesting is wrong, your agent could be setting himself up to look like a partial to complete douchebag. A good agent will explain the pros and cons of your offer in light of the market and the specific property. He will explain that someone else might outbid you but that outbidder might be paying a schmuck price. He will explain that he will do his best to present all the excellent aspects of your offer—no matter what the price. He will set himself up to be a winner with you, no matter whether you get the house or not. In doing this, he will set you up to be a winner too.

SORTAFacts™

Studies show that people like to win. When they don't win, they like to blame anyone other than themselves. Reframing losing into winning helps make 10 out of 11 people feel better.

—*Courtesy of Sortafact*

TrueSTORIES

I was approached by some potential buyers, Wayne and Tina, who had bought and sold a few homes in the past with

ADVANCE READING COPY. NOT FOR SALE.

another agent. In their final transaction with her, they decided to make an offer that was significantly lower than the asking price. Their agent told them that the offer would never fly with the sellers. Yikes. They proceeded to have her write the offer as they wished and present it to the sellers, but the agent had set herself up to lose, lose, lose. When their offer was accepted, there was no way for her to recover her winner status, no matter how you define a winner. Thus, Wayne and Tina became my clients for the next transaction and the one following that and so on (and so on... because those two love themselves some movin').

Low O (And I Hear They're Working on a Drug for This)

Yes, it's uncomfortable when our clients suggest a much-lower-than-likely-to-be-accepted offer. In this case it is best to ask enough questions to ensure they understand how their offer might be received. Note my wording: *ask enough questions.* This is very different from telling them how you think their offer will be received. You could be wrong, so don't climb out on that limb. In the event that they are adamant about writing the potentially uncomfortable offer, frame the conversation and the presentation so that you are the hero if that offer is accepted.

You don't want to be the loser, however, if it isn't accepted. It's best if your clients don't feel like the loser either. If the sellers don't take the offer, the sellers are the losers. If someone else's offer is accepted, they were more willing to overpay and your clients were saved from making an uncomfortable purchase and potentially a bad investment.

Say, "Okay, this is a long-shot offer, but it would be most excellent if we were to get this deal done. I will do everything in my power to work my magic to try to make this happen. If the seller wants to wait until someone who will overpay comes along, that's the seller's prerogative. By the way, if you found out someone would pay $X, would you be fine with it or would you wish that you had come up in your offer price?"

If they say they would be fine with losing the property, there is no way you can lose. If they say they would not be fine losing the property, remind them that there is always a chance that there will be someone who is more desperate, won the lottery, or has

ADVANCE READING COPY. NOT FOR SALE.

bigger *cojones.* This will either inspire them to up their price or feel okay about losing out to a fool. Support them and tell them how well equipped you feel going to war for them on a field where whatever the outcome is, y'all will be the winners. That's the American way, after all.

When Write Stuff Is Wrong

Buyers who want to write personal letters to accompany their offers are often given free rein to do so in the real estate industry. They also often request having their agent present those heartfelt letters. Do not let your buyers do this and don't abide. Ever.

Do not let them submit photos either. Not only is it tacky, but it can also be discriminatory. If you have done your job and talked to the sellers' agent about the sellers and have looked carefully through the home for clues as to what kind of people they are, a blind letter from your buyers will never be better than what you, as a savvy agent, can present in an in-person meeting.

If you absolutely cannot present the offer in person, then *you* write the offer letter to ensure it matches what is important to the sellers. Never let your buyers write that letter.

SORTAFacts™

Selling a random something to an anonymous someone results in a successful sale less than 13% of the time.

—*Courtesy of Sortafact*

TrueSTORIES

As I was reviewing offer-accompanying letters with my seller clients, Stacy and Addison, we encountered one that really set my clients off. The letter, written by the potential buyers themselves, waxed on and on about their involvement in a fruit-tree-saving organization. They also included a loving photo of themselves on their honeymoon, and they indicated that the yard would be perfect for their long-desired chicken coop.

"Over my dead body will they put chickens in my newly landscaped yard," Addison yelled. "I would rather take less from

ADVANCE READING COPY. NOT FOR SALE.

someone else." She had a few other choice words that made me nearly pee my pants from laughter as she ranted that she didn't like this couple whom she had never met and probably never would meet.

That worked out well for the clients with the second offer. Their letter went on and on about their intense love for the home and the neighborhood. It sounded more like a "Dear *Penthouse*" than a "Dear my future house" letter with all the mentions of luscious carpets and hard woods, but it made its point. Although this letter was also written by potential buyers, it did not give any indication as to why they were offering a price a good chunk lower than the asking price—in a multiple-offer situation, no less. This can be a good thing or a bad thing depending on the scenario, but in this case, it made the overly gushing love letter seem disingenuous.

The third offer was written by the buyers' agent, Toni, on behalf of her buyers. It was the lowest offer by a slight margin. Toni had called me ahead of time to ask questions. Smart. She then presented the buyers exactly in a way that she had determined the sellers would like her buyers best (carefully avoiding discriminatory landmines).

I cracked up when Stacy and Addison expressed how much they liked the buyers presented by Toni. Both the chicken coopers with their highest offer and the *Forum* letter writers with their sensual prose thought they had a slam-dunk acceptance in their future. They didn't.

Present to Present

My real estate partner and I were totally shocked when we called to set up a time to present our buyers' offer, only to be told that it was the first time in years that this prolific builder had a request from a buyers' agent to physically present an offer.

I think the precise words of our response were: "You're fucking kidding me?!"

Okay, those weren't my partner's words because she doesn't have quite the potty mouth I do, but we were both shocked.

The art of selling has been so greatly diminished, initially by the fax machine and now by email and other expediting technologies, that the idea of having to actually present an offer in person

ADVANCE READING COPY. NOT FOR SALE.

has become foreign and terrifying to many agents. If you claim to be too busy to present your offers in person, confess that to your buyer because they deserve to know. If you claim that is not how it's done in your area, make sure that "how it's done" is not an institutionalized laziness and unwillingness to work cooperatively with the "cooperating" Realtor. If you think that technology is a replacement for selling, think again. As a buyers' agent, your goal should be to physically present offers whenever feasible. Of course, before you do this, you have to study, understand, and practice the art of delivering O's.

ADVANCE READING COPY. NOT FOR SALE.

PART 3

EMBRACING

Sell-U-Rite

Embracing Sell-U-Rite*

Although popular, loud, happy buyers can work a bit like sold signs, they're much harder to plant in a lawn than actual signs. If you make the shift to allow a significant portion of your business to come from representing sellers, your chances of tremendous riches will be better than a reality TV show on cable. In general, working with sellers is the higher-hanging fruit, but the pickins can be juicier.

SORTAfacts™

Real estate sellers like to expose themselves in public and on the internet 97% more often than buyers. National real estate advice blogs suggest agents provide trench coats for 3% of their buyers.

—Courtesy of Sortafact

Why So Seller-ious?

There are lots of reasons to work with sellers. Take your pick!

- Lots of people see signs emblazoned with your name.
- People like to work with people whom they perceive as understanding them and their 'hoods.
- Marketing cool properties anchors your brand to cool properties.
- Sending out collateral to market a property is a softer sell than marketing yourself directly.
- People can see that you have been selected.
- You can control open houses where you'll meet customers and future clients.
- You can blast listing information and then sale information to your target markets, creating two points of contact.
- You use less gas.
- It's a chance to test your creativity.
- You can publicly talk about your listings but not your buyers.
- You can target people and publications that might be outside of your own sphere.

Are you sold on being a seller yet? Read on to learn Sell-U-Rite secrets of the trade.

*My rapper name.

CHAPTER 16

To List Is Bliss

As you might have realized by now, this book isn't like other real estate books that teach you to employ systems for great success. Like AA sponsors, those books guide you to do the shit you should know to do and to avoid the shit you know you should not do. If slogans and constant reminders work for you, great. However, I don't believe that you have to ape your clients' answers or continuously use their name at the start of every sentence. Those old-school sales tactics trigger my gag reflexes like…well, never mind. But I tend to forget names easily, so perhaps that's my lame excuse for not repeating clients' names constantly.

I view that traditional sales stuff like I view a healthy lifestyle: I will do the best I can as long as I can do it on my terms and with coffee, tequila, and chips and salsa. However, there are some mental templates that are more positively associated with success than others. One such lesson states that trying more things is more positively correlated with succeeding than waiting to try one seemingly perfect thing is. You can spend your whole career doing nothing but waiting for perfection. Hell, this has profound implications for life too, but we don't want to veer too selfy-helpy here.

The point is, try some of that stuff out. Other people might laugh at you—hell, you might laugh at you—but go ahead and spew out some of those dorky scripts and see if they work. If you prime your curiosity and turn your gears so the template works for you and your clients, you'll be positioned for the greatest level of success. You will also be best prepared for wearing the listing tiara.

TRIALS&Titillations™

Plenty of other books cover the deal flow system, but if you're feeling ripped off that you spent your entire real estate education budget on this book, make yourself a handy chart that spells out how much you want to earn. Use colored pencils, or don't. Figure out the average price range of the houses you want to sell and divide by the commission rate you charge. Divide that number into how much you want to earn. List that many houses.

Follow up when you say you will, and do what you promise to do. Follow the good advice in this book. Sell your listings. Then you can afford to buy more books, read them, and follow that advice. If those systems don't work, practice saying the following: "Do you want fries with that?" Remember, you can't easily hightail it to the unemployment office when you're self-employed.

Listing Appointment

The listing appointment should be a two-step process. First you find out what you're going to sell and who you're going to work with. Then you present how you're going to successfully do it. This is advantageous not only because you can learn a bit about the property before pricing and marketing but also because the process gives you two times to interface with the sellers. This is particularly important for your clients with bipolar and multiple-personality disorders. They might hate you during the ebb of the first meeting and love you at the flow of the second. Don't miss this fun opportunity. Explain your two-step process before the first meeting. You don't need to mention your appreciation of the medicated mentally ill, though.

First Meeting

The first meeting in the duo of listing appointments is all about the sellers. They should come away from that meeting feeling like you have enough time and attention for them, that you will be pleasant and competent, and that you liked what you saw. There is one major reason, beyond lack of perceived competence and other obvious factors, that agents lose out on listing appointments: they

ADVANCE READING COPY. NOT FOR SALE.

do not give the impression that they buy into (like) the property enough to support the price.

The first meeting also serves to help you see if you'll be a good fit for the property. The best salespeople aren't the best for every product…real estate included. Even I have experienced moments like this when the sellers were smart enough to perceive a truth that I didn't admit to myself.

TrueSTORIES

I really want to say that this story is not about me, but… If this gives you a sense of superiority, I certainly don't blame you.

I went to a listing appointment for a property that I had tried to sell a few years prior in a tougher market and with a less motivated seller. My impressions of the house were clearly tarnished by the negative feedback we had obtained when the market sucked and the now-dead cat was stinking up the joint. Although the house was of a style that was not my favorite, that generally did not affect my ability to successfully market a property. But this time, this detail paired with my past experience with this property led to a lackluster vision on my part. In addition, because the client and I had worked with each other in the past and knew each other well, I was not as crisply objective as usual.

My client was really smart and sensed that I did not like the house and, therefore, would not be the best for listing the property. The price I believed in was less than the price he ultimately listed and sold for with another agent. The truth was that I had treated the house like an old fuck buddy instead of as a sexy beast to be unleashed onto the market.

SECRETSforClients

When you are realistic in your analysis of the sales data and you find that the listing agent you are considering does not seem to like your property, ask the proper questions to find out whether or not this is true. Every property has someone who would appreciate living in it—even squatters need a place to come out

ADVANCE READING COPY. NOT FOR SALE.

of the cold. If your prospective agent cannot convince you of a price that reflects the market, and if you feel that this agent is not excited about your property at the price you truly believe to be reflective of the market, you should get another agent.

This works with prices that are too high as well as prices that are too low. If the agent is presenting a high price but you know he doesn't believe in the price, he could be buying the listing— enticing you to get you to sign the paperwork. He has every intention of asking you to reduce your price to a more realistic level later, when you are under contract to stick with him as your listing agent. You need to extract what your agent truly believes because that will influence his intentions…and your ultimate real estate future.

Prepare for the first meeting by familiarizing yourself with everything you can find about the sellers, the property, the neighborhood, and the market details of all competing properties. Bring a listing contract and a notepad. Be sure to find out in advance if the sellers have any reasons that require you to be extra discrete so you know if it's okay for you to arrive five minutes early and stand outside taking notes and photographs. This can be important if, for example, the seller is a bigwig in a public company and her transfer has not been announced or if the witness protection office has not finished the paperwork.

If you can't do this work in advance, arrive two minutes early for your appointment. You'll seem professionally on time. After pleasantries, explain that you will be walking through their property while taking extensive notes. Explain that the level of detail you like to obtain is important and you will want an even finer level of detail before you put the property on the official market. Ask them how much time they have for you to get really detailed for the most accurate analysis. Tell them you also will speak with them about their short-term and long-term plans and anything they would like to share about what they love about their property, what they would change, and any improvements they have made. Then, give them a choice of what they would like to do first—walk through or sit down to talk.

ADVANCE READING COPY. NOT FOR SALE.

During the sit-down at meeting number one, there are some absolutely crucial bits of information you must learn from your sellers:

- Why are they moving?
- How far are they in the process?
- What, if any, other companies are they considering?
- Who else, if anyone, are they interviewing?
- What price are they thinking? Why?
- What is their timing? Why?
- What are their expectations?
- Where is their goody drawer?
- What are their past real estate selling experiences?
- How were they referred to you?
- What drew them to the house?
- What air freshener do they prefer to use to eliminate the pot odor (this is particularly important to my friends in Washington State)?
- What did they discover about the house that they didn't realize before they moved in?
- Who do they view as the target buyer?
- Are there seasonal aspects to consider that might not be apparent?
- Are there any other things that you think should be pointed out, explained, or emphasized?

Be curious, and casually and unapologetically **ask**.

SORTAfacts™

86% of real estate agents admit that they forget to ask vital questions at listing appointments 91% more often than they shut their tongues in a lockbox and 33% more often than they return from a listing appointment to find a piece of lettuce lodged next to their front incisor.

—*Courtesy of Sortafact*

ADVANCE READING COPY. NOT FOR SALE.

True**STORIES**

       I arrived at an initial listing appointment for a couple I knew fairly well. Josh and Sandy had been married for over fifteen years, and I had sold them their home back in the day. I remembered the couple well because they were darling, of breeding age, and adamant about not needing to consider future kids or pets when they were first looking for the perfect property. They wanted their lives to be about travel.

When Sandy called to set the initial listing appointment, because I felt a dangerous level of familiarity and she seemed in a hurry to set the appointment and get off the phone, I scheduled the first meeting without much fanfare. The next day at the house, I immediately began to compliment them on all the improvements they had made to their home. I was excited to see that they had really done "the right things," and I wasn't shy about telling the couple. In my excitement to connect with the sellers and encourage them that the projects they did together were going to result in a great return, I skipped the part of finding out why they were **really** selling. Josh and Sandy had mentioned that they might be moving out of state, but I didn't take the time to get to the real reason behind the move. I could make the excuse that I didn't want to pry, but that would be a total lie—I always say that the right kind of prying is in the best interest of the client.

I also failed to see the initially subtle nonverbal clues that should have screamed at me to tone down my enthusiasm. It wasn't until I opened the closet and saw an entire side emptied of women's clothing that I shut my complimenting piehole long enough to shift gears. Switching from blabbermouth, friendly sales mode to appropriately curious mode, I was able to recover enough to see the tears in Josh's eyes.

We continued out to the backyard. Stepping in number two at meeting number one shed a little more light on the situation: husband number one and his dog were soon to be replaced by petless partner number two. If I hadn't caught on to the nonverbal clues by then, I would have quickly understood as Sandy launched her

ADVANCE READING COPY. NOT FOR SALE.

"I told you dogs are disgusting" tirade. Entering a marriage with a pet can be tricky if the dog-owning spouse doesn't like to pick up dog shit and the dog-adopting spouse doesn't like dogs... or men, really. My association with the happy times in their lives and my happy-bunny constant reminder of those times cost me the listing.

While it's important to obtain answers to the aforementioned questions, asking the questions takes some finesse. An especially tricky one is finding out if the sellers are considering other companies or agents. Although the National Association of Realtors reports that, more often than not, sellers interview just one agent, it's wise to know if you have some competition. It is even better to find out who you are in competition with. If you do find out, say something nice about your competition before you begin to highlight your beneficial differences and the benefits to hiring you will be perceived as more sincere. If you ask your potential patrons where they are in the getting-ready-to-list process, you might just extract this information without making them feel like fools for not considering multiple agents. Don't come right out and ask them who else they are considering—that's enough incentive for them to consider calling in a few competitors. Instead say, "I'm excited to work with you." Then watch their face for a guilty expression. If they don't answer, "Me, too!" you might be safe to look surprised and say, "Where **are** you in the process?"

SECRETSᴘᴏʀ**Clients**

A good agent will appreciate the fact that you are interviewing other prospective listing agents. It will make them work harder. It will also benefit you by exposing you to different approaches. Once you feel totally confident with a prospective agent, that's when you should go for one more interview. Again, do not choose agents based on the highest asking price unless they can prove that they have real market data and believe their incredible ability to achieve that price.

ADVANCE READING COPY. NOT FOR SALE.

You should also find out the most important factors for them in choosing a real estate expert. You can ask this casually while walking through the property or more formally during the initial sit-down. This will help you highlight where your skills intersect with what's important to them. If you don't have those skills, take the time between the two listing appointments to scamper and bone up.

Whenever you're gleaning information of any sort, write it down. Pause and listen and think in a way that proves to the sellers that you are really analyzing and strategizing. Some clients are impressed with computerized note taking, and some agents even go so far as to video this walk-through. That's not a bad idea because watching the walk-through later will allow you to strategically analyze what exactly was discussed as well as how things were said. This also helps compensate for your dementia while giving the seller the impression that you really care about the built-in Bingo ball selector they installed in the daylight basement for Nathan's bar mitzvah party in 1978.

Extracting the sellers' impression on price can be extremely tricky, but it is critically important. In spite of their claims to the contrary, most sellers do have a price in mind for their home. They might not know if it's realistically high or dismally low, but they have a benchmark of desire. They might know more than you do—after all, they've lived in the house and are privy to all the details that you are yet to uncover.

Some sellers think they should keep their price impressions to themselves in order to obtain your objective analysis. You can mitigate the effects of this seller paranoia by preemptively addressing their concerns. Say, "I will still come up with a crisp and accurate analysis from the real market data at our next appointment. In the meantime, what are you thinking about price?" If they claim not to know, don't believe them. Make a joke about what they would say if they had no choice but to pick a price. Or ask them to pick their dream price. Once they give you that, ask them to pick their realistic dream price. Foxy. Explain that it won't affect the price you will suggest but that it's always good to know whether you're presenting good news or bad.

ADVANCE READING COPY. NOT FOR SALE.

If you have found out that they are interviewing other agents, you have found out where they are in the process, and you have found out that they have received market analyses already, so you have some ammunition. You can express confusion over the fact that the competing agent produced the plan at the first substantive appointment rather than digesting and providing a custom plan for their specific home. Explain that all your marketing is customized (and be sure that's the truth). Then find out what they were told about price, terms, timing, marketing commitment, everything, but promise that you are far too experienced and stubborn (wink) to have that affect your analysis and plan.

Keep in mind where they said they are in the process. They could be in the early stages of considering a move, packing their bags tomorrow, interviewing you as the last of six agents, asking for your advice on the best time to move, or planning for a transfer that is not due to take place for several months. When you know that you have competition for the listing, you can strategically tweak your second-appointment presentation to be the last (see "Bit O' Science"). This is generally the best timing, especially when you have found out who is competing for the listing and you feel that you are not in the most formidable competition. If you feel that the competition is fierce, you might want to go first when scheduling your presentation appointment so you can successfully seal the listing contract and, hopefully, completely cancel the other appointments.

If you have done your homework to learn a bit about the sellers and the property, you can provide just the right materials to leave with the sellers at the first appointment. If your second appointment is scheduled for several days out, you can email or mail them this piece along with a note thanking them for the first meeting and confirming the second. This material should anchor you to aspects of similarity.

What the hell does **anchor you to aspects of similarity** mean? Let's say you're attempting to list a horse property and the sellers are 4-H fanatics who are trying to sell their horse farm. You can send them a copy of a relevant article or a marketing piece from another horse property that you've sold. If you are attempting to

ADVANCE READING COPY. NOT FOR SALE.

get into the luxury market and you have never sold a luxury-priced home, you can do the same thing with a fun or informative article. Pluck something about luxury real estate from an excellent article that you read. If you're not reading articles on luxury real estate, you probably shouldn't be trying to sell it. Sometimes an effective and unusual marketing piece from out of town is a deal stealer. Effective marketing ideas spread like STDs in local real estate markets, so if you can find one that's not overdone in your area and that your competitors aren't likely to have laid their paws on, you'll be cemented into the sellers' minds.

Research

Between the two meetings, fill in the holes in the sellers' information with your own research. Not only must you understand market trends, neighborhood features and changes, important details about comparative properties, financing trends that might affect the sale, and all of the pertinent details about the house, you have to make sure that your facts are accurate. Delve into sellers' proclamations and correct potential inaccuracies with finesse. Often sellers will claim a certain square footage, insist that they have a new roof, or swear that the leaky oil tank was removed. They will also tell you all the details of the sale of their neighbor's house. While they might mean well, you can't rely on their anecdotal stats.

SORTAFacts™

Men over thirty who dismiss the fact that their mother answers the phone when you call and yells, "Honey, are you still asleep down there?" claim they make 78% more money than their W-2 tax forms show.

—*Courtesy of Sortafact*

These know-it-all pronouncements that sound dismissive of potential inaccuracies are triggers for your fact-checking tentacles to start twitching. Turn those twitches into the benefit of working with you. If the tax records indicate a different square footage or they have added onto the house without an official measurement,

ADVANCE READING COPY. NOT FOR SALE.

you can offer professional measuring as part of your service to protect them and to fend off future discrepancies with appraisals. The new roof could be ten years old, so prod in a co-conspiratorial way to see if the word **new** should actually be **newer**…or not even mentioned. Was the oil tank removed or decommissioned or never there? Offering to look through their paperwork to help avoid misrepresenting the situation is another service you provide. Sometimes your clients are totally correct about the neighborhood data, sometimes they are full of shit, and sometimes they are testing you. Knowing the actual data and details of a neighbor's house rather than going off of neighborhood lore is vital for representing your sellers well. Just as important, how you deliver corrections to sellers' data can make the difference between winning the listing and watching someone else pound their sign into the sellers' yard.

TRIALS&Titillations™

Log in to your favorite social media site and post a contest for the best real estate marketing materials for selling property. Give away something substantial for the winning submission—expensive concert tickets and trips to someplace wonderful tend to work well. When you steal the best idea (and this exercise requires that you do), the commissions you make will more than cover the expense of the prize.

The Second Meeting

The second meeting should also feel like it is all about the seller, but the truth is that it should also be about you and your plan. There is no substitute for hard work in preparing an accurate market analysis and a uniquely compelling plan. Do not be lazy. Make a gorgeous presentation packet. Leave it with the sellers if you like to give them something to refer to. Or take it with you so they'll have to call when they have questions—and so no other agents can copy your genius. Make it strictly paperless or not. Either way, it must be gorgeous. Include a lovely, full-color analysis of the market, current tax information, market trends, a detailed marketing plan, examples of your marketing materials,

ADVANCE READING COPY. NOT FOR SALE.

stuff about your company and its greatness, and your bio with testimonials and other convincing information. There are so many books, DVDs, worksheets, and videos describing what to put in the marketing packet that I'm not going to go into detail about what to include—this is focused on the how and why.

Assuming you have statistics and materials to support all that you are trying to convey, it's time to delve deep to find out the best way to convey it to each particular seller. Let the sellers know that you have covered every detail and analyzed every factor, and that you have the unique and necessary experience to achieve their goals. Inform them that you are aware of their busy lives and respectful of their time.

Tell the sellers that you always tailor your presentations, and focus on the information that is most pertinent to each seller—just like you tailor each marketing plan to best represent each property. Your goal is to be so smart that your clients feel smarter. The sellers will feel like schmucks if you let them feel that they are less thorough in their review or that they are wasting time on things that shouldn't require mental masturbation. Give them options. Show them the physical representation of your work (the thick, sexy booklet or the latest electronic device of analysis, for example). Tell them that you have several options and they can choose how they would like you to proceed with the presentation. For best results, present the options in this specific order:

1. If you have enough time, I can go over each comparable property and all the features. I can go over the entire plan, and you can ask questions along the way or at the end. (I generally don't suggest ending with, "Do you have to be anywhere tonight?")
2. If you're in a hurry, I can buzz through the marketing plan and you can flip through the comparable properties and ask me any questions. I have cleared my schedule for you, so I'm good either way.
3. Together we can go over the most important aspects of the plan and the most important comparable properties. We can discuss and you can ask questions as we go. This is what most people prefer, but I want to be respectful of your time.
4. Or you can list the property with me right now. (Smile for this one.)

ADVANCE READING COPY. NOT FOR SALE.

End with, "Which would you prefer?"

Beware of nonverbal communication—both yours and the clients'. Often people in couples will have different decision processes and responsibilities. It's easy to be drawn to the partner who is most engaged and to ignore the quiet, less sparkly partner, but do so only at your peril. When you leave, the quiet patron won't necessarily stay quiet about how he or she feels about working with you. Position yourself so that you can see both their faces. If they can make faces about you to each other and you can't see them doing this, it means that you have not orchestrated the seating arrangement correctly. If they disagree in front of you, acknowledge both points of view. You can save your incredulity for after you leave and have made sure that your cell phone has not butt dialed them (yes, that bit of advice comes from an unfortunate experience).

After you've covered the information, ask if they have any questions. If you know they've interviewed other agents, ask if there was anything covered by those agents that you did not go over. I once forgot to do this and later found out that I lost the listing because the other agent offered to pay for a freaking home warranty. That shit cost $350—nada when you consider that my forgetting to ask cost me a listing.

If they haven't committed to you already, ask them when they will be making their decision. Check to see if you should call them in a few days. Thank them and tell them that you would love to work with them. Let them know that you like them and like their house. They don't need to be your best friend, but clients don't hire real estate professionals they can't stand.

Before you leave the second meeting, you should have a good idea whether or not you are in the running to get the listing. If you don't have any vibe about it, you probably didn't get enough sleep the night before, but most sellers don't want to hear all about that.

Sellers think that the interview process for listing their property is their interview. A great real estate professional knows that this is not exactly true. If you approach the process with curiosity and artful inquisition, your questions can lead both you and the sellers to the right answers.

ADVANCE READING COPY. NOT FOR SALE.

CHAPTER 17

FLUIDS

Although I always recommend drinking coffee while working with buyers—not only is it delicious but it also keeps you awake when your buyers are yammering on about their cousin's incredible impersonations in the neighborhood talent show—alcohol is by far the more important fluid when it comes to working with sellers. If you drink a couple glasses of water between the coffee and the alcohol, you will have a decent chance of getting a part-time job as a cosmetics salesperson when the market gets shaky. If not, Botox is getting cheaper all the time.

TRIALS&Titillations™

Start a rumor about a supersuccessful, spunky real estate broker who manifested her shit-to-shine story by embracing the Camel Diet. Count how many friends you can get to start their day with thirty-two ounces of water on an empty stomach. See if you can be the first to buy the domain name. Write a book and create a clothing line.

TrueSTORIES

I met a couple at an open house, and they decided to interview me as a possible broker to list their home. I did not have any prior relationship with these people, but I liked Nick and Wendy immediately. The feeling continued when I arrived at their house for the initial meeting at 4:00 p.m. on a Friday. After walking through their home together, we sat down to chat. They started to make themselves, and offered to make me, what looked to be some delicious tequila sunrises.

I know it's totally unprofessional to accept a drink at the first substantive meeting with clients. This is the time to discuss and disclose—I'm talking about real estate facts, not truth-or-dare stories. It's usually great, however, if *they* engage in consumption (except the time I came to the appointment to find my potential client passed out on the front sidewalk, but that's an extreme example and, shit, he'd sign anything).

The tequila sunrise is such a vacation-y, tropical drink, and we were in the midst of a long stretch of rainy, depressing days. I'm not making excuses but, damn, it was pretty much the perfect trifecta: Friday at 4:00 p.m., dismal weather for days, and… well, a delicious tequila-filled beverage. With my inability to say no to a perfect trifecta, there was no hope.

As the first drops sped down my gullet, Nick and Wendy looked at one another and said, "We're listing with her."

As it turned out, they had interviewed several other agents, and none of them had dared even a drop of the proffered tequila. I imagine them, week after week, interviewing agents at the witching happy hour on Friday, looking for their imbiber-in-arms. I got that listing by being a lush. Aren't you proud of me?

SECRETS foɾ Clients

Although our mommas taught us all that when you invite someone into your home, it is nice to offer them something to drink, from time to time we forgot that this should apply even when we are inviting contractors in. Often your real estate professional has been going from appointment to appointment, and she has a parched throat. Help a gal out.

SORTA facts™

Studies show that people who enjoy books with references to oral sex enjoy laughing over self-pity 4 to 1. 89% of people surveyed understood why this important statistic was included

ADVANCE READING COPY. NOT FOR SALE.

in this chapter, but only 56% understood why this chapter was included in this book.

— Courtesy of Sortafact

What is the takeaway from this? Hell if I know. Maybe the lesson here could be that you have to cloak your professionalism in a layer of authenticity. When working with people, know that there is enough business to go around. Not everyone will love you, but that doesn't mean that you have to become someone else.

I don't, however, suggest making the first move and bringing a Bob Marley CD and some homemade brownies to the listing appointment, nor would I suggest pulling out tarot cards to show how in touch you are with future market trends. The real lesson is to read this whole book with a gigantic grain of salt. Just be sure that it's resting around the rim of a delicious Cadillac margarita.

ADVANCE READING COPY. NOT FOR SALE.

CHAPTER 18

ON YOUR SIDE

If only there were magical glasses. When everyone warned me that my life would change when I hit middle age, I just knew I would be different. This was an experience where I really wanted to be different, or at least the same as those other fabulous people who never seem to age. I nearly screamed when I was dancing naked through my empty house once and saw my mother's cottage-cheesy thighs in my mirror. And I don't believe in ghosts. I know the skin dangling from my neck is not a waddle but instead is due to the fact that I sometimes forget to apply moisturizer. I have the wrong concealer. It's because I haven't had Botox (yet). That's all. I'm totally different.

My husband's clutter is art, as are our family photos. My fuchsia living room is sophisticated. My dog doesn't smell (okay, even I know that's bullshit, but I'm trying to make a point here). Riiiiight. As unique and wonderful as I hope I am, my home is, my kids are, my career is, I hope my husband thinks I am, my best friends claim me to be…I'm not. As Charles de Gaulle said, "The cemeteries of the world are full of indispensable men." And sellers, like all people, believe they are indispensable.

Indispensable *and* normal. Real estate transactions are not a time when people want to be unique. It not the best time to let your clients feel like you have never encountered a situation like theirs. They especially don't want to hear that their house needs more Botox than the average ranch-style home or that they're the only clients you've ever had to remind to flush the toilet. People want to know that even Bob Dole uses Viagra. They need to know that even fabulous and famous movie stars have to prepare their homes for sale.

Whether they're moving out, scaling down, or vamping up, sellers will find preparing a house for sale is personal. And embarrassing. It's almost like going to the bathroom—we all must do it. As real estate professionals, we get to see a whole lot of personal.

Outsiders' Eyes

Our sense of superiority is quickly stifled when we, ourselves, consider becoming sellers. It wasn't until I took my most blunt and observant best friend, slightly drunk and therefore very candid, through my house that I realized how my clients must feel. "It's like *Storage Wars: The Home Edition*," he said. His harshness was the dose of honesty I needed, but I must admit that it secretly pissed me off and hurt my feelers.

What They See
- The allure of authenticity

What We See
- Dirty bras
- Debris of a failing marriage
- Gifted children's bad report cards
- Dog hair tumbleweed
- Foreclosure notices
- K-Y jelly
- Pink slips
- Man-size pink slips
- Torn linens
- Shower curtains covered in mildew
- Frayed toothbrushes
- Dorky inspirational notes
- Long-empty bathroom-soap dispensers

I'm still guilty of traipsing through potential sellers' homes waving my arms like I have a magic wand that will make their home appear in its most sellable Disneyland-alicious delight. The trick is to magically orchestrate the transformation by strategically revealing it in a way that makes the suggested transformation seem commonplace.

ADVANCE READING COPY. NOT FOR SALE.

I don't suggest admitting to the sellers that you, too, had to clean up the contents of your goody drawer before going on the market because, well, that's private. It's okay to tell them that you had to finally toss the Oxycodone left over from your carpal tunnel surgery, but it's best not to tell them that you also had to hide the Vicodin that your friend gave you after her boob job. Tell the sellers to clean up their shit in a way that says their shithole is not the worst you have ever seen. Often, this means the absolute truth must be tweaked a wee bit.

SORTAFacts™

Painkillers are the most commonly stolen item from open houses throughout most of the country. Earmuffs and firearms are the number one and number two most swiped in Alaska.

—*Courtesy of Sortafact*

Our clients need to hear that the way people live in a home is almost always different from the way they sell a home. Let them know that they're not doing anything wrong by living like they're living. They just can't sell like they're living.

Once a filthy housekeeper of a client asked me if the home needed more staging and cleanup than the homes of most of my other clients. Her house was such a sty that I had to stop and really look deep into her eyes to make sure she wasn't bullshitting me. Did she really think everyone lived with dog-shit stains on a twenty-thousand-dollar rug? No, most people don't have twenty-thousand-dollar rugs. The accouterments of wealth might make others forget that anyone can live a squalid lifestyle, but as real estate salespeople (and because even rich people have untalented cleaning help), we aren't as easily fooled.

TRIALS&Titillations™

Find someone with an opinion that is 180 degrees from your own. Try hard to internalize his belief and discard your previously held belief. Read three things on the internet that support your new belief. Pat yourself on the back because that pissed-off

ADVANCE READING COPY. NOT FOR SALE.

feeling is your confirmation bias fast at work. See? Getting on their side is not as easy as it sounds.

To the extent that they are miserable, sadists know only too well that misery loves company. Your miserable sellers must know that many people find selling their home to be an invasive, emotional, and all-around pain-in-the-ass experience. They must also know that getting their house *ready* for sale can be equally wrenching. Explain these emotions before your clients become familiar with them. Leave room in your explanation for the remote possibility that they will enjoy the process, but let them know that, whatever they experience, they are in a club with plenty of like-minded members.

Delicately test to see what camp they think they will end up in, and then share a personal story that puts you into that tent with them. If your client's house smells like dog, you can share how you always need your dogless neighbor friend to do the preparty sniff test because you can't detect the dog smell in your home either. If your client is going through a divorce (and you're not pissed at your husband for something like making nonrefundable plane reservations for a wedding that is not taking place in the same month as what is printed on the tickets), you relate another divorce that ended successfully.

SECRETSForClients

Remove personal photos from your house when you are ready to sell. I know your family is the cutest and you have no other art for those walls, but it is imperative that your beautiful family does not distract buyers. Jealousy is not the most common emotion to coax offers out of buyers. Unless you're selling your darlings along with the house, take down those portraits.

If your agent is gentle with you and lets you keep the litter box in the kitchen, the invitations on the refrigerator, and the potty chair in the master shower, that's not a good thing. It probably means that your agent is too nice to be honest with you. Nice is good—just not in place of honesty in this case.

ADVANCE READING COPY. NOT FOR SALE.

Premature…You-Know-What

Want to hear a supertrue stupidstition? Don't mentally spend your commission before you close. One of my cohorts put together a very lucrative deal on a high-end property. A few weeks into the transaction and quite a bit before closing, he decided to test-drive a fancy car that he intended to buy with the commission he was to earn. The next day, the transaction unraveled. He swears that every time he mentally spends his commission before he officially earns it, the deal doesn't close. I asked him to please never do that when he's working on a deal with me—or I will cut him.

Why can't we just enjoy a little success? What harm is there in cracking open an effervescent bottle of a little something with our sellers upon signing a sale contract? There is no damage in sharing tequila, scotch, or even a beer, but a celebratory drink like champagne is forbidden at this stage. Getting to this stage is a biggie and took a tremendous team effort by you and your sellers, but it is just one major hurdle in the race to a successful close and a payday for you and your sellers. Real estate contracts come with contingencies. Some stand like mini–speed bumps on a neighborhood street at midnight, while others block the way like a country club gate. Sales can fail. Transactions can unravel even after a contract is made. Sellers can feel as vulnerable and rejected as a man dumped on a third date because he wore his Speedos in an icy pool. Rejection after attraction can feel worse than no attraction at all. Be sure to balance your sellers' excitement over buyers' attraction with the reality of potential rejection.

This balance is particularly critical in a market where external factors like economic uncertainty, global political instability, newly instituted regulations, and local job insecurity are wildly at play. Beware of the moment when typical markets become atypical. Understand the history of these shifting markets and use a walk down Memory Lane to prepare your clients.

"It's not always about you!" my mother used to constantly harp. She was right. Be sure your sellers understand that. My favorite way to do that is with the Share and Tell list:

ADVANCE READING COPY. NOT FOR SALE.

1. Prepare sellers for potential buyer requests — from the common to the outrageous.
2. Share how you have personally felt when confronted by these annoyances.
3. Explain how shoving your feelings aside has helped you achieve success — just like they'll achieve when they do the same.

External factors causing failed sales can be the most frustrating. You can often take a wee bit of blame when these take you by surprise. Distressed sale situations often involve banks. As much as we hear that corporations are people too, we know that type of "people" doesn't generally move as fast as real people. Banks often move at a snail's pace, for example. The slow response from banks can tamper buyer enthusiasm like a suspicious smell in tight quarters. That's a tough one for an agent to combat, but you should at least expect it. Perhaps the sale failed because the buyers were too demanding with repairs, leaving the sellers feeling overwhelmed and nickel-and-dimed. (Hell, I would rather be nickel-and-dimed than hundred-and-thousanded, but whatever.) You do not have the luxury of claiming that unrealistic expectations of buyers and sellers caused a sale to fail; you are the one responsible for managing those expectations.

SECRETSforClients

Ask your agent what she has personally done in situations similar to your own. Ask for a specific example. By recalling a similar situation, she will either have to admit that she has not personally experienced anything related to what you are experiencing (and she'll be more understanding from then on) or she will let you learn the right or wrong strategy from her success or failure.

It's good for your business to assess each and every sale fail even though self-honesty is hard. Focus on assessing the ultimate outcome of each of your client relationships instead of focusing solely on the transactional analyses. What does this mean? If your relationship with your sellers is still outstanding after a sale fail or

ADVANCE READING COPY. NOT FOR SALE.

two…or three, you have done your job. The transaction that failed to close might have been a shittier deal for your sellers than the one that actually closed…or not. The point is if, during the failed transaction(s), you and the sellers remained teammates in action, the ultimate outcome is not much of a factor in your ongoing relationship with your client. Monthly and year-end assessments of each transaction should go beyond the outcome of the transaction—closed or failed—and extend to the outcome of the client relationship. Can you count on those clients to call you for their future real estate needs, questions, and referrals? Your business hinges on the answer to that question.

SECRETS for Clients

There is a saying among real estate professionals that is frequently repeated: "All real estate is local." The saying is catchy and helps create a positive spin, often accurately, on bad national news. What it comes down to, though, is the fact that shifts in larger markets often become shifts in local markets. If your agent's head is so in her 'hood that she doesn't notice national shifts, market changes can catch both of you unaware and unprepared. If your agent suffers from provincialism, it could cost you.

Keep Your Cool

The buyers' agent may be about as professional and charismatic as Snooki. You, your clients, or all of the above may sincerely hate him. But when you're working with other real estate professionals, do not make them opponents.

Sometimes it's hard not to mentally vilify them. Just make sure you do not do so verbally, and never in front of your clients. You will work with a lot of annoying people throughout your life. I annoy myself sometimes (okay, often), so there is no way in hell that I can claim to never be annoying to others. In real estate, however, you are a facilitator and not a principal. This means that, as an agent or broker, you are not a party to the contract or transaction so you had better not internalize the situation as if you are. It's like being a marriage counselor—don't actually participate in the three-way.

ADVANCE READING COPY. NOT FOR SALE.

SECRETSforClients

Unless your agent's name is on the deed to your property, do not let her make decisions for you as if it were.

Sometimes other agents really frost your ass. It takes all your willpower not to retaliate in the face of this kind of frustration, but you must know that you're out on thin ice. If the buyers' agent's behavior goes beyond douchebaggery and into the realm of unprofessionalism, the ice becomes even thinner. Massive unprofessionalism certainly needs to be shaved from the glacier of our industry, but simple bad behavior is best numbed by a cocktail on the rocks and some sympathetic friends visiting from Iceland (so they're less likely to know the jerky agent involved). It's not worth having the asshole tell her biased side of the story and potentially taint your stellar reputation.

Your relationship with other real estate practitioners is almost more important than your reputation with your client sphere of influence. Your clients will lose if other agents hate you. Your clients will win if other agents perceive you to be smart, agreeable, helpful, honest, and fun to work with.

SECRETSforClients

When choices are abundant, buyers' agents can create subtle clues to steer buyers away from viewing your property if they hate your real estate agent…or you.

Your reputation can compensate for a less-than-stellar reputation of your client. This rarely works in the reverse.

TrueSTORIES

One of my agent friends, Mark, told me of his soon-to-be sale fail. The buyers got too greedy on repairs after gouging the sellers on the initial price negotiation. On top of that, the buyers were using an agent the sellers had previously hired and then fired,

ADVANCE READING COPY. NOT FOR SALE.

and they hated him. When attending the inspection, the hated agent, Vernon, had the extreme misfortune and audacity to track a few leaves into the house. All of this sent Mark's sellers into fits of anger. The sellers were clearly under more life stress then generated by the need to rake. They decided not to do a single repair in order to kill the sale and lose the buyers represented by Vernon, leaf tracker. Mark was beyond frustrated. He knew that when Vernon came over that weekend to present the repair addendum, it would not end with a commission.

I suggested Mark buy a gift certificate from a cleaning service and present it to his sellers while sort of letting them think it was from Mark's buyers. This prevented the stink from the sellers' dislike of the buyers' agent from sticking on the buyers. This is a form of re-triangulation. The technique has saved many transactions, and it saved this one too.

Sharing stories with your clients about the ineptitude of other agents only complicates transactions. Keep their ineptitude a secret as much as humanly possible. Chances are, the sellers have already conjured negative images of the "bottom-feeding, nitpicky, demanding, spoiled" buyers as effectively as the buyers have conjured negative images of the "greedy, out-of-touch" sellers. You don't need to add to this by blurting what a dolt the other agent clearly is. Adding emotional eye of newt to an already simmering caldron can make your brew bubble over. Resist the temptation to vent your frustrations about the other agent to your client. When all else fails, re-triangulate.

No One Will Ever Know

When your sellers are embarrassed about their true motivation to sell, it can be challenging to achieve the outcome in their best interest. Maybe you saw your Junior League client mackin' on her friend at a girls' night out and then again at a WNBA game, but if her husband doesn't share that with you, you must play dumb no matter how much he claims they're moving to get into the proper parish.

When faced with this tough situation, the third-person story technique can be helpful. It is a way to stand by and simultaneously

ADVANCE READING COPY. NOT FOR SALE.

illustrate to your clients what their behavior looks like to others. It's a way of foreshadowing a likely outcome in the face of an immovable position. Often this most likely outcome is not becoming to your client.

TrueSTORIES

My partner and I were representing a seller, Iris, who really *needed* to sell her gloriously customized penthouse. Iris was posturing to appear nonchalant and unmotivated in order to hide the fact that she was plagued by evil financial demons. Because we had done our own research, we knew she was not presenting the true picture, but we didn't let on. It's so much easier when clients fully open their kimonos, but some people value privacy more than I can understand. Pretend to believe those private clients, but remain true to helping them achieve their undisclosed goal.

In this situation, a competent agent representing a well-qualified buyer presented an offer below the asking price. We knew the responsible thing was to make Iris seriously consider this offer before her plight became too obvious to ignore. But she was digging in her heels and refusing to consider any offer below her asking price.

We strategized with Iris by reminding her that we would stand by her position and tell the buyers' agent she did not have to consider an offer in this price range. We would tell the buyers' agent that the seller had the luxury of waiting out the market for months or perhaps years and years and years until she got the price that would recoup her investment.

As we said this, it was clear that Iris was picturing just what those months or years might look like in light of her true financial situation. We painted this honest picture without being preachy or didactic—and without letting on that we knew how dire her situation was. She knew that we would stick by her through months and years. She knew she didn't have the luxury of that time. She was then able to look at the offer reasonably while we remained trusted advisors on her side to help her control her own destiny.

ADVANCE READING COPY. NOT FOR SALE.

As the minister told his parishioners during a Sunday church sermon, "You would never cheat, lie, or steal, but someone in your pew might." As Misty told her fellow pole artist in the dressing room of the Clit Cat Bar, "I can't believe Saucy offered a lap dance to Marvin, my best customer. You would never do that!" Same general idea.

Your job is to strategically place your buyers in the role of the sellers and the sellers in the role of the buyers while still remaining on your patrons' side. Think: I'll show you mine if you show me yours.

ADVANCE READING COPY. NOT FOR SALE.

CHAPTER 19
OPEN HOUSE

The history of the open house is a fascinating one. I have read a couple of false histories about some cave-maker jezebels sending the *Homo fabulous* from the tribe out to find the perfect pelts while opening their "caves" to tribal *Homo erectus,* but those stories are vicious rumors. My uneducated guess is that the first open house was in Levittown, New York, in 1947. The initial attempt was a flop because the attendees were all neighbors who lived in the exact replica house down the street. Several years later an ingenious agent decided that sneaking out of the office and into someone's home might give the edge on capturing prospects. This method proved to be very effective, as holding open houses became the most popular weekend activity for anyone with a scuffed briefcase and a comb-over.

The right open house can be hugely beneficial to your career and life. Here are some components of the most effective open houses:

- Good visibility with lots of signage potential
- Seller bakes well and shares
- Appropriately priced
- Easy escape in case of visitor with a hatchet
- Your outfit matches the pretty exterior
- Reflective of the type of homes you wish to sell

Even if you prefer to enjoy your weekends, there are plenty o' reasons to drag your sorry ass out of bed to host an open house:

- To find a buyer for that home
- To find a patron who will tell the ultimate buyer about that home

- To find a buyer for your other listings
- To set up a buyer consultation for a new buyer
- To get a date
- To meet neighbors who want to list their homes
- To get your name out
- To get feedback to discuss with your seller
- To make your seller happy

SECRETSꜰᴏʀ**Clients**

Some agents like conducting open houses because they give their business exposure—they can pick up buyers and sellers for future transactions. An honest agent will confess this to you. If they tell you this is the *only* reason, it might be because they don't know how to successfully hold an open house to benefit you. Many agents have tremendous success with open houses because they're good at them. If they placate you by sticking an untrained, warm body agent in the house so they can tell you that it was open but didn't sell, perhaps it was due to the lack of talent of the warm body.

Personal Preparation

How well you capitalize on the open house is determined a lot by what you do ahead of time. Remind yourself of all the property's special features. Scope out the nearby parks, restaurants, shops, schools, and liquor stores. Check out the houses for sale in the immediate neighborhood and make yourself some cheat sheets on the features, prices, market information, and condition of those properties.

If the house is a great representation of the type of business you have, or would like to have, anchor yourself to that house like the coattails you love to grab. Send out postcards or strategically blast social media. Invite people to come and see you. Call a few people. Personally invite any neighbors you know. Actually, tell them to ask any of their friends who might be in the market to buy or sell to come visit you and see the cool abode.

When you're trying to build your business, holding open houses for more experienced and prolific listing agents is one of the most

ADVANCE READING COPY. NOT FOR SALE.

excellent ways to launch yourself. Host open houses that match the kinds of listings you want to have and to meet potential sellers and buyers to snare as your clients. Preparation gives you the bounciest launch pad.

Dress for the 'hood. Don't wear your Hillary pantsuit with spectator pumps in a neighborhood of liberal artists, gays, and lesbians. I'm not suggesting cargo pants, a Prada tool belt, and a beret would cover all of your bases either. Just be aware of the jewelry you choose and the clothing you wear. As Marisa Tomei sarcastically put it in one of my favorite films, *My Cousin Vinny* (and notice I call it a film and not a movie), "You blend." This is something to strive for. It is true if you are marketing high-end McMansions, city estates, suburban tract homes, whatever. Just think about it for a few minutes and then try to blend a bit. If you're the in-house agent for a slumlord, make an effort to wear something that doesn't clash with the squalor. Have all your information about the neighborhood with you. Have all the information about the house in your car. Hidden. You need to have memorized those stats before the day of the open house—or at least hide your cheat sheets for discrete reference.

Preparation H

The get the property ready for an open house, there are some absolute must-dos. Flowers, cookies, and bribe money are secondary. Do these first:

> Clean (interior and exterior)
> Deodorize
> Replace all burned-out light bulbs
> Add light where necessary
> Get the temperature right

SECRETSforClients

Ask your prospective listing agent what she thinks about an open house. Many sellers fear having their house open to the public, but if you feel this way, don't reveal this right off the bat. Be open to discussing the pros and cons. You might have

ADVANCE READING COPY. NOT FOR SALE.

valuable possessions that will entice thieves. You might fear an intelligent criminal casing the joint for future attacks (or maybe I just put that in your head). Put away your valuables and pop your benzodiazepine—you'll get through it. Listen to why open houses might be an important part of the marketing plan for your home.

Open Wide

When the house is fully prepped to be in the spotlight, don't forget to unlock the door. I know that sounds incredibly obvious, but a few times I was so busy turning on lights and making a rush for a last-minute bathroom break that I forgot. Greet each guest with a laid-back smile and a handshake. State your first and last names. Don't squander an opportunity to get your name out there in the public. Look them in the eyeballs, or in that general direction, and listen for their names. If they don't say them, get them by smiling and saying, "And you are?"

Those victims who immediately give you their first and last names are the least suspicious and the most comfortable with you as a salesperson. They are also probably the most successful, so mortgage loan underwriters should pay attention to this detail, but they don't.

Those who give you only their first name might be a little reticent, but they might just be religious and not want to give it up on the first date so soon after church and before Denny's. The first name will do. For now.

SORTAFacts™

Studies show that the most confident people use their first and last names when making business introductions in person. Online, however, people tend to introduce themselves by the name of their first dog and their current computer operating system.

—*Courtesy of Sortafact*

If you can't even extract a first name, figure something major is going on with that person, like:

ADVANCE READING COPY. NOT FOR SALE.

- Just had a fight with significant other
- Doesn't have a significant other
- Just experienced a repressed memory
- Doesn't like salespeople
- Doesn't like you
- All of the above

Remember that people often act like assholes, and that might have nothing to do with you…at all. It's only all about you to…you. As my mom always reminded me, "We are all the stars of our own show." Holy shit, people *are* clueless (but not us, right?).

SORTAfacts™

This one's more than just a Sortafact: 90% of Americans classify themselves as smarter than the average American. 61% of Americans think they are more attractive than the average man or woman.

— Courtesy of Dr. Frank Luntz[1]

Position matters (but you know that). Once introductions are out of the way, you want them to know the bullet points of the property. I like to say, "The cheat sheet is on the table for your viewing pleasure." It's a little unusual but not too clever. Tell them that you will be in the next room if they have any questions. If they are receptive, leave it at that. For now.

Some people will keep up the asshole routine even after you pleasantly give them space. If they are avoiding you, even if you are so interested in why they are being assholes, this is not the time to ask. Just smile and say something like, "Actually, I'm here for any of your *easy* questions." That is a little bit of safe self-deprecation, which is a very important element at this stage in your relationship with an open house customer. It creates a friendly and confident but not cocky sales demeanor. Now go to the next room and listen.

---

1. Frank I. Luntz, *What Americans Want…Really: The Truth About Our Hopes, Dreams and Fears* (New York: Hyperion, 2010)

ADVANCE READING COPY. NOT FOR SALE.

If you have throngs of people at your open house, you might deem this a successful open (I don't necessarily agree) and decide you don't have time to go to the next room. Just repeat your flyer and question lines with each person, but pay attention so you're ready for when the second point of contact should occur.

Say you have moved to another room. As the people enter the room where you are strategically stowing away, they are now be coming to you. Acknowledge their approach with a mellow smile and with, "Are you looking to buy in the neighborhood?" This will determine whether they are future buyers for your listing, future buyers to work with later, or representatives of a potential future listing opportunity. If they are rude and stand-offish, fuck 'em. They would probably be a pain in the ass to work with anyway.

But if they're pleasant, listen to the answer to this question—and notice *how* they answer. These clues direct you to what your next move should be—to move away or to move in for a deeper relationship. If customers sheepishly state that they are "just snoopy neighbors," praise them and tell them that neighbors are the best source for finding new owners. Ask them to please help sell the house to their friends. They might like you and do just that—or remember to call you when they want to sell their home. If they are receptive and indicate that they are, in fact, looking to buy in that exact neighborhood, smile and ask them if they want to buy *this* house. This is especially effective if they have toured most or the entire house before coming into the room where you are poised.

Other tricks that I have employed with varying success involve postures. If it's crowded, you must stand. I say this with sensitivity toward people with vertical limitations, but do your best to prop yourself. If there are only one or two people in the house, sit in your stowaway area and when they come into the room, leisurely stand up. It will give them the subconscious feeling that they are important to you but you're not overly eager, and you will get a little exercise in the process. If attendees seem to have a sense of humor, I sometimes say, as I'm standing, "I'm working so very hard today." This has sort of a conspiratorial effect as you're "sharing" that you were caught being a little lazy on the sellers' behalf.

ADVANCE READING COPY. NOT FOR SALE.

SECRETS for Clients

When an offer comes in days or weeks after your last open house, don't automatically count out the open house as the catalyst for that offer. Time has a way of tricking our analyses of results.

True STORIES

Collecting contact information, that later leads to a sale, is the next best thing to writing an offer on the spot. Of course, offers on the spot are rare beasts. In fact, it's only happened to me once and that was at my very first open house, when I didn't know any better.

I'd had my license for one day and asked an agent in my office if I could host an open house at one of her listings. I carefully photocopied the contract with all sorts of notes so I knew how to fill it out, and I brought a blank form too—just in case. I was ready.

I eagerly greeted each open house visitor, and when I saw that one couple had the requisite stars in their eyes, I asked them if they would like to buy the house. They said, "Um, yes." So...with throngs of people walking through and wondering what the hell this idiot agent was doing, we sat at the kitchen table and wrote up the offer. When I returned to the office with the full-priced offer, I told the listing agent that I sold her house. Brigit, too, looked at me wondering what the hell this idiot agent had done.

She said, "We don't sell listings at open houses!"

I asked her much wiser self, "Then what do we do?"

Brigit explained that the open houses are only to appease the seller. Coming from a retail buying background, I was utterly confused. Now, I was probably a total dolt for writing up the offer at the kitchen table *during* the open house. I could have hooked the buyers for later contract writing and cultivated more offers from other buyers too. But because I sold a listing at my very first open house, I still disagree that open houses are not for selling.

ADVANCE READING COPY. NOT FOR SALE.

Ask the Big Q

Open house visitors will be very surprised when you ask them directly if they want to buy the house. Why they think you are sitting at an open house on a weekend if not to sell a house, I have no idea, but they always seem surprised. This tells me that most people holding open houses do not ask the one question that seems to be most obvious.

Or perhaps it's just that the attendees think it's as much fun to hold open houses as it is to tour them. I might not have the most exciting life, but I assure you that I could find more stimulating things to do than holding an open house if there is zero chance visitors will be interested in buying the house, another house, or listing their house in the future.

Whatever the reason for people's surprise, I have obtained business with this question many times.

Good to Know

Bring a snack or you can get grouchy. Be careful to avoid green and brown snacks, as it is generally not good to have those particular colors stuck in your teeth when you're trying to be professional.

It is not unheard of to have no one show up at your open house. Even during lulls in the traffic you can make use of your time. Try these exercises:

- Squats in place (particularly good where the carpets are a little less clean)
- Walking lunges (but too much furniture can mess you up here)
- Sit-ups (better with a clean floor and when there's no chance of anyone walking in on you)
- Push-ups (similar to sit-ups but can be done with a little dirt on the floor—just wash your hands afterward)
- Jumping jacks (not recommended in condos or without a supportive bra or manssiere)
- Sales pitch practice in the mirror (check for hidden cameras and talk quietly in case you miss a customer coming in)
- Jump on trampoline (I was once caught doing this in the backyard and was probably deemed a little less than professional. See point on bra or manssiere.)

ADVANCE READING COPY. NOT FOR SALE.

Pilfering Intel

When the visitors are preparing to leave, ask them if they have any questions. If they say no, ask, "Not even an easy question or two?" Smile so they know you're being chill and fun. Usually they will respond with a joke and an easy question that can be found on the cheat sheet. Then, enthusiastically answer the question with the same attitude as though you have scored a three-point basket. They might be shy and interested. They might be nice and disinterested. They might be dumb. All of these can make them future clients.

If they ask you a good question, they are interested in the property—or in you as an agent or as a date. No matter what their motivation, these good questions make them eligible for a real answer, which means you might have to get a quick email off to them the next day. This is where you employ the trick to getting their contact information. Many people in the real estate training realm tell you to have a fancy sign-in sheet. The one time I did provide that sign-in sheet, I had Mickey Mouse, Oprah Winfrey, and Mylong Schlong all sign in. Now I dig out a notebook that is clearly my working pad, and I ask them to jot their email address down so I can email them some insider information. Look carefully at their contact information and confirm that you can read their writing. Thank them by the name they just wrote down. This can be somewhat embarrassing if they wrote Mike Hunt or some other snarky nom de plume, but you must confirm.

SORTAFacts™

Clients don't like when you fail to get back to them as promised, and 77% of the time they don't acknowledge that it is due to their sloppy handwriting.

—Courtesy of Sortafact

If you obtain just one contact, it is enough to deem the open house successful. Create a little pneumonic for yourself so you can remember who the person is. Mine often sound like "lady with hose tucked into her underwear" or "man with mismatched toupee." Okay, okay, sometimes even I go with "hot broad in great

ADVANCE READING COPY. NOT FOR SALE.

186 AROUSING THE BUY CURIOUS

sweater" or "twinkly eyes." Be careful to assess whether or not to reveal your helpful descriptor when you follow up later.

If inquiring customers don't want to write down their information, I tell them that if they want to buy the property, they can easily call or email me, as my name is conveniently placed on the flyer, and I *promise* to get right back to them. They think it's funny when I state the obvious.

True**STORIES**

I was holding an open house in a newly converted condo project. It was a typically rainy winter day and, after two hours of guzzling coffee in the model unit with not a single visitor, I decided to sneak in a bathroom break. I locked the front deadbolt so no visitors could come in and, planning to be no more than two minutes and hoping to hear if there were any visitors at the front door, I left the bathroom door open. When I was in midstream, I heard the deadbolt turn as the developer and owners, the only other people on the planet with keys, entered the condo. What were the chances?

After the Fact

Now follow up. The *very next day.* If they call you, return their calls. Not returning phone calls is a woefully common problem, and it's a quick way to lose clients. Instead, communicate in a way that potential buyers will love you and want you to work with them.

Obviously, you will have already covered many of the basic perks to the listing, but you'll have left some of the juicier information for following up. This is akin to showing just a bit of cleavage but not flashing the whole tit while still at the first-conversation phase. As new as your breasts…um, er…*listing* might be, you don't need to go for the reveal immediately. Use these tools to get what you want—in this case, contact information.

SORTA*Facts*™

Real-life scientific studies measuring the bodily response to various stimuli indicated a peek o' cleavage yields a 76% more

ADVANCE READING COPY. NOT FOR SALE.

positive response than the whole boob does. This success is less profound with moobs and even less so with butt cracks.

— *Courtesy of Sortafact*

Your sellers' interpretation of the success of the open house will be based on the information you glean and what you do with that information. Always call the sellers immediately after the open house to give feedback. No matter how many times sellers have been told by friends, family, and their superknowledgeable real estate cousins from out of state that houses don't sell at open houses, they still put emotional eggs of hope in the open house basket. If you have any inkling that some excited buyers will surface with an offer, be sure to let the sellers know that you are hot on the follow-up trail with them or their agent. At the same time, temper your excitement so you do not overcommit and under deliver.

Much of what you learn at open houses is not obvious. Share your synthesis of the information with the seller. If it was a lonely open house on the first sunny day in months, you can infer that the weather affected the traffic and you might want to aim for another open house the following week. If only a few families showed up and they shared that the yard was too small, you might discuss tweaking the next ad to reflect the one-level living and the easy-care yard and aim for empty nesters.

SECRETSforClients

Expect your listing agent to provide feedback without constant prompting. Even if there is little or no activity to report, a good agent will report back anyway. He should research inactivity and provide data to help you understand whether there is something you can affect. Appreciate bad news more than no news at all but also don't be afraid to be a squeaky wheel. A great agent won't require that you squeak, and if you do squeak, he should correct his approach so you are a well-informed partner in the selling process. If he doesn't check in with you consistently… find a better agent.

ADVANCE READING COPY. NOT FOR SALE.

CHAPTER 20
OLD SCHOOL

Once the property is listed and your sellers are reasonably aware of the need for them to pick up after themselves, it's time to sell, sell, sell. These delicate real estate techniques are as old as the art of selling itself. According to New York municipal records, in 1866 four Jewish peddlers set up the first pushcarts on Hester Street, ushering in the era of the traveling salesman in America. These salesmen carried the selling techniques from old Europe to the New World like they carried their wares on their backs. I have spent my life learning them too. I consider them precious and valuable gems handed down to me from my ancestors, and I like to share.

Your Shtick
I come from a long line of Jewish scrappers. Recycling is just a newer, greener way of doing what my ancestors have been doing since they came to this country. They were also auctioneers, liquidators, and appraisers. That meant that they knew the value of stuff and how to sell it. My dad taught me that everything is merchandise until it is sold. Before stuff is sold, it can never be considered junk. This is lesson number one of the world I grew up in.

Although this has not been thoroughly vetted, it is a commonly held belief in my family that my grandfather, applying old-school techniques taught to him, invented the concept of the charity auction. He was an industrial auctioneer who spent a lot of time in the philanthropic world. He came up with the idea of having items donated and then auctioned off. Sometimes I'm pissed at him, as I have to spend weekend after weekend at such auctions, wading through tables full of baskets. It takes a couple hours

189

before the passing appetizers make me thirsty and the resulting cocktails make me desirous of baskets of stuff that I don't need. I also don't like my competitive nature manipulated so easily. It's not the philanthropy that bugs me but the requirement that I publicly display my desire to win. I usually like to keep that on the down low.

Auctions, like real estate, require merchandising. Merchandising requires a whole bunch of other skills. My father is the king of auction merchandising, and his brilliance in this arena taught me the skills that fed my early career in retail. First, he always starts an industrial auction with a wrench. Sometimes he has to race off to the hardware store to buy a wrench when there are no wrenches in the sale merchandise. He auctions off the wrench and then moves on to other tools. At some point, he might be selling huge tractors, but he always starts with a wrench. It's his trademark.

Trademarks are useful in developing your brand. I don't mean this in the intellectual-property sense of trademark but rather in the creation or use of something that defines you—a *shtick* (sometimes there is nowhere to go but Yiddish). With the right shtick, clients can identify you, and you can attract the clients you desire. A camera is all you need to get started. Then post pictures on your website (yes, you should have one of those) and work your theme discretely into your social media (feel free not to embrace this advice and you can remain a well-kept secret).

Here are some great professional head shot shticks that stick:

- You with your dog (size matters)
- You with an instrument (generally best when instrument is musical and not one of torture)
- You in an art gallery (be sure it is real art)
- You in a police lineup (best with other agents in the lineup and your sign saying: "Guilty. Sold.")
- You in preppy attire in front of an exclusive club (best with an expression that says, "Oh, this old thing.")
- You doing volunteer work (see what works for politicians and copy)
- You on a bike (put the seat on it first)

ADVANCE READING COPY. NOT FOR SALE.

There are so many ways to create a shtick that it is a *shandeh* (look it up) not to have one. You should be able to effectively market a variety of properties while still letting your personal vibe shine through.

Even if you're just getting started, the brand of the agency with whom you affiliate might be enough to create the kind of business you intend to have. Research of top agents throughout the country provides evidence to suggest that agent distinction is best achieved by co-branding with a like-minded company. If the company with whom you are considering affiliating is established as a heritage company with deep local roots in historic property sales and you want to specialize in plantations, this might be the perfect fit. If the company with whom you choose to work has a kiosk in the holiday bazaar every year and sponsors the milk-tasting at the 4-H competition and you intend to represent young, professional athletes looking for large new homes with practice courts in the suburbs, you might have a harder time reconciling those two brands.

The types of properties you sell will inform your brand in the same way the specialty pickles on a kosher hotdog pushcart do. When you're new to real estate, the more time you spend strategically planning what you want your brand to be, the better you'll be able to tailor your business to support that brand. If you want to brand yourself according to the clients you'll work with, identify the key players in that market and try to get an endorsement. My friend's great-uncle had the best watch pushcart on the Lower East Side. He built his business by offering all the fancy-schmancy men in the storefronts a huge discount for wearing his watches. When you plan to attract a certain clientele, just remember that like-minded people tend to congregate; then place yourself in a position to be the salesperson to that congregation.

The Perils of Judgment

I cleaned machines and tools in freezing cold factories. I drove forklifts and four-on-the-floor trucks long before it was safe for me to do so. I saw enough ball scratching to last a lifetime, only to then give birth to two boys. Just because I was a girl with painted

ADVANCE READING COPY. NOT FOR SALE.

toenails didn't mean I couldn't hold my own with the men. More important, I learned that the guy in the dirty overalls could have a significant wad of cash that could buy and sell the guy in the leased BMW many times over. The prejudging bug in real estate has stung me when I forgot this important lesson.

SORTAFacts™

Studies show that the more people have to draw attention to their wealth, the more transient that wealth tends to be. The opposite is true for poverty.

—Courtesy of Sortafact

Fee Plea

Know what you're worth and don't undercharge. If you're worth less, charge less. Remember that negotiating skills are critical in real estate. If you simply stink at negotiation and, therefore, you can't negotiate favorably for yourself, don't expect people to think you'll be able to negotiate on their behalf.

As my self-proclaimed-genius husband says, "Whaddya want, 100 percent of a phone booth or 1 percent of AT&T?" The contrast here is increasingly obvious as phone booths approach extinction.

TrueSTORIES

My grandfather and his protégé, my father, dragged themselves to Bumblefuck Middle o' Nowhere to assess and bid on a door manufacturing plant. The plant was under contract with the US government, so the owner had to keep his desire to retire secret from his employees and the Man until the contract was fulfilled.

My father and grandfather told the owner that the eventual sale of the plant should bring around $100,000 (them's the good old days) and that they would charge 15 percent plus $7,000 in expenses to set up, market, and conduct the auction. They all agreed to proceed at the end of the year when the government

ADVANCE READING COPY. NOT FOR SALE.

contract was up, and they sealed the deal in the usual way: with a handshake.

A few months went by, and they got a call from one of the few employees aware of the plan to sell. She warned my grandfather that she had seen a sleazy-looking auctioneer lurking about the plant. My father was dispatched to investigate and found out that, yes, the owner had decided to renege on his handshake and hire someone willing to charge only 5 percent and $5,000 in expenses. After a few choice words were directed, my father made plans with my grandfather to attend the auction anyway.

The big wooden, spray-painted signs advertising the directions up the dirt-and-gravel road leading to the plant didn't differ at all from what my grandfather and father would have employed. But the auctioneer's wide-brimmed Stetson and foreign twang revealed it all: Mr. Owner had hired a cattle auctioneer.

"Aw shucks, fellers, this here planing-type machine looks to be a doozy. Not entirely sure how it works, but let's start the bidding at $500."

When the bidding for the $5,000 item ended at $750 and the buyers' chuckles collectively declared, "Sucker in our midst," my grandfather and father started the long road home.

Several weeks later, Mr. Owner appeared at my grandfather's office angrily demanding to know whom he should sue. He was furious that my grandfather and father had specifically told him that the auction would bring $100,000 and it only brought $23,000! In response, my grandfather and father enjoyed teaming up and berating the man for hiring a cut-rate cattle auctioneer to sell factory equipment. My father, always good with a quick mental-math calculation, praised, "Good for you. You saved $15,850." Granted, his buyers also saved—in the ballpark of $78,000—but Mr. Owner didn't need to be reminded of that.

Mr. Owner still wanted to know who he could sue. My grandfather kindly told him to walk over to the frame on the wall and tell him what he saw. Mr. Owner scowled into the mirror and growled, "Me!"

"That's who you should sue."

Remember this story when you're negotiating your fees.

ADVANCE READING COPY. NOT FOR SALE.

TRIALS&Titillations™

Pour yourself some liquid and begin to sip. Read on, thinking about these stories and how they might be relevant to the betterment of your business and the enrichment of your life. If you get stumped, throw this book at something that won't break and call three people to vent your frustration.

TrueSTORIES

My father used to marvel at one of the greatest auctioneers in the country. He was charismatic for sure, but Sol was also really smart and full of tricks.

An auction was underway in a large industrial compound that required the crowd to physically move from one item to the next as each was being sold. After a particularly successful part of the auction dealing with the lower-priced merchandise, the auctioneer needed to move along to sell some large machinery. The crowd was loitering, not moving on to the location of the pricier machines.

The auctioneer, despite this, began the sale of a tractor. I say it was a tractor because all industrial machines that move are tractors to me. The tractor was worth $20,000 to $30,000, and its sale was to be followed by even larger tractors. The auctioneer began the sale at $10,000 and immediately received an unenthusiastic bid. He shouted, "Sold!"

What an idiot, right? He clearly lost a minimum of $10,000 in his haste to git-r-done. He also pissed off the people who intended to jump in when the sale got closer to the real bidding-to-buy range.

When the people griped about losing out on a fantastic deal, they weren't even aware that the auctioneer's actions had told them this sale would have fantastic deals. When the auctioneer responded in an unapologetic and chastising way that he didn't have all day to wait for them, he was telling them that they had better pay attention. They learned that waiting to bid would not result in a better deal but rather in no deal at all.

ADVANCE READING COPY. NOT FOR SALE.

Bossy Advice That May Change Your Life

Pay attention to stories around you and watch how people react to them. Try to apply lessons from outside the world of real estate to your business. Pollinate your brain across people, families, industries, and time. Listen to your own family folklore and learn from the stupid things your family and friends have done. Think like a storyteller so the lessons will implant for longer and on a deeper level. Temper your smugness so you don't fail to see brilliance. Brilliance is there among the most successful *and* the least successful. Sometimes the only difference between these two categories is time. I was always told that advertising icon David Ogilvy said, "Good ideas don't care who they happen to." Since I can't verify that he said this, I'll take the quote for my very own.

ADVANCE READING COPY. NOT FOR SALE.

CHAPTER 21

Mmmm Word

One of the great things about working in real estate is that you really do get to use a lot of different skills. As much as we must be unabashed salespeople, we also have a huge opportunity and responsibility to understand marketing and the four delightful P's: price, place, product, and promotion.

Price

As real estate sales professionals, we spend a lot of our time on price, specifically strategic pricing issues. Here's a handy-dandy tactical tip: avoid automatically latching on to nine. We see that so many products are marketed in prices ending in a nine, and we think, *Yippee, that's what we'll do too.* Even though the internet search engines for many real estate sites have preset pricing categories and few, if any, have numbers ending in nine, the vast majority of agents would still price a home at $599,000 instead of $600,000. Think of how many buyers miss the hit as they're searching from $600,000 to $700,000. Probably many. Think of how many buyers miss the hit as they're searching from $500,000 to $600,000. For sure, none. Wouldn't you rather also target the buyers with the bigger budget?

TRIALS&Titillations™

Ask any and all of your family members, friends, and clients if they look up real estate on the internet. Ask them what price range they search. If they're not current clients, they might be coy because they think you're prying into personal stuff. You'll hear, "Oh, I look way beyond what I can afford." Assure them that you're just doing an experiment: "The price isn't relevant, just how you're phrasing it."

They might have a top number and not a bottom number, or they might have a bottom and not a top, but if your experiment turns out like mine always does, they will never have a nine beyond the second number. Think about this and price accordingly.

SECRETS for Clients

Even experienced real estate professionals can make mistakes. Sometimes you will get lucky pricing your home outside of the parameters of what your agent suggested; many times you will not. In robust markets, pricing your home higher than what was suggested and selling for that price will give you a sense of relief that you trusted your instincts. It will also give you a sense of superiority over your agent. Pat your own back gingerly and be glad you don't know that you *could* have made even more money on your house with a lower asking price (*see* "Multiple O's").

There is a bit of a science to pricing. Pricing a home in a market with a lot of sales data points and in a homogenous neighborhood is fairly easy. The general idea is that you match the features that are similar and then deduct for the lesser aspects and add for the better. But pricing homes is as much of an art as it is a science. When analyses go way beyond granite kitchens and stainless appliances, it takes experience to understand nuances of value. Many scenarios call for understanding price elasticity, scarcity of comparable houses, pricing relative to unique features, high-low techniques, and when supply and demand don't matter much.

If you just follow the science of pricing and don't pay attention to finessing your art, you'll see varied results. You help your sellers price a home, brilliantly market the hell out of it, and then sell it, so you use that sale as proof of your competence. If this keeps happening, it is easy to get blinded by the glow of self-importance.

ADVANCE READING COPY. NOT FOR SALE.

Then…the market shifts and that glow dims. What do you do with price when the market has leveled off and you get asked to market a unique home?

Think Outside Your Industry

The information on the psychology of pricing would fill several libraries. Thinking outside the industry can give you many tidbits that will catapult you right over the masses of agents who never take the time to study this stuff. Here's one nugget to entice you: when you have a unique house with a perceived higher but unknown value, you are better to start the price higher—even if you have to ultimately take a price reduction. It will anchor the value to a higher price point and create a framework within which to drop the unique house. But this doesn't work when the unique factor is that the sellers have created an indoor terrarium out of Plexiglas for their exotic reptiles. You need something more like imported tiles with amber fossils lining the floor of the cupola overlooking the ocean.

Place

The physical place of the product is usually pretty well set when it comes to real estate—unless you're selling mobile homes. In the case of mobile homes, it's only considered real estate if the land beneath the mobile home is owned. See how well we paid attention in real estate school? There is place consideration that transcends the physical location, though, and this ties in directly to product.

Product

The product encompasses the home, lot, neighborhood, building, school…you get the point. Try to consider all aspects of your product. If a minimum-security correctional facility (for men who spent too much time hanging around toddlers-in-tiara pageants) is being built where the park currently stands, you will need to know this and figure out the best positioning.

By tweaking positioning, the actual product can change. Properties with spectacular views might not be view properties forever. You need to know this for both your sellers and your buyers. Trees,

ADVANCE READING COPY. NOT FOR SALE.

vacant lots, and other blockages can change your product from a view property to a property that requires you to come up with other features to emphasize. Depending on what you find most important to a potential buyer, these could include something like lot size or location near shops and restaurants—something less likely to change.

Buyers might point out product issues that they'd like to be addressed. You can acknowledge and deflect with something like, "The railroad track being laid behind the master bedroom means you'll be able to buy this house for half of what it would have cost a year ago and, because of all those Black Sabbath concerts you attended in your youth, you won't hear a thing." (It works best when the part about the concerts is whispered). Or "The neighborhood used to be teeming with free-range meth heads, and now you can feel confident knowing they will be all cooped up in the halfway house next door—just like your chickens under the new homeowner association guidelines." Be careful about being too apologetic for elements that you perceive to be a product detriment. If you offer an allowance to replace the carpet, that might be the first time the buyers ever realized the carpet was a remnant from the Age of Aquarius.

Promotion

Flyers, social media, traditional mailers, signs, signs on signs, e-this and that, and your effective yapper are all valuable tools for promoting property. Plus, it seems like every day new applications and products are being developed to promote real estate. Some of these ideas leave me annoyed and sad for the poor fools who invested time and money. Still, I like to keep an open mind because some of these fads could actually become the next go-to technique for effectively promoting properties.

When it comes to promotion, you can't bore people into buying your product. The word *charming* appears in 72% of all real estate listings, but what does it really mean? After all, people described Ted Bundy as charming. When I read *Freakanomics* and its claim that *charming* can mean many secret things, I thought, *Oooo, they caught on to the secret real estate Illuminati. Now they know that flyers are part of the bigger subliminal advertising conspiracy.* I felt like I did

ADVANCE READING COPY. NOT FOR SALE.

when I read how Robert Frost marveled at the way people discovered hidden meaning in his poetry that he never knew he put there.

Let me fill you in on a secret: if there is a secret and coded meaning in these words, I didn't mean to put it there...or did I?

I really don't believe that there is (much) of a hidden code among boring real estate words. Sometimes you just can't get your clever juices flowing and you resort to boring—we all do it from time to time. The bottom line is that many salespeople are simply too lazy to come up with something other than *charming* or *gourmet* or whatever other words those *Freakanomics* guys rightly accused real estate salespeople of overusing. This same, boring language is the one we use among ourselves. It's not a code; it is laziness. Now, here you might think I'd look in that book to come up with more examples, but I'm too lazy—see, just like you!

This is what I hear at sales meetings: "I have a new listing coming up. I had it on the market during blah, blah, but now it is staged and ready to go." Or even worse, "Now it's dialed and ready to go." (Yuck.) Did you notice that the "new" listing was negated by "had it on the market"? No wonder we tune out at sales meetings. And the drivel continues, "It has granite countertops and stainless appliances and this wonderful water feature and gleaming hardwood floors. It has four bedrooms and two and a half baths." This might be followed up with the recitation of useful information, but after all these years in real estate, I'm bored. And if your clients have spent any time on real estate porn, they've heard all this before too.

Start with something intriguing and attention grabbing. Subliminal sex often works if you're good with the smart double entendre. Constantly adjust your phraseology. If you're good at making up descriptive words and phrases, this is where you can have fun. Personally, I love the words we hate.

SORTAFacts™

Exercises that piss you off and make you want to shut a book are proven to be 72.5% more effective in generating creative writing than emotion-neutral exercises.

—*Courtesy of Sortafact*

ADVANCE READING COPY. NOT FOR SALE.

Mouth It

Practice saying these words in the mirror:

- Moist
- Cunt
- Dandruff
- Mucus
- Clot
- Labia
- Slacks
- Cock
- Vomit
- Globule
- Pussy
- Moist (It *does* bear repeating.)
- Goiter
- Smegma
- Panties
- Pustules
- Ointment
- First husband

TRIALS&Titillations™

Feel free to use a handheld mirror if that makes the exercise more engaging. Now start writing your real estate ads.

SORTAFacts™

Mind-blowing research has indicated that self-righteous indignation spurs people to action 88% more effectively than inspiration. This tops 98% when cringing is involved.

—Courtesy of Sortafact

One of the greatest acceptable prejudices is the universal hatred of words because of their meaning. It's fine to hate them based on their sound because they brought that on themselves. However,

ADVANCE READING COPY. NOT FOR SALE.

their meaning was given to them—like religion or bad grooming habits. It's not their fault. Embrace these words and become familiar with them apart from their meaning, and they will bring you a kind of freedom that can come only from telling your clients that, yes, they are pussies for not making a decision before it became too late, but they're still better than the goiter of a client you worked with yesterday whose girlfriend was a total cunt.

Having a few of these universally hated words in your lexicon is also good in the shock-the-shit-out-of-them exercise. This exercise is best performed with someone you secretly dislike.

Shock the Shit Out of Them

Make up words when you want to give your clients an *idea* of what you mean but still keep it a little fuzzy. This can also help you cover your butt when it comes to having your statements read back to you in front of a pesky mediator.

Replace boring phrases with spicier language. Here are some examples of replacement words or phrases that you can play with to get your superior creative juices flowing:

Old	New or Different
Fabulous	Screams "you want me"
Gleaming	See your reflection
Clean	Lick-able
Double-headed shower	Recreational shower
Self-closing drawers	Anger-management drawers
Large master bath	Coma-inducing, spa-like bathroom
Charming	Little Red Riding Hood optional
Gourmet	*Kitchen Confidential* will take on new meaning ;)
Elegant	Dignified indispensability
Dramatic	Drama-queen inspiring
Grand	Centerfold of the neighborhood mosaic

These examples are pretty dramatic, but even a slight word switcheroo can miraculously change how an event is perceived and remembered. It can change how *your product* is perceived and remembered.

ADVANCE READING COPY. NOT FOR SALE.

The words we use affect how *we* are perceived and remembered. All of this lumped together means that the words we choose change how history is perceived, remembered, taught, and ultimately passed down.

The words we use matter. We quickly type emails in anger and frustration, and then we hit send. We read rude texts from our friends with an angry intonation that does not exist in the written word. We post, like, tweet, retweet, comment, and share with little or no analysis of the fine detail of word choice. In doing this, we are speeding up history. Our words, therefore, have greater significance than they have ever had. Thinking through each word can take a long time, but it can also work wonders in implanting the right history and in helping you aim your communication toward the right bull's-eye.

SECRETSForClients

It is dangerous to assume that the buyers for your home will be just like you. It is, however, important that your real estate broker understands what drew you to your home in the first place. Challenge her to come up with primary, secondary, and tertiary target buyers but also to remain flexible if an interested party completely misses the bull's-eye. If you have interactions with potential buyers, do not drill them to see if they qualify or meet your assumption of who the future buyer might be. Make sure your broker doesn't make that mistake either.

Target Practice

Figuring out the target buyers for your listing will often help you emphasize certain features and aim your four P's for the bull's-eye. I used to do this with more of a commitment than I gave to most other aspects of my life—until I got burned. Selling a seven-thousand-square-foot home to a single woman and her dogs cured me of being too committal with my focus on the target buyer. That said, I do think that with any product, you have to target your promotion—just not to the complete exclusion of prospects outside your bull's-eye.

ADVANCE READING COPY. NOT FOR SALE.

This is where there are no great shortcuts for understanding the market. If you emphasize a rumpus room fit for Bunco and clown birthday parties that flow out to a grassy soccer field of a yard, this is great if you're targeting breeders. It is not quite as great if the house is in a neighborhood of suboptimal schools, hip restaurants, a preponderance of Prada. It might be better to think of something more spicy than sparkly, but still without being so committal. If you just start by working to understand the neighborhood dynamics and the buyer profiles, this will go a long way in helping you know the *what* and the *where* to promote.

Four P's and an M

The m-word (*marketing*) applies as much to the price, place, product, and promotion of property as it applies to you personally. Most accurate real estate books confide that, while it is honorable to work in all price ranges, über-rich real estate professionals tend to position themselves to sell the higher-end homes. Beyond this, the rich real estate agents tend to be more focused on listing clients than on clients who are buying. Tackling this segment of the market takes a very strategic and tactical positioning of *you*. It takes a very strategic physical positioning of you as a brand. If you are uncomfortable hanging and playing where the deer play, the buffalo roam, and the rich people mingle, you are not going to be able to successfully position yourself to work with those creatures. Don't despair; a lucrative and fulfilling career can be had in all price ranges. The lower ranges will just require you to do more blatant real estate work during the hours that you would otherwise be golfing, playing tennis at the club, and attending charity events.

The brilliant Polish writer Stanislaw Lem said, "Cannibals prefer those who have no spines." I assure you, however, that cannibals do *not* make the best clients. In marketing yourself, you benefit from having the backbone to walk away from some business in order to position yourself with meaning. This is hard when we're all swinging from the commission pole, but I promise it's a good idea if you plan to not get eaten alive in this business. Because I tend to get bored focusing on a narrow set of neighborhoods or

ADVANCE READING COPY. NOT FOR SALE.

a small sphere of clients, this has never been my strongest suit. Talk about spineless, I'm even too commitment phobic to get a rub-on tattoo. From my earliest propositions, *no* was not a word that flowed from my lips with the greatest of ease. Because I have always liked to say, "I'm versatile," it took me longer to strategically assume my favorite position...in the market.

There are people who like to preach that the four P's of marketing is a dead concept. Really? If you don't have a product at a price people will pay and a place to obtain that product, your promotion might get you tons of Twitter followers but, ultimately, you're just a twat.

ADVANCE READING COPY. NOT FOR SALE.

CHAPTER 22

PARTY PEOPLE IN THE HOUSE

There is not a party in any room above ground level in America where real estate does not get discussed. Everyone needs a place to live, and we love to talk about it. Therefore, everyone is a potential buyer, seller, renter, or cardboard-sign holder. If you are selling jewelry, it's different because it has been said that we can all live without jewelry.

To survive as a real estate pro, it is imperative that you know the market. You have to know *and* understand your business. Knowing and understanding are two different things. You can know statistics inside and out and still not understand your business. For example, you can *know* that the market is up 6.5 percent, but what's the understanding behind that? Does that mean that prices are up 6.5 percent this month over last month, this year over last year, or this month this year over the same month last year? Or does it mean that 6.5 percent more properties sold than…when, what, where?

SORTAᖴacts™

83% of top media futurists surveyed felt that a market would go up 9.3% in the future.

— *Courtesy of Sortafact*

At the risk of exhausting you before you even get started, I'm going to tell you that you also have to know what potential clients and customers know and understand. That's a lot of work. Here's the snazzy new math to use to really connect with real estate lovers:

Knowing + Telling = Turnoff
Showing + Telling = Reality Show
Understanding + Telling = Getting Blindsided by Data
Knowing + Understanding + Showing + Telling = Real Turn-On + Data = SOLD

Activity Book Experience

Please stop skimming this book for a moment because here is an activity book experience that you won't want to miss.

Dinner parties are wrought with opportunities as well as pitfalls, from the second you say, "Yes, what can I bring?" to the moment you say, "I guess this means I should go."

Close your eyes and picture getting dressed up for a dinner party or gala event. If that image creates terror in your mind's eye, for this exercise pretend all your insecurities are in your past and you just have to figure out how to cinch the perfect outfit over your waist. Now, assume you look good—real good. Off you go. You arrive at the party and start to work the room, dropping subtle and intelligent hints about real estate. In doing so, you achieve your goal of luring the perfect prospective client into asking, "So, how's the market?"

Answer: _____
_____ (You will be held accountable to this no matter what special ingredients were in the brownies you consumed fifty-seven minutes before.)

SECRETSForClients

Approach a real estate professional you know. Ask, "So, how's the market?" How she answers is critical to knowing how well she will communicate on your behalf. It might also tell you whether or not she is in bullshit mode.

When you need to answer that question, you must first seek to understand—and the best approach to that is to ask direct questions. In this way you can find out a bit about the question askers

ADVANCE READING COPY. NOT FOR SALE.

before expounding in a way that could make you look like a bore or a fool. If you have indulged in a little preparty social media porn, you might know enough about the partygoers to have some ideas for the best direct questions to ask. If not, follow their question up with an indirect question to clarify. For example, when you ask what *they* have read about the market in the media or what *they* find to be the best media source of real estate information, you are less likely to later be blindsided by what they have learned, what they value, and how they interpret that information. Ask them if what they read about the market seems to accurately reflect what they or their friends are experiencing. You will then begin to categorize these potential client partiers. They could be:

- Statistic spewers whose knowledge of the market increases with every martini consumed
- Magazineoholics trying to understand how every article boasts conflicting facts
- Doctors who are used to people thinking they know so much that they believe it
- Neighbors who feel market research is thoroughly conducted by walking the dog
- Nobel Prize–winning economists with twelve bestselling books on real estate

Once you have them appropriately pegged, you can tailor your answer to deal with their test question accordingly.

If one of my teenage sons asks about the market, he probably has very different motives than my friend who writes for a national business magazine who is asking the same question. My son probably wants to know whether our family vacation will be spent in Spain or Spokane this year. My writer friend might want to know if his article about falling interest rates and their resultant huge surge in the market was completely ill timed. You need to know who is asking and why the question is being asked so you can turn the situation into a money-making opportunity. Understand what is being written in the publications that you think your target clients might pretend to skim. Understand how that relates to your business.

ADVANCE READING COPY. NOT FOR SALE.

In short, find out what they think about the market and how they're trying to frame that information. How does their knowledge of the market relate to their personal life and what they dream of accomplishing in their world of real estate? You might then find a place for yourself in that very world.

TrueSTORIES

I was preparing to attend a party in support of the arts. Now, I love myself some arts, but I am hard-pressed to explain why that toilet in the Pompidou is behind Plexiglas. Knowing this party was to be chock-full o' potential buyers and sellers who were also art lovers, I spent an hour reading a few current art blogs and sites. I was looking for points of reference that tied the market of the art world with my experiences in real estate. There were a few interesting facts that would be lucrative crowd pleasers at the party.

There was a cool article about people who had moved from day-trading to real estate speculation to art speculation when cash became king. Aha, there was my tie-in. Truthfully, I found it interesting, so I wasn't just prepping for pimping—I was also learning something in the process. Still, I had to internalize the information so it didn't become, as my father always warned me against, *le bullshit.* I needed to maintain sincerity at all times because nothing stinks stronger than the bullshit of pretension.

At the party I was approached by a denizen of the art world who asked me the polite question, "So, how is the market?"

I followed with, "I was just going to ask you the same thing about the art world." Deflection is great, especially when you've had a lot to drink.

"Well, it's tough," she confided.

I always try to get them to explain as much as possible be- cause then it gets easier to appropriately tailor my answer in a way that it will remain relatable and relevant. In this case I asked her if it was tougher for artists, dealers, or buyers. She indicated that it was tougher for artists and dealers because the prices had softened tremendously. She also indicated that there had been a

ADVANCE READING COPY. NOT FOR SALE.

surge in nondiscerning buyers who were looking at art as more of a commodity. I asked her how she was dealing with that and what her personal thoughts were about longer-term prospects in the art world.

From there it was an easy segue into her thoughts and plans for her art space and her home. It was clear that she was thinking of selling her large home and scaling down to a condo pied-à-terre. Now I had my angle and could appropriately and honestly suggest that it was a better time to purchase an owner-occupied condo than any other time in recent history—provided it was the right condo with strong reserves and, because of some new lending guidelines, the buyer should have a longer-term strategy in mind. I both *understood* her situation and *knew* recent trends and lending guidelines in the condo market. Yay for me that time.

SORTAFacts™

My all-time favorite real estate line—courtesy of my old-school Jew crew—is: "The best time to buy real estate was ten years ago." My favorite response to market predictions that don't benefit my needs is: "Beside every better-than/worse-than expected result lies the rotting carcass of another worthless prediction."
—*Courtesy of Sortafact*

Join the Party

Even if you love your slippers and robe so very much, don't forget that attending parties and charity events is very important for your career if you are attempting to create a higher-end portfolio of real estate business. It is assumed that if you have a modicum of success, you will talk about your profession from time to time. Parties are the perfect atmosphere for it.

Keep a good balance, though. Don't go into hardcore sales mode, but do subtly anchor your conversation to valuable tidbits of information or a respectful mention of an interesting aspect of a property that might be of interest to people in attendance. If you are new to real estate, this is a good opportunity for a career tie-in. You can talk about a highly interesting property you are showing

ADVANCE READING COPY. NOT FOR SALE.

to indicate that you play and work in the same sandbox as your target audience. Name dropping can be a valuable tool too, but use discretion. If you have not perfected that art form, you'll come across as inauthentic and pretentious. You might not be aware of the business you lose while you're obnoxiously clinging to coattails.

Perfect preparty preparation involves digestion of:

- *Vanity Fair*
- *The Economist*
- *People*
- A few key websites or blogs

If you find yourself unable to keep up with some basic fun facts about the very industry in which you work, it's best to stay home and do a little studying. Know your stuff, have some idea of who will be at the party, find out where the guests are coming from, and weave the conversation from there. When you're asked a question, tailor your answer accordingly.

I want you to know I'm your friend and I always want you to party as much as I love to party—so my suggestion to stay home and cram for the next one actually hurts me more than it hurts you.

ADVANCE READING COPY. NOT FOR SALE.

CHAPTER 23

GREASING THE SKIDS

Hearing something for a second time is not as exciting as hearing it the first time. It's also not as scary. It's like porn—you get immune (or so I hear). That's why in real estate it's so important to tell people what might happen, tell them how they might feel when it happens, and tell them what you'll do to make them calm the hell down when they call you freaking out. I even predict what time they'll want to call me freaking out so I can tell them *not* to call me in the middle of the night. I swear to you, before I did this, they *did* call in the middle of the night. Twice they were drunk dials, though, and I can forgive those for the humor they provided.

There are so many things that commonly surface in real estate that there is no reason not to go over some of those possibilities with clients—or as I like to say, to grease the skids. Don't scare the shit out of them, but do prepare them. It is best to use stories so they can relate without feeling like you're telling them bad things will happen because they are bad people. In this stressful time, they want to feel like their good and common experience is the best one possible.

SECRETSforClients

An agent who preemptively shares scenarios of what might happen and provides plans for several eventualities will be better equipped to handle the even smaller things that always come up in real estate transactions. If you meet an agent who is more of a don't-worry-be-happy sort, he might not know what to worry about in the first place. This is fine if you're lucky, but it's best not to depend too much on luck.

Offers—The Down Low

There is no reason for sellers to be angry about offers below their asking price. If your sellers are angry about an offer, you have not done your job. I know that sounds harsh, but it's usually true. Sometimes people like being angry or they are displacing anger that is really a result of their too-tight pants. The people who like to be angry don't want you to take that away from them, but you should still try, if just for torture's sake.

If you go through the scenario of what you and your clients will do in the event that a low offer is presented, there should be a conspiratorial moment if the story becomes reality. I suggest that you use a pretty extreme example of a low offer to drive home your point and desensitize the sellers.

Here's how you do it using an asking price of $800,000. The sellers say, "I'm not interested in having some bottom-feeder come in and lowball me." Sound familiar?

You say, "I know how you feel when they come in with a low ball, and all it makes you want to do is toss the contents of a high-ball in their face. We won't splash them right away, though, and here's why. Let's say they throw us an offer of $500,000." Listen for an audible gasp but keep a straight face. "We will say, 'Thank you so very much for your offer.' We can then use the existence of their offer to encourage any other fence-sitting potential buyers to get off the stick. We will certainly be careful not to scare these fence sitters away by being too aggressive and pushy. You can then make a counteroffer of $799K. That way you will give the distinct impression that you are willing to deal but that you will not open your kimono to a price much lower than your asking price."

Now that you have vaccinated your sellers against one of their most feared diseases, you have provided the antibodies to the dreaded lowie. With a reinforced immune system, the sellers shouldn't develop the rash of frustration that could cost them a sale. If one of those objectionable bids does come your way, the sellers will know you're smart and they should not feel insulted. They will feel empowered and strategic. Just like disappointing blind dates, immunity to low offers does build up. If this scenario does not happen, your sellers will be so relieved that they just might love you.

ADVANCE READING COPY. NOT FOR SALE.

Other events to grease the skids for include crazy local or global happenings that can affect the market in unforeseen ways. The reality is that the worst-case scenario is when the sellers don't get an offer of any sort. People who have never experienced this kind of dry spell in the past think it can't happen to them. Sharing an example of an event that caused offer impotence (like 9/11) can illustrate how even the sexiest, best prepared property can go a long while before even getting to first base. Even a property that's never been a wallflower can suffer involuntary abstinence as a result of these unforeseen events. And the longer the gestation period, the harder it is to get offers up when they do come in. Explain that market contraception does not last forever and whatever happens, you and your clients will be prepared.

SECRETSforClients

The first offer is not always the best. Sometimes it is, and sometimes it isn't. Challenge your agent to explain this to you. Ask her to tell you very specifically what she will do if a strong offer comes in immediately after you place your home on the market. Ask her what she would advise you to do.

A Quickie

In a robust market, prepare sellers for the possibility of multiple offers. This is a delicate dance, as you don't want to promise but you want to prepare. If you don't do this and multiple offers do come in, they might think you priced their home too low. That misconception is fine when you're working with buyers but not with sellers. The sellers, with the input of your strategic advice and infinite knowledge, are ultimately who determine the asking price of their property, but if anything goes wrong, they love to play Pass the Responsibility. In reality, a multiple-offer situation handled properly with prepared sellers can mean that the pricing strategy was perfect. If this is explained to the sellers only after the offers have poured in, they'll feel that you are being defensive. If you share this before, they will feel brilliant for working with you—and they should. (*See* "More than Two to Tango.")

ADVANCE READING COPY. NOT FOR SALE.

SECRETSForClients

Ask your listing agent how he handles lowball offers. Feel free to test him by saying how much a low offer will piss you off. If he does not give you the distinct impression that he will graciously handle any offer a potential buyer might make, he could cost you thousands of dollars when it comes to the final sale. Agreeing with you now could result in something that is disagreeable to you later.

SORTAFacts™

Preparing people for severe negative experiences tends to lessen the negative effects of regular ol' negative experiences 92.5% of the time. Repeating this exercise at least three times generally results in negative experiences being perceived as positive experiences…or loss of consciousness.

—Courtesy of Sortafact

Invitation to Invade

Prepare sellers for how they will feel when people traipse through their home. Tell them that the one day they don't make their bed after days without a showing will be the one day that a hot buyer prospect will want to see their home.

Prepare them for when a buyers' agent calls to set an appointment and they scramble to hide everything in the goody drawer after an out-of-town visit from their hot partner only for the friggin' agent and buyers not to show. Tell them to put away their Oxycontin. They never know when a certain right-wing political radio talk show host might come through an open house.

Feedback on showings can hurt sellers' feelings. They can feel invaded after people have walked through their house. And if those same people didn't like the glamour shots, well…unprepared sellers may feel like tone-deaf contestants on *American Idol*. Calmly point out that because their glamour shots are enthusiastically applauded by their partners or visitors of special internet sites,

ADVANCE READING COPY. NOT FOR SALE.

the glamorous shouldn't feel insulted if the people touring their home don't appreciate their all-too-adorned beauty.

Explain that some agents have bad manners. Some might leave lights on or open closets and drawers. Tell your sellers to get over it. Tell them that security alarms can be tricky for some of the more challenged among our industry's professionals and they shouldn't be surprised when ADT calls to say someone named RealProf is in your home. Once in a while, the agent doesn't leave a business card, leaving the sellers to guess—and hope—that whoever left the fridge open was the Realtor and not the transient they refused to give money to that morning. Explain to the sellers that sometimes buyers' agents run out of cards. This is another get-the-hell-over-it situation for the sellers, and it's easier for them to get there if they are told in advance. Be sure they hear it before they experience it.

Explain how showings can result in various uncomfortable situations.

True**STORIES** (Except the End)

Fifteen brokers enthusiastically swung open the front door for a scheduled open house for brokers. Margot forgot that her home was on brokers' tour that day and was luxuriating in the bathtub when the group walked into the bathroom. Screaming and splashing ensued. Later, Margot tried to blame her broker for not informing her of the scheduled tour. The email trail proved her wrong, but she stopped fussing when a reasonable offer from a buyer of one of those same brokers came in. The offer was accepted. The next time the seller put a home on the market, she commissioned a naked glamour portrait of herself to expedite matters...and remembered to wax.

SORTAꜰacts™

Artwork featuring vaginas ranks slightly below taxidermy on the Professional Stager's List of Quick Tricks.

—Courtesy of Sortafact

ADVANCE READING COPY. NOT FOR SALE.

True**STORIES**

A forever-single fifty-six-year-old seller, Bonnie, did not want her cat boyfriend to be let out of the house under any circumstances. He was, however, a sneaky cat that would try to escape (I didn't blame him, but that's another story), so she was adamant that her home could only be shown during confirmed appointments for which she could remove the cat.

When Bonnie left for two days to a wood-whittling convention at the beach, she was unable to take her boyfriend cat. A particularly hot prospect buyer was in town and wanted to see her home smack dab in the middle of that whittling event. After much drama by her and many promises by the listing agent, Bonnie reluctantly agreed to allow her house to be shown.

The buyers' agent was thoroughly versed in the importance of not letting that sneaky cat anywhere near an exit. Upon leaving the home after a hypervigilant home tour, the agent saw the cat in the front yard and freaked out. She then spent the next two hours coaxing the cat back into the house with tuna and food and cat ganja, ultimately grabbing the cat and bring it, hissing and scratching the hell out of her, into the house. As she knelt to set the hissing asshole cat down, there, staring at her from across the room, was the exact replica of the hissing cat, watching amused as blood dripped from the poor agent.

If the sellers have a pet, tell a story about a sneaky ferret that escaped in spite of heroic methods of prevention. Then they will understand that asking the showing agents to kindly tell Squeakers to stay on the couch is not really a reliable method for handling a cat in the mood for a walkabout. If the house smells bad, explain that, although you love cats and are unable to smell their shit piled up in the litter box, you have had clients literally lose tens of thousands of dollars by being immune to odors that were totally off-putting to people with, I don't know, noses that work.

TRIALS&Titillations™

Go to your nearest strip mall. Go around the nail salon

ADVANCE READING COPY. NOT FOR SALE.

to the back where there is a real live palm reader's neon sign. Step inside the shop and try to get a discount from the psychic for predicting the events of only the following week. Proceed with the week. Make a checklist of the surprising things that happened that the psychic predicted.

Sellers are worried about a lot of things. Remember selling your home and having people judge every aspect of your life? You don't? Try it soon, and it will cure you of any residual smugness. Even if some of us are less worried about being walked in on while practicing commercials, naked, in front of the mirror than others might be, we are all worried that we are leaving money on the table by selling for less than we could.

Playing with Others

Tell your sellers in advance what they should do if a coworker or neighbor expresses interest in their house. If the sellers question your value because *they* found the potential buyer, they're going to need to be educated. They should realize that they're partnering with you—and that there is a deep chasm between expressed interest and a closed sale.

Just as sellers sometimes don't play well with others, agents can be just as guilty. Agents might try to steal clients. Stealing buyers is more common among unscrupulous agents when there is not a buyer's contract in place. Explain to your patrons how to sniff out those scoundrels. It's good to go through scenarios with your clients so they recognize the signs when agents are trying to steal a listing or a buyer. Real estate among the top agents is really more collaborative than cutthroat competitive. It is competitive, for sure, but the best agents and brokers understand the value in cooperation. This should be explained to your clients so they don't envision vultures picking at client carrion while digging their talons into the closest sniffing buzzard. That's scary.

SECRETSforClients

Ask your prospective agent whether she views her business as primarily competitive or primarily cooperative. Understand

ADVANCE READING COPY. NOT FOR SALE.

that too much opponent-speak can be even worse than too much cronyism.

Morning Woe

Remorse is not for buyers only. Sellers often experience intense remorse the night after they accept an offer. Assure them that this is normal. They might not ever meet their buyers. They might meet the buyers and find out that they are very different from what the sellers hoped. They might have a loan delayed, so they should create some cushion in their moving truck plans.

Closing

Guidelines, regulations, guidelines, regulations—all leading to intended and unintended consequences. A sale that comes to fruition requires satisfaction of a three-way sort. For the more easy-to-blush among us, it is classier to refer to this as balancing a three-legged stool. It is important to educate clients on all of the decision makers who prop up that precarious stool:

- The buyers
- The appraisers
- Those pesky underwriters

Buyers have to want to buy. They also have to be able to afford to buy.

Cash buyers eliminate the need to worry about two of the three legs because they don't need appraisers or underwriters, as they are avoiding a bank loan. But most buyers need or want to obtain a loan. Loans require appraisers, who need supporting information to justify the price. The lender's underwriters review the appraisal and the buyer qualification details to make sure it all conforms to the current lending guidelines. Explain to sellers how simply preparing their house for buyers to fall in love is not always enough.

You might find buyers willing to pay a price that is not supported by the appraisal data. Discuss this with your sellers. Also let your sellers know that you understand that the opposite can

ADVANCE READING COPY. NOT FOR SALE.

occur. In this scenario where the appraisal is more than the purchase price, the sellers can feel ripped off and the buyers can be thrilled. Help your sellers see the data that the appraiser will use before you list the house. Discuss the fact that there is as much art as there is science to pricing a home for sale. There is no way to be absolutely sure that every leg of the stool will be of the right length to keep the transaction from toppling, but to the extent that you can consult and conspire with your sellers, the more prepared they will be for creating a sturdy relationship with you.

Review what the sellers will do if their home doesn't sell under the conditions and price y'all establish. Have a plan, but remain flexible enough to groove with the gyrations of the market.

True**STORIES**

I was approached to interview for a listing with an otherwise savvy lady who had previously had her home listed with a less-than-scrupulous agent for over $800,000. She had also obtained an appraisal that must have been conducted by Homer Simpson and valued the house at $900,000. Meanwhile, our analysis put the optimistic value of the home at $500,000.

The market *was* appreciating. Although market appreciation is not always the case, this seems to be a lesson that we need to relearn generation after generation. Her lofty projection of the market trajectory, however, showed a divorce from reality. She was adamant on selling for $800,000. Upon inquiry, she had no alternative plan for selling for less than $800,000 and likewise no compelling reason, beyond desire, to stick to that price.

I told her that, yes, we could get that price for her. Assuming the continued rate of appreciation, we would simply have to wait about six years. I suggested that the listing might drag on too long to make it feasible to start the marketing immediately and that we should give it about five years while carefully watching the market.

Sometimes sellers are fearful that they're not selling for the maximum dollar amount, and sometimes sellers are fearful of not

ADVANCE READING COPY. NOT FOR SALE.

selling at all. They won't be fearful that they're paying you too much commission if you help them navigate and alleviate those fears. Warning signs are the first step in preparedness. Warn away.

ADVANCE READING COPY. NOT FOR SALE.

CHAPTER 24

MORE THAN TWO TO TANGO

If you're a lover of the multiple O, you should do all you can to have your sellers achieve one.

Handled correctly, multiple offers give your sellers a great chance to obtain the highest price and the best terms. Still, not all sellers love to be the recipients of multiple offers. It is more stressful to them than you probably realize. If you haven't greased the skids, they may think that you have underpriced their home, and if you didn't play your cards well, they might be right. It is up to you to make them see that it is only because of *your* fabulousness and their willingness to comply with your brilliant suggestions that they have received multiple offers. Make sure it's true and let them see how hard you've worked to achieve those offers. If they can't see you in action, tell them and congratulate them. Together you've hit that sweet spot—you know the spot.

Maximum Extraction

If multiple offers pour in without much work on your part, chances are there might be more offers in the wings that could possibly be extracted. You must have a system of tracking showings and feedback so you can delicately let other agents know that there is a game on and they might want to play.

I recommend a few easy tricks for maximum extraction:

- Keep a feedback log of each of your listings and their showings. Indicate when each agent has shown the home.
- Put in a pinch of sass and a dollop of humor as you call each agent for feedback within twenty-four hours of the showing (remind him of a few details of the house).

- Log the feedback and whether there is interest or a need for further follow-up. ("Husband coming back to town next week and wants to see" should go straight onto your calendar to jog your forgetful mind or your assistant's.)
- If there is interest, ask the agent if he would like to be notified of price reductions or offers. When you call him back about this stuff, you are then doing him a *favor* and fulfilling your promise to follow up.
- Keep track of all communication so you have a goody bag to dig into for a backup offer.
- Use a web-based tracking system so your entire team can access feedback and communication. Most real estate teams break the work into buyers' agents, sellers' agents, closing coordinators, office managers, and other functions. It's not a bad idea in theory, but I have called those teams before only to find out that the members available to chat have no clue about the history of the property or prior conversations that I have had with other team members. This is suboptimal for your clients and, therefore, for you.

It totally sucks to find out that an agent planned to write an offer on your listing later in the day but you've just signed the first and only offer that came in. You missed out on even knowing that you could have had more than one offer. Take the time to track and follow up.

SECRETSforClients

A good agent will understand how much the idea of multiple O's can create visions of more than just big wallets. He will help you balance between greed and practicality so your excitement does not cause premature withdrawal and so you achieve a satisfying...closing.

SORTAFacts™

With the proper finesse, people who take credit where credit is due see only 77% of the success that they would achieve if they also took credit when credit wasn't due.

—Courtesy of Sortafact

ADVANCE READING COPY. NOT FOR SALE.

If you approach potential buyers or their agents too aggressively about the intense level of interest in your listing, some dangerous overselling outcomes might crop up:

- The threat of multiple offers could cause potential buyers to back away from the competitive scenario.
- Pushing the fact of tremendous interest can cause a rash decision to buy. Rash decisions to buy can later lead to rational decisions to not close.
- An intense competitive bidding environment might push the price beyond the ultimate buyers' comfort or qualifications.
- If an above scenario plays all the way out, an accepted offer might not stick. Other offers are likely to lose interest because they are lemmings.
- If the accepted offer doesn't stick after a few days, other offers are likely to have moved on to buy something else.

In contrast, if you're too timid, they might miss their chance. The best way to balance this is to gauge interest from the beginning. When you called the agents after they showed the listing and they indicated that their clients might be interested at some point, that's a green flag to ask if you should keep them apprised of other offers. When you call back to tell them of the latest offer, they will feel grateful rather than hounded.

SORTAFacts™

79% of people feel 97% more comfortable with a decision that most people would make. Misery loves itself some company.
—*Courtesy of Sortafact*

TRIALS&**Titillations**™

Call twenty top agents in your market and tell them they have been selected to participate in a little survey for a fancy institution of higher learning. Don't tell them you're fancy or institutional. Ask them how they handle multiple offers when representing a seller. Write down exactly what they say. See if

ADVANCE READING COPY. NOT FOR SALE.

there is any commonality between their responses and whether you agree that their techniques are in the best interest of the seller. Copy where applicable.

The way you handle this delicate situation will determine how well you represent your sellers. It will also determine how your peers perceive you. This will, in turn, determine how well you represent future clients.

When a buyers' agent is informed of the existence of other offers on a property his buyers are considering, he might claim that his buyers do not want to get into a bidding war. If you leave it at that, you might deprive your sellers of seeing the best offers. You might also be depriving the buyers of getting the property of their dreams. Explain that multiple bids do not have to constitute a bidding war. Tell the agent to have his buyers simply present the offer price just below the threshold where they would gladly step aside and not buy the property. The buyers might assume the other offers are strong and be willing to outbid, they might think the other offers are weak and lose out by offering too low, or they might figure out the price that works for them and offer accordingly. Without offering at all, the buyers will never know, and the sellers will not have the option of understanding where the market stands. It is your job to make sure good communication provides fertile ground for harvesting the best deal.

Make sure to communicate to all of the buyers' agents who are presenting offers that there are multiple offers. They need to know when your sellers will be considering and deciding so they can arrange their schedules to present their offers. Encourage buyers' agents to submit their highest and best offers. This is a delicate jig. Many times listing agents aggressively oversell, and this can backfire.

Offer Presentations

When the bidding buyers have written their offers, there are different ways of getting the offers in front of the sellers. As antiquated as face-to-face interaction may seem in the age of techno-mania, I still recommend physically presenting offers whenever possible.

ADVANCE READING COPY. NOT FOR SALE.

In-person communication and the effort portrayed to set that up shed positive light on the offer, generally benefiting the sale as a whole.

Many real estate how-to books suggest that it is *not* in the best interest of the sellers to have the buyers' agents present offers in person. The books often suggest that the sellers' agent should not allow this to happen. Sometimes it's illegal. In states where attorneys handle much of the negotiations, the buyers and sellers come together only in the attorney's office to sign. In other states, the buyers and sellers never meet. The sales processes and methods of offer presentation become standardized, and that's fine—after all, you're not going to challenge the legal code in your state just to have an in-person meeting. But sometimes the buyers' agent is just lazy and emails the offer with no fanfare, warning, or explanation. When the seller is out of town, email might be the only option, but this distanced communication method rarely leaves a positive impression when personal communication is an option. Don't allow processes to be standardized just for your own lazy practices.

To the extent that it is not legally dictated, it is important that you are not unilaterally making the offer presentation decisions for your sellers. Selling is a collaborative effort, and the decisions lie with the principals involved—not you. If your sellers are total jerks in front of strangers, having buyers' agents present offers to your sellers might backfire. The buyers' agents should not leave their presentation feeling like they made the born-again sellers finally understand how abortion could be a good thing. In general, however, when representing sellers, I strongly suggest keeping yourself open-minded to having your sellers see you in action working with the buyers' agents. It can also alleviate a lot of curiosity and concern when multiple offers fly in quickly.

And if you suck, this is also a good way to get schooled in front of your clients. Bone up before you're boned.

First, get organized:

1. Take multiple manila folders.
2. Take a pen—or a label maker if you're OCD.
3. Label the folders 1, 2, 3…

ADVANCE READING COPY. NOT FOR SALE.

These folders will be your quick-and-easy organization system for the many offers your clients will receive. It may seem silly to take these steps, but there are lots of reasons to do it:

- It is a lot easier for people to remember single-digit numbers than multisyllabic names.
- It will be easier to attribute the terms and conditions of the various offers to the various numbers.
- If a buyers' agent presented in person, it will be easier to forget that his fly was down if you don't refer to the offer he presented as Tighty-Whitey. Likewise, Dog Lover with Unibrow is not a good defining offer name.
- Numbering the offers will allow the sellers to review the offers with more emphasis on price and terms like down payment, closing dates, opportunities to rent back, and request of personal property, for example.
- It is easier to keep away from factors in the offer that a seller cannot legally consider. (*Offer Number 3* is more legally allowed than *Spinster Nurse Offer*.)
- It is easier for you to keep track of all of the stuff pertinent to each offer.
- It is fun for the seller to feel like a rock star or a rhinestone cowgirl (although I recommend reserving the glitter for your drag queen clients).

During and after the presentation of offers to the sellers, the buyers' agents should be on standby, available by phone or in person to answer quick questions that might be necessary to achieve mutual acceptance. Ask them, pretty please, to do this. The communication takes finesse and balance. You might be going for first-place and second-place offers.

You have to be careful not to help your seller accidentally accept more than one offer with only one house to sell. You have to be careful not to lose all buyers to timing or contract screwups. That is bad.

It feels so good when people want you. Clients like this special feeling as much as we do, and it can be stimulated when someone

ADVANCE READING COPY. NOT FOR SALE.

wants their home. When you are responsible for this arousal, your patrons will see you as the fluffer that you are. Once you move them beyond that powerful, sexy feeling to the climax of a successful close, there will be no other partner in this real estate rendezvous than you.

ADVANCE READING COPY. NOT FOR SALE.

PART 4

WORK IT!

Work It

Although most of these pages are loaded with real estate specifics, the truth is that most of the data are part code for helping, seducing, persuading, assuring, selling, prompting...you know, arousing the buy curious. Things that you need to do with buyers are not so tidy that they don't relate to sellers too. Buyers become sellers, and sellers become buyers. Face it, nothing is ever exactly by the book; nor is there one best operating system.

Technology is part of the real estate world. Books about technology might make both you and your mother bored, but we know that we need to embrace the gadgets that will rule the industry. You can and should buy lots of cool applications and use technology like it's going out of style...because it is. The latest and greatest technology will propel you along, and it's important not to be a Luddite and dismiss. Brag about going paperless...and actually do it.

Technology will eventually fill out a listing, analyze data, pick a price, create a buyer profile, send the buyer on a tour, and create a fill-in-the-blank contract to be e-sent around. If you dismiss technology, you will lose.

However, if you dismiss yourself, you will lose worse.

Who Needs You?
No one...if you think that technology can replace you.

Everyone...if you understand that there's an art to communicating persuasively.

So download until your screen is full; click until your fingernails chip. But keep in mind that the technology that works for everyone today will look kitchy and nostalgic tomorrow. Should you embrace it anyway? Obsoletely. Want timeless? Skills of persuasion that work for you today will last your lifetime. Work it.

CHAPTER 25

BIT O' SCIENCE

You might have noticed that this book teeters on the inappropriate precipice. As much as I'd like to apologize for offending delicate sensibilities, I realize that if people are ever going to remember any information that might be remotely useful, they have a much better chance when the lessons are infused with humor and sex—the two things most positively correlated with memory. My altruism should not be mistaken for tacky classlessness. I do it for you, because I want you to remember. Science has taught us a lot about human behavior and memory, and what we do involves a heap of human behavior, so it might be a good idea to take off your chastity belt so you can remember this shit.

I have a little nerd in me—not right this minute; my husband isn't even home now, and he would refute the "little" part. What I mean is that I really do like science—particularly the science of psychology. If I hadn't been careful, I could have ended up tucked away in a dusty lab somewhere or asking people, lying on a couch, to tell me about their childhood. I still recommend asking clients about their childhood because it can be interesting. And, you know, there is psychology in real estate.

Ordering You Around

Do you remember second dates? How about third dates? I suppose you would if you were not a horny slut and you actually went on a few dates before *that* date. Most of us remember the first date or the last date or the first/last date (when the two are one and the same). There are actually some scientific factors at play that determine why you remember those dates better. The same can be said for what your clients remember about the houses you show them. There are three effects related to memory and the order of presentation:

1. Primacy: Referring to the enhanced recall of items presented at the beginning of a list (peppercorn, coffeemaker, atlas, glove, locksmith, manhole, sock, gerbil, ringworm — we would remember peppercorn)
2. Recency: Referring to better recall for items at the end of a list (from the list above, we would remember ringworm)
3. Middlin': Referring to the shitty recall for items in the middle of the list (not a real effect, but you get the point)

Studies on primacy and recency showed that while memories tend to be stronger for the first and last items in a list, memory is also affected by the time between exposure to the first and last items and the time that elapses before the list recall is required.[2] These studies are as old as shit, but they form the basis for a huge amount of the most current, snazzy memory research.

So why should you give a rat's ass about this? Think about how we show homes. It stands to reason that the more time there is between homes tours, the harder it will be for clients to remember those homes. If you want your clients to remember, and you don't want your gas guzzling weekends to go to waste, you better pay attention to these memory techniques.

When you are working with new clients, you will be judged by the houses you show them. Once they have explained all their desired criteria, they will assess how good you are by whether you are able to expose them to properties that excite them. This is how they will decide if you listened to their wants and needs. The burden is far greater when you don't have a prior relationship by which they can judge you. They will anchor their belief in your competency by how well their desires are met.

---

2. Bennet B. Murdoch Jr., "The Serial Position Effect of Free Recall," *Journal of Experimental Psychology* 64, no. 5 (1962): 482–488; Murray Glanzer and Anita R. Cunitz, "Two Storage Mechanisms in Free Recall," *Journal of Verbal Learning and Verbal Behavior* 5, no. 4 (1966): 351–360.

ADVANCE READING COPY. NOT FOR SALE.

What should you do? If you have set up a tour of homes to show, show the very best one first. The first home will be tied to their impression of you and will establish the kind of relationship that can comfortably get you through the less desirable properties in the middle of your tour. They will know that you get them. You can then make fun of the other properties together as you go. End the tour with the second-best property. The first and last properties will be the ones they will really remember. You capture primacy and recency memory effects and maintain the best shot at selling them something on the tour. If it's a multiday tour, still start the tour with the best and end the first day of the tour with the second best.

There are two memory factors at play. One is the order in which you show the houses, which affects the clients' memories of the data. One is the quality of the order, which anchors you to their evaluation of your success. The piece of information that they latch on to most will be what they remember. Help your clients anchor how they perceive you to the quality perception that you want them to carry.

SORTAꟽacts™

Real estate scientists have concluded a huge worldwide study, and the results conclusively show that the experience at the closing of any real estate transaction determines how the transaction is viewed in the future.

— *Courtesy of Sortafact*

Price Anchoring

Studies show that people moving from more expensive areas tend to anchor their spending to the area they are moving from.[3] People moving from less expensive areas will often squeeze themselves into smaller homes to match their lower price anchor. This factor is independent of the buyers' personal financial picture. The

---

3. Uri Simonsohn and George Loewenstein, "Mistake #37: The Impact of Previously Faced Prices on Housing Demand," *Economic Journal* 116, no. 1 (2006): 175–199.

ADVANCE READING COPY. NOT FOR SALE.

longer they are exposed to the new market, the less they see this anchoring effect. Explaining this bias to your clients can help them make better long-term decisions.

Strap It On

If you have a long tour of homes, you will need to work harder to help your clients remember details about the tour that will be helpful in their decision-making process. You can influence what they remember by pegging some fun trait or behavior to the property you most want them to remember.

TRIALS&Titillations™

Look up an online claim that is backed by a study—any study. Look up the citation, if there is one. Follow the citation to blogs that cite blogs that cite blogs. See if you can find an actual study at the end of the bloggit hole. In the unlikely event that you find a study, read it and see if it says what the blogs claim it does. Swallowing these claims may require you think twice before you claim that you don't swallow.

TrueSTORIES

I was spending an entire Saturday touring a family of five that was moving to the Northwest from the Midwest. The kids ranged in age from five to twelve years old, and their parents did not believe in medication. The market was tight in that there were not a lot of houses that matched their list of needs and wants. They did, however, want to spend the day looking at as many homes as possible in order to understand their soon-to-be new city. I knew, therefore, that they would be frustrated once we were done touring the few houses that actually came close to meeting their criteria, and I didn't want them to perceive me as the source of their frustration. I set up the tour as best I could.

I thought I was showing them the best house first, but I had underestimated their bohemia, and they deemed it too fancy for their taste. This made me reevaluate—the one house that I realized might work was scheduled for the middle of the day, not the best

ADVANCE READING COPY. NOT FOR SALE.

for memory implantation. With no way to reschedule the tours, I needed to figure out a way to cement the memory of that house.

The middle daughter, Ashli, was a gymnast and more disrespectful than I, as a parent, would allow. The family dynamic revolved around dreams of Ashli's Olympic gold and her incredible cartwheel prowess. We toured the perfect boho home in the middle of the lineup, and I agreed to try my best cartwheel on the front lawn for the gymnast. This provided the perfect mnemonic device to help the family remember the house that would normally be forgotten in the middle of the pack. Because I suck at gymnastics, my efforts not only grass-stained my outfit but also cemented Ashli's superiority. I became a good-sport co-conspirator. The favorite home was dubbed "Mrs. Cartwheel," and they were able to indulge the favorite child by buying Ashli's special house.

Ask your buyers to give each house a name to help them create an intentional memory. It's a proven mnemonic device that will produce sustainable memories. This becomes more important the lengthier your tour becomes—the longer the time is between seeing/experiencing and recall, the further it slips from short-term memory. If you're like me (i.e., bad at gymnastics and unable to do cartwheels), find as many sensory opportunities to move the best house into your buyers' longer-term memory as possible.

Playfully telling your clients that there will be a quiz after the tour also greatly increases the chances that your clients will remember the properties. Intentional recall is far superior to unintentional recall.[4] This is a fun test disguised as an exercise to engage the children who are grumpy about being dragged along for the property tour:

> **HITCH (House Intelligence Test Counterbalanced for Buyers, Children's Edition)**
> - Which house would inspire you to follow your passion?
> - What candy do you want as a prize for telling your parents to buy this house?

---

4. George Mandler, "Organization and Memory," in *The Psychology of Learning and Motivation: Advances in Research and Theory*, ed. Kenneth W. Spence and Janet Taylor Spence (New York: Academic Press, 1967), 1:327–372.

ADVANCE READING COPY. NOT FOR SALE.

- Which bedroom do you want to have as your own?
- Which fabulous house do you predict your daddies will like best?
- How many more houses do you want to drag yourself to before your parents buy you one?
- What are the names of the last three houses we saw?
- Which house had the best pet?
- What did your mommy like best about that toilet with front and back oscillating bidet features?

This was inspired by the BITCH, Black Intelligence Test of Cultural Homogeneity, also referred to by my professor Robert Williams at Washington University in St. Louis as the Black Intelligence Test Counterbalanced for Honkies.

If you happen to have a good sense of humor, you might be glad to know that there is also a humor effect that you can take advantage of. Make your descriptions of the homes fun and funny, and clients will have an easier time with recall. This enhanced recall with humor is often attributed to an increased cognitive processing time and an emotional arousal associated with humor.[5]

SECRETSforClients

Take notes when you're touring properties. Write down the pertinent things your agent tells you. Because your agent has to be professional, the burden falls on you to come up with humorous names for properties. When used properly, humor affects memory more than anything else…except sex. Just because a house with ceiling mirrors and velvet posters of dogs playing pool cannot be called the Penis Palace by your agent, there is no reason that you cannot christen it accordingly.

---

5. Stephen R. Schmidt, "Effects of Humor on Sentence Memory," *Journal of Experimental Psychology: Learning, Memory and Cognition* 20, no. 4 (1994): 953–967.

ADVANCE READING COPY. NOT FOR SALE.

Abracadabra

There are magical numbers when it comes to memory. Seven hits the sweet spot of human memory. This comes from one of the most highly cited papers in psychology, published in 1956 by George Miller, called, "The Magical Number Seven, Plus or Minus Two." Many have argued about the full meaning of what has become Miller's law, but it basically says that the number of objects that can be stored in an average person's working memory is seven, give or take two.

Internalizing how this information might affect how you conduct your business can only help. I usually try to tell people who want to see an exhausting number of homes on one tour that clients tend to get house rot and make suboptimal decisions after seeing more than about seven homes. Taking Miller's law literally, I try to leave myself a sludge factor of two so we can tackle nine if necessary.

Even after I've carefully educated stubborn clients, they often want to see more than Miller's Magic Number of houses. The best way to handle this is to chunk. I don't mean that you should feign illness by throwing up to get out of the rest of the tour. Instead, chunk the houses into groups of the magical number. You can split the day into the first batch of seven-ish properties followed by break in the day and then the second batch. For memory maximization, show no more than two chunks of five to seven properties.

True**STORIES**

If you have a bad sense of humor, a laboratory in the bowels of a college basement where experiments are conducted could be a good place for you.

I actually spent quite a bit of time in those collegiate bowels conducting some pretty cool scientific research on human behavior for my master's thesis. Never mind that when I read my thesis now, nearly blankety-blank years later, I hardly understand a word of it. What the hell is *regression analysis*, and how did that ever relate to my life? My research attempted to use Martin Fishbein

ADVANCE READING COPY. NOT FOR SALE.

and Icek Ajzen's theory of reasoned action in a practical application. This is to say that I was hoping to find a mathematic tool for predicting behavior.

The nutshell explanation is that a person has beliefs about certain behaviors that are weighted differently, like exercise or taking public transportation. Let's say you're considering taking public transportation. You have a friend who does this and loves saving all that money and feeling like a greenie. You also have another friend who has taken public transportation only to sneeringly describe the self-proclaimed messiah who preached that deodorant was an instrument of the devil. You will weigh the importance of those opinions differently. If you relate to the snobby friend more, you will shy away from public transportation. These things will affect your intention. Intention will determine behavior.

You can apply this theory to predict your clients' behavior. Try this:

1. Ask the sellers if they intend to list their home within [*insert the time frame here*].
2. Ask if they were referred to you by someone whose opinion they value (a salient referral).
3. Ask them if they intend to list their home with you. This is subtly different from asking them if they are *going* to list their home with you. It gives distance between intentions and actions. Because we are judged on our actions more than on our intentions, this question packs less perceived judgment but tons of insight.

You can influence behavior if you're able to find a salient referral to tell your potential clients that you are the rock star of real estate. This is why so many books focus on asking for referrals. It's not, however, just the number of referrals that will influence the intention of a particular client but rather how important that referrer is to the recipient of that referral. You might think all referrals are created equal, but if you want to represent corporate executives, for example, you should be grateful for the referral from the executive secretary and orgasmic-ally grateful for the referral from the CEO. In that

ADVANCE READING COPY. NOT FOR SALE.

scenario the CEO referrer is your orgasmic ally. If you can identify the type of business that you want to have, you can strategically target the people from whom you would like to extract referrals.

SECRETSforClients

If you have a good friend who is looking to buy or sell real estate, you have a lot of power. Your real estate agent will have a great chance of working with your good friend if your good friend values your opinion and you extol the virtues of your agent. Real estate professionals can do all the self-promotion they want, but your opinion and recommendation are what will count when it comes to your friend.

TrueSTORIES

I was showing high-end condominiums in the urban core. While plugging the parking meter, I unknowingly dropped a few business cards on the street. Someone who lived in a permanent state of urban camping strategically picked up one of my cards. This happy camper had obviously seen me drop the card and was able to make a loud and slurring referral to my client as she parked up the street and scurried to meet me in the lobby of the condo. Although we both laughed at the fact that this homeless person had referred me as "the best Realtor in the business for finding the perfect home" (under the bench by the bocce court on the Norsh Park Bloxsh), the referral was not the most meaningful coming from this particular referrer.

SORTAfacts™

Most highly impressive studies from schools with high undergraduate tuition find that past behavior is the best indicator of future behavior. This has been scientifically supported by divorced second wife ex-mistresses.

—Courtesy of Sortafact

ADVANCE READING COPY. NOT FOR SALE.

Research Says

Blah, blah, blah and so what? When clients come to you with a stated intention, like listing their house with you, you can measure the relative strength of their intention. You can also affect the strength of their intention by asking their cherished friend or influencer to recommend you. Look into their relevant past behaviors and you can predict whether you'll get the listing. If this doesn't work, crystal balls are not prohibitively expensive.

Science pulls back the curtain on the secrets of why we do so many of the things we do. To the extent that we can find practical applications to make science useful, it can become a secret map to effective communication and sales superiority.

ADVANCE READING COPY. NOT FOR SALE.

CHAPTER 26

When you're in a negotiation, it's best to breathe through your nose.

I love myself some Jewish proverbs and so often wish that I could embrace them as my own original ideas. An old scrapper, Babe, taught this one to my friend Rick, who instructed me to breathe through my nose when I wasn't and should've been. I have shared this with many of my friends when they, too, were not using it and should have been.

One of my great friends has given this advice in her negotiation training sessions with wide success. She related to me that she tells her trainees that when they are negotiating, they need to shut their mouths and breathe through their noses. I told her that is not the proverb. She insists that it works because the idea of shutting up in negotiations is the revelation. I agree that shutting up is the revelation, but this steals the aha moment from the listeners as they try breathing through their nose and only then realize it can only be done by shutting the fuck up. Jewish proverbs simply aren't so obvious. You still have to work a little to understand, for G-d's sake.

Rates

Praise people for asking if your fees and commissions are negotiable. Then firmly tell them what you charge with a pleasant but unapologetic look on your face. Look them in the eye. Then... breathe through your nose.

If you feel you are charging more than you're worth, adjust your fee accordingly. If you feel you are really worth what you are charging, write down the reasons why and, in the privacy of your own bathroom, work your justifications out in the mirror. Or do it in the car. The good thing about Bluetooth is that you can now practice many of these techniques while driving without looking lithium deprived. Well, you might, but so does everyone who's actually talking on the phone.

One key here is that your justification for your rate is not about you and what you have to spend or how hard you have to work. It is about how your clients will benefit from paying you what you're worth. I am burying this comment in the middle of this boring paragraph and here it is: good sales always assume that you do what's in the best interest of your client or customer. I will only say that once because it's annoyingly obvious. It's not pithy, distracting, or memorable—just obvious.

SECRETSforClients

Ask your agent what she charges in commission. Then STFU. Have a bowl of Chex Mix next to you if you will feel the need to fill the dead air with noise. If she answers confidently and succinctly, move her into the contender camp. Then ask your agent why she charges what she charges. Then STFU. Her answer should be convincing and unapologetic, and the focus should be on the benefit to you...not on how much it will cost her to be effective.

Even if you are willing to bend on a few numbers, don't make it too easy for your potential clients or they will question your ability to negotiate on their behalf. Some agents offer additional marketing materials like fancy home books, videos, advertising in national publications or local glossy magazines that sellers can choose to pay for over and above the commission. Instead of offering a dissy'd (discounted) commission, give them one of these extras as a freebie. This will allow you to be viewed as confident in your worth but not entirely inflexible. Plan this in advance and don't offer it until they actually earn it. If they don't ask for it, don't waste it.

ADVANCE READING COPY. NOT FOR SALE.

What does all of this have to do with breathing through your nose? If you're not careful, it could have nothing to do with it at all. Breathing through your nose can only be successful if you are confident enough to say what you need to say and breathe. In the case of commissions, answer the question but do not prattle on beyond that.

TRIALS&Titillations™

Listen to someone waxing on about an opinion that you know is complete bullshit (save politics and religion for advanced Trials and Titillations). Place a pleasant smile on your face to give the appearance of agreement. Stay quiet and smile. When he is completely done with his inane diatribe, think about saying, *Don't we wish that* we *were always right?* But don't.

Simplication

If someone asks you a simple question, answer it. Don't try to guess why she might be asking such a dumb question or you can screw up by trying to answer more than what she's asking. After all, you don't need to reveal more than is necessary (*see* "Let Them Do the Undressing").

For some incredibly stupid reason, open house attendees often ask me, "Um, er, are the sellers moving?" My inclination is always to say, "No, they are so hoping that whoever buys the house won't mind them staying," but I refrain. I usually just say, in the friendliest manner I can possibly muster, "Yes." Then I breathe through my nose with a fake smile on my face. If they don't have the balls to ask why the sellers are moving and what the scoop is on the sellers' move, then they don't deserve to know.

When the nosey neighbors or potential buyers ask if the sellers are flexible, I always answer, "Yes." I then pause for effect and might follow up with, "How did you know? Although, I'm not sure if they prefer Hatha or Bikram." Of course there are many other ways to answer that question while still appropriately representing your sellers' best interests and not alienating buyers, but I usually go for the humor shtick.

ADVANCE READING COPY. NOT FOR SALE.

The efficacy of these scenarios is measured by the shut-up factor. If you ramble on and on, the effect is lost. If you don't shut up, the people with whom you're negotiating invariably will, and you'll miss everything they would've divulged. Also, always try to maintain a pleasant smile so you don't come across as the snarky bitch that you are.

SORTAFacts™

People who are quiet and have good posture and a pleasantly sane smile are 16 times more likely win in negotiations than blabbermouths with a giant smile and food in their teeth. This disparity is even more marked with hunchbacks.

—*Courtesy of Sortafact*

Offers

This quiet technique can also be very effective when an offer is being presented to you, especially if it's in person. When someone presents you with a ridiculous offer, you have a useful arsenal of eyebrow arches (make sure you maintain a good, crisp wax for maximum effectiveness), eye narrowing (this is getting decreasingly useful as my eyelids continue to droop into a permanently narrowed range), pursed lips, and head tilts. An ambiguous, "Wow," is also effective. By shutting up, you allow room for the other person to launch into a diatribe of justifications that will line your purse and your clients' pockets.

When *you* present an offer below what you believe the sellers will be expecting, don't let them know that you believe this. Once they sense that you feel that your buyers are making an offer lower than what is expected, you have inadvertently alienated your very own clients. Practice your story ahead of time and anticipate what you will *not* say when they say what you think they'll say. Then, present your offer and breathe. Often, the sellers or their agent will reveal exactly where this negotiation will go next, and you can steer accordingly. If they respond in an unfavorable way, remember that you don't need to start filling the silence with verbal justifications.

ADVANCE READING COPY. NOT FOR SALE.

True STORIES

One time distraction took over my STFU philosophy, and I actually purposefully made an offer without shutting up... initially. After presenting what I actually thought was a pretty good offer to a couple and their agent, the husband angrily swiveled his chair to turn his back to me. Both his wife and their agent were mortified.

I was gleeful because I'm a masochist for these kinds of situations. Because I have a little sadistic element to my masochism, I decided to present the rest of the offer, including all of the boilerplate boring parts—specifically, seriously, and directly to this husband's back. I put the type of smile on my face that one would expect to see on someone who is presenting a full-priced offer to a thrilled seller. On and on I went, never once diverting my eyes from the nerdy trade-show logo emblazoned on the back of this guy's T-shirt. When I was done, I turned to the wife and the agent with a big, satisfied smile, and I...breathed through my nose. And, yes, we did put a deal together.

Email

There is an email equivalent to breathing through your nose: not responding to every email. You can return an email with a phone call if necessary, and you can cover your butt by leaving an email trail stating that you will call.

"My client feels..." emails from other agents are often best left unanswered. It's really fun when you have people who are scared of a little interpersonal repartee. They might continue to send emails regarding things that should truly be discussed voice-to-voice or in person, and they'll often write out the issues as if stating facts but then they won't ask any questions. If you ignore the emails that aren't asking for a response, these people will continue to send emails that make the intensity of their clients' desires more obvious.

Sometimes a simple reply of "Thank you" or "Thanks for making us aware of that," without any additional editorial, will cause enough angst that they will open the email kimono even further.

ADVANCE READING COPY. NOT FOR SALE.

They can't hate you for thanking them, but they can dislike themselves for being the pesky prattler, and that dislike is a good place to find common ground when you're bored.

Breathe, sit back, and enjoy. Although I have so much more to say about emails, this is another time to STFU.

TRIALS&Titillations™

Look at one of your many annoying emails. If you have to wait more than a day or two to find one, go back to one of those Get Up, Show Up, Follow Up seminars because, with enough business, annoying emails should be a regular part of your in-box. Let's say the email describes why a particular buyer feels that the repair addendum she presented is very fair in light of the overall inspection. Type a long and somewhat bitchy but intelligent response to said annoying email. Be very careful not to do this after your requisite evening cocktail(s) or you might accidentally hit send. Now sit back, read it, and laugh. Sign it, "Yours in dipshittery."

Now delete it and retype, "Thank you for your time," or "I see," or "Wow," or "Got it," or "Thank you." There are so many ambiguous responses, and it can be fun, fun, fun to see how the recipient of one responds.

TrueSTORIES

There are one or two or three or…agents I've worked with who were simply not my favorites. One in particular was actually well respected and didn't suck at her job. Several times we were the finalists in a seller's robust interview process for a listing, and several times she won. I only tell you this so you understand that I was a little hostile and a wee bit jealous.

I had a listing that I was yearning to sell, and she had buyers with desires that were aligned with my yearnings. Thinking she was being a shrewd negotiator, she decided to call me to ask about the sellers' motivation.

Usually when people ask me if my sellers are motivated, I prefer to switch it up and cheerfully say, "I'm motivated!" This time,

ADVANCE READING COPY. NOT FOR SALE.

though, when she called, I could tell that she had me on speaker-phone in the office with her clients quietly (sort of) lurking beside her. I could totally hear them snickering in the background like co-conspirators—in a Peter Sellers sort of way. Speakerphone is fine and handy in certain scenarios, but I feel it's rude to put people on speaker without letting them know, and it's stupid to allow the "secret" listeners to share their excitement over their sneakiness so audibly.

This time I replied to her speakerphone insinuations of the sell-ers' price being too high in an equally conspiratorial way. I told her that no matter what the price, she should be proud of her reputation for getting her buyers to come up in price. She was *so* good at that, I said, and she had such skill in convincing her buyers to write offers on the houses she wanted to be able to say she sold. Then I breathed through my nose.

I heard an immediate fumble and—surprise of surprises—the speakerphone was quickly clicked off as she promised to call me right back. You know…technical difficulties and all.

Now, I would never satisfy my retaliation desires if they would in any way jeopardize my sellers. This was the kind of market where I knew that nothing would discourage those particular buyers away from my listing. I was safe to set free my snarky, vindictive self.

Shutting up can keep you out of trouble. You don't want to be seen as the opponent of the "other side."

I'm not proud to say this but, although it is important to make other real estate professionals your allies, sometimes it's really hard because you simply can't stand them. I mean, they drive you fucking crazy. You should, however, always remain a facilita-tor—the more you can enjoy working with the agent for the buyer or the seller, the better. Really. The result of shutting the fuck up should not be that clients or other agents hate you but rather that you elicit the information of what it will take to consummate a successful deal. The key is to get without too much giving—we all know it's really better to receive than to give. Come on.

ADVANCE READING COPY. NOT FOR SALE.

CHAPTER 27

EAST TO WREST

Sometimes there's just no room for naughty humor to steer a conversation back on track. This is where nice replaces naughty as we look to martial arts—the movements and sparring—as a metaphor for communication.

Lately every strip mall big enough to have a nail salon is training ground for future martial arts stars. Suburban parents with a dangerously unscheduled five minutes in their children's week drag their little Connors and McKenzies to bow, punch, and shout their way up the belted ladder toward black. Most never make it. The lessons are lost, and the uniforms are discarded for soccer cleats and cell phones.

But the truth is that the lessons go deeper than a wrist twist to punch or a side-block pivot kick. In witnessing the effectiveness of the moves, we begin to learn that there are many ways to spar. If we learn some basic facts about how we all think and apply an understanding of how traditional moves, *kata*, work to distract, attack, and defend, we see these respectful dojos as laboratories for learning great negotiation, communication, and sales techniques. What a great alternative to a deluxe pedicure.

You know that your clients and other agents are not against you, but it doesn't always feel that way when they attempt to spar with you. Meditate your way into your inner dojo and remember that martial artists work *with* their opponents. They respect the abilities and energy of their opponents in a way that provides great lessons for dealing with clients and other agents.

Simple Truths

Before smugly tightening our soon-to-be-black belts and donning our bonsai pruning shears, we must focus on two simple facts. The first: we all have a pretty good reputation with ourselves. Because we look for confirmation of our excellent reputation and ignore all the notes on the bathroom wall to the contrary, we build ourselves up until we know that we are better than average. With that kind of self-esteem, we have every reason to believe certain bedroom friends when they promise to still respect us in the morning. Science proves that most of us think this way. Those of us who do not think we are better than average are in psychological disequilibrium. We hate it when this happens, so we try to fix this disequilibrium through therapy and with drugs and alcohol. If most of us view ourselves as above average, we should be grateful for the fools holding down the fort at the pathetic end of the bell curve. A hardy thanks goes out to them. Successful communication relies on understanding that our clients and colleagues are just as susceptible to these self-serving biases.

The second simple fact is that we all accept more responsibility for successes than we do for failures. As a real estate professional, you will be seen as either a partner in your clients' success or the cause of their failure. You have to know that we all possess these biases—even you and...gulp...me. This is a challenge because as a salesperson, you will have to set aside your own biases in order to maintain a helpful ninja role in the story of your client's life. This is especially challenging when your client is wrong. Every time you tell someone they're wrong, you lose. It is like a karate chop to their sense of self. But what if they need to be corrected?

SORTAFacts™

95% of people who like to argue emphatically claim that they don't like to argue. Coincidentally, 95% of winning an argument against these deniers involves convincing them that they're right.

—*Courtesy of Sortfact*

In addition to several broken ribs and a tiny scar, I gained a lot of life lessons from two influential senseis in my life. They taught me to extract greater meaning from seemingly irrelevant

ADVANCE READING COPY. NOT FOR SALE.

information. Sparring is a type of communication where the lessons can be lost without the intention to learn because emotions run high. Martial arts can be seen as the physical representation of verbal repartee (VR), so I really have to bow to my senseis when I admit that I learned a lot from embracing my inner grasshopper. There are many forms of martial arts, and each has its own lessons.

Karate

The karate style of martial arts involves attacks and counterattacks. Karate-style VR tends to be the most commonly used method of negotiation. Novices can spend so much time preparing for the counterattack that they neglect the self-control necessary to find power in stillness. Advanced karate is so much more than kick, punch, and block. In real estate when we use a misunderstood karate chop response to correct our client's errors, we do so at our peril.

True**STORIES**

One Sunday I was hosting a very crowded open house even though my sellers had received several offers earlier that morning. A boisterous man took one step into the house and asked, "Do you think this house is overpriced?"

The initial mental karate chop response was to defend the price like Daniel-san would defend Mr. Miyagi. Remembering my attempt at a *zuki* punch that resulted in my broken ribs many years earlier, I refrained and asked, "Do you?"

Mr. Boisterous shouted for all to hear, "I would never pay this much for this house!"

I said, "What price *would* you pay, and we can write a back-up offer."

In this way I was able to allow him to save face by using a respect-and-correct technique. I blocked his punch with a respectful question and allowed him to take a second punch. I was ready with the counterattack—that the market had spoken louder than his bellowing annoyances—respectfully letting him know he would still be eligible to make an offer for what he felt was a reasonable price. He would, however, have to get in line behind the other offers.

ADVANCE READING COPY. NOT FOR SALE.

Tai Chi

Proponents of tai chi (I am waiting until my octogenarian years to join this camp) claim many health and meditation benefits in addition to the more traditional one—avenging your master—that other martial arts provide. The more you understand the art of tai chi, the more you see its use as a form of kicking ass. Many experts claim that tai chi is a fighting and self-defense martial art only at the highest levels of understanding; before that it is more of a form of meditative exercise. Experts learn to study change from the outside world and then to yield and use incoming energy instead of opposing force to deal with their opponents. I suggest that this is the very best martial art to consider when dealing with contrarians.

True**STORIES**

     I was working with a very smart and fun contrarian buyer. If I accidentally voiced any opinion, he would meet it with a counterpunch opinion. If I switched to agree, he would leap back to my original position. There was no getting on his side—unless I *stealthily* got on his side.

Because there is some mystery surrounding commissions, it is understandably common for buyers to wonder why an agent would work to get them a better price when doing so would result in less commission for that agent. The commission is often a percentage of the sales price of the property so the lower the price, the less the commission. It is not hard to see why this might be perceived as a conflict of interest when agents represent buyers.

This contrarian buyer was keen to toss out the challenge of this potential conflict of interest in the form of a roundhouse kick-of-a-statement: "You have no incentive for getting the seller to take a lower price from me because you'll make less in commissions."

Stop reading. You can handle this roundhouse kick. How would you answer? Wait, you were supposed to stop reading! I knew you were an overachiever.

ADVANCE READING COPY. NOT FOR SALE.

True STORIES The True Story Continues...

I responded to Mr. Contrarian's roundhouse kick with, "You're right, I will make less in commission." Then I breathed through my nose. At the exact moment that he felt satisfaction in catching me in his trap, I said, "If you love me and tell all your best friends to hire me, I will make more, more, more in commissions."

The agree-and-deflect technique is as old as the tai chi masters in the park.

SECRETS for Clients

Successful real estate negotiations depend on your real estate agent being able to handle many players in the ring. The best test of how she will handle tough situations on your behalf will be how she handles tough situations with you. Give her a test. Ask her how she would handle a question posed as a punch to the gut, like, "Why would anyone buy this house?

Martial Arts Masters Know:
- When to hold 'em
- When to fold 'em
- When to walk away
- When to use a hand (or a mouth) as a lethal weapon
- When to run

Judo and Aikido

Judo and many of the grappling sports use opponent energy more than opposing force to win the day. Using the least amount of physical strength necessary to throw an opponent is the "gentle way," which actually is the meaning of the word *judo*.

Approaching sales like a judo king can work a lot like a tai chi approach, except with judo you get a chance to jump on top of your opponent. If your client is hot, you might want to think judo.

ADVANCE READING COPY. NOT FOR SALE.

258 AROUSING THE BUY CURIOUS

Aikido is based on the principle that when your opponent strikes, your opponent leaves part of his defense vulnerable. Silence often works best when practicing the aikido equivalent of VR. Steven Seagal knew to use his attacker's momentum against the attacker instead of resisting. Too bad that knowledge didn't extend to the fact that balding and ponytails are two great things that don't look great together.

Hi-Yah!

All the martial arts teach us to use our opponents' energy to benefit us. Whenever one opponent in the ring punches or kicks, it's easy to see that she left an opening for the defender. Her opponent also has an opportunity to use the energy from her punch or kick to slither aside and pull her in for a counterattack.

Studying these time-honored Eastern traditions can give you tremendous sales insights. Use the momentum from a verbal discussion to slither onto the side of your clients. If they are presenting challenging misinformation, understand that they are leaving themselves vulnerable to a punch of truth.

In real estate—unlike in martial arts, where you are dealing with opponents—you are dealing with clients, proponents who sometimes act like opponents. Because you do not want to be seen as an opponent to your clients, you can use diversionary and deflection techniques to strategically correct while still allowing your clients to respect themselves in the morning. Study the nuanced differences in the martial arts to see what form works best for you. Sometimes you should approach sales challenges as a gentle and wise tai chi master. Sometimes you might want to go straight to judo and grappling on the floor.

The more you know about the real estate process, just like the more you know about martial arts, the more you can anticipate your clients' objections and concerns. Being well practiced will develop your sales muscle memory. The martial art form you choose can greatly contribute to your quest to achieve the sales black belt of your desires.

I love working with know-it-alls, inquisitive people, highly educated and analytical people, people who test me, people much

ADVANCE READING COPY. NOT FOR SALE.

smarter than me. I also love working with artistic people, people who know that they need my expertise, people who feel like they don't know what they're doing (sometimes the smartest people, actually). With all of these types of people, I find that what works best usually involves more tai chi than karate. It goes back to the argument against eagerly and intensely combating all objections instead of using the conspiratorial dance of language and energy to channel, redirect, and steer clients' energies, ideas, and desires in the best direction. Then, and only then, can you secretly call yourself a sales sensei.

ADVANCE READING COPY. NOT FOR SALE.

CHAPTER 28

THE ART OF OFFERING A BLOWJOB

When I ask my husband to do a favor for me, I often follow it up with a specific promise—usually of a blowjob. I learned this technique from a very important book called *The Sweet Potato Queens' Book of Love*.

I've been married for a long time by today's standards, so there's no doubt my husband has learned by now that my promises are often empty. I counteract this by committing to the blowjob in front of other people. This gives him embarrassed pleasure but also brings in witnesses to *his* commitment to do the favor for me. He has never asked for the same witnesses to the fulfillment of my promise, but I suppose that's just not what he's into.

This technique is a form of disruption. And it's not just for significant others. It can be used on clients too (and I so want to leave it at that, but this is not *totally* that kind of book). After all, one of my assistants did meet her future husband at an open house—but far be it from me to suggest which disruption technique she used to nab him.

Offering a blowjob might not be within your comfort zone in communicating with clients, but the technique is still applicable even in the most professional settings. The right kind of humor can be used in serious situations when distraction is necessary. Don't dismiss it.

TRIALS&Titillations™

Think of empty promises that you can make if people do favors for you. Here are a few to get you started:

- Profess to love them for the rest of the day/year/their lives.
- Vow to buy them a winning lottery ticket.
- Say you'll provide Doris Day parking for a year (optional variation for your straight friends: rock star parking).
- Pledge to plant them a real-live money tree.
- Promise to buy them a gift certificate to Backdoor Clearance, A Colonic Center.

Now add a few of your own:

-
-
-

The Psychology of Disruption

There are two psychological factors in effect with these types of promises. One capitalizes on the art of distraction, and the other addresses the effectiveness of provocation—you know, getting a little inappropriate. The issue of distraction is top of mind in our culture of data deluge. Distraction has gotten a bad rap, and it can certainly offer an excuse for not getting shit done. Used effectively, however, it can inspire creative genius.

How does this apply to real estate? A focused mind might be focused on the wrong things. There are so many preconceived notions in our wonderful world of real estate that a fixation on those notions can result in a lack of creative problem solving and intractable positions of negativity. Let's face it, ours is not seen as the most respectable, innovative industry. Provocation by definition is stimulating. Stimulation produces results. Distraction with provocation directs thought and behavior in a strategic direction that the distracted, provoked listener wants to go. Open the mind and stimulate.

Curiosity is a kissing cousin to distraction, and provocation and is a most excellent motivator. In the real estate industry, there are vastly different levels of knowledge and smarts. This isn't obvious in people's titles like it is in a more structured corporate environment. We're all Realtors, real estate agents, or brokers. It's hard to know what you don't know, and it sucks having someone

ADVANCE READING COPY. NOT FOR SALE.

with your same title point it out. It feels different having the CEO of your company suggest a better way to conduct your business than it does having a peer do so. So when you need to correct a less experienced or less knowledgeable agent whose cluelessness is causing a transaction to unravel, use sensitivity to help soften the blow.

The best teachers and trainers know the value of curiosity. In 1994, George Loewenstein, a behavioral economist at Carnegie Mellon University, found that curiosity occurs when we feel a gap in our knowledge.[6] New knowledge sinks in much better when we pry open that gap a little more while providing the information necessary to fill it. I call this opportunity the hinge, and the best way to install and activate that hinge is to incite curiosity.

People don't like to feel stupid, so creating curiosity is much more effective than telling an agent with whom you are working that he fucked something up. Distracting with a funny and provocative hinge to widen the gap of knowledge will result in the right kind of curiosity to soothe fragile emotions and impart knowledge so the deal can close successfully. This handy true story will illustrate.

True STORIES

A very experienced real estate broker friend, Suzette, was representing nice, accommodating buyers on their purchase of a five-thousand-square-foot home. Amy, the sellers' agent, was very inexperienced. Her part-time job at the mall should have been at least sort of a clue for her hapless sellers, but they were old and tired, and they relied on their sixty-eight-year-old daughter from out of town for the referral. Since the sellers were both over ninety years old and had compiled a lifetime of valuables from their craft-bazaar-attending addiction, a good sellers' agent might have considered how much time they'd need to clear out of the house as she was negotiating the offer.

---

6. George Loewenstein, "The Psychology of Curiosity: A Review and Reinterpretation," *Psychological Bulletin* 116, no. 1 (1994): 75–98.

ADVANCE READING COPY. NOT FOR SALE.

Suzette took note of the glorious crafty collection and appropriately inquired about the length of the closing, but Amy dismissed her concerns pompously. Suzette kept pressing, asking if the sellers would need a longer closing or a rent-back consideration in order to move out completely, but the sellers' agent's dismissal gave the impression that it was all under control.

Two days before closing and the buyers' possession, the inside of the house was still piled high in a maze of telltale hoarder trails between the stacks—not one item had been removed.

"When should I swing by and pick up the keys so the buyers can meet their moving van on Thursday?" Suzette called to ask.

"Oh, I don't know because the sellers won't be out of the house this week," Amy replied from the stockroom of her part-time job.

"How much room do you have in your stockroom or at your house for pornography film equipment?" my friend wisely asked.

"What? What do you mean?!" Amy inquired with a never-before-displayed zest and interest.

"Well, since you have negotiated a legally binding closing and date of possession for your sellers, and my buyers have acted on faith that you knew what you were doing, they have arranged for filming to begin this weekend. Setup should take about a day. Facilitate the sellers' move out today or expect a special delivery on Thursday. I doubt they need more actresses this go-round, but if your minimalist attention to real estate contracts continues, you might be in need of a second job on their next film. Do you own furry handcuffs and kneepads?"

What Suzette really wanted to do was scream at this mentally comatose agent. The only time she seemed to pay attention was when distraction and provocation were employed to create a modicum of curiosity. As she imagined having to explain a certain delivery to her boss at the mall or her teenage daughter, she was spurred to action. Although she and her daughter and all of her daughter's friends did not sleep for two days, the sellers were miraculously out by Thursday.

ADVANCE READING COPY. NOT FOR SALE.

TRIALS&Titillations™

Figure out what you want from someone. Ask, "What can I do to get you to be my slave?" (If a sort-of-appropriate substitute is necessary, ask, "What can I do to get you to fulfill my every desire?")

SORTAfacts™

Studies show that adding a provocative component to an otherwise banal question results in levels of Peak Curiosity (PC) reached within three seconds, often coinciding with the listener's question, "WTF?" and eventually followed by an answer.

—*Courtesy of Sortafact*

For Favors

The art of disruption is good for getting people to do favors for you. In the Heath brothers' book (they are so friggin' cute), *Made to Stick: Why Some Ideas Survive and Others Die,* the authors talk about a clever flight attendant, Karen Wood, who was futilely trying to get people to pay attention to the safety instructions. Finally she announced:

> If I could have your attention for a few moments, we sure would love to point out these safety features. If you haven't been in an automobile since 1965, the proper way to fasten your seat belt is to slide the flat end into the buckle. To un-fasten, lift up on the buckle and it will release.
>
> And, as the song goes, there might be fifty ways to leave your lover, but there are only six ways to leave this aircraft.... The location of each exit is clearly marked with...red and white disco lights along the floor of the aisle.
>
> Made ya look!

Here, the favor was paying attention. You'll need to come up with your own favors to ask of your clients.

ADVANCE READING COPY. NOT FOR SALE.

TrueSTORIES

Back when I was a retail buyer, nearly every month we would head to New York and make our way to the Garment District to pick from the latest and greatest trends. It sounds sexy and glamorous, but the truth of the matter was that it was a total grind. In addition to viewing the new fashion offerings from our vendors, one of the main goals was to go after financial assistance to liquidate the merchandise that needed to be marked down to sell. This means making a certain kind of friend.

I remember the first time I went, my boss told me I needed to pack something special: kneepads. She addressed this specifically to me first, and then she shouted to all the buyers, "Get on your markdown kneepads. We're going to market!" This was an environment where, and a time when, that behavior wasn't quite out of the realm of possibility. After long enough in the industry, though, I no longer needed those wimpy pads — I had developed calloused knees. That means great negotiating skills. Again, I have to pull your mind out of the gutter.

For Memorability

Using these disruptive terms helps remove a certain amount of monotony from the boring tasks we ask of people we work with. For example, if a buyers' agent has shown your listing, you need to call him within twenty-four hours to elicit feedback. As the agent probably showed his buyer more than just one listing, remind him of something about the property that stands out in an unusual way. Those of the scientific persuasion call it the Von Restorff effect, a bias in favor of remembering the unusual. This effect does not elicit a memory for the little cottage with the vegetable garden, a nice view, and the kitchen with stainless-steel appliances. It does, however, work if you're trying to trigger a memory of that tidy hobbit villa with a yard for surviving end-of-world food shortages, a view of that phallic high-rise, and check-the-dirt-in-your-teeth shiny appliances.

Or make yourself stand out in his mind. Instead of leaving a message of the "I'm just checking in; please call me back" boring variety, I often claim that if the agent returns my call, he'll win

ADVANCE READING COPY. NOT FOR SALE.

the lottery. The odds of that happening being only slightly less than the odds of me making good on that certain promise to my husband, the results are surprisingly similar.

For Diffusion

Osmosis deals with diffusion of water in much the same way that disruption can work as a diffusing salve, calming a situation that is heating up from a slight simmer to a vigorous boil. Abstract language works best in these circumstances, as it sends the steam of the drama into the calming atmosphere. If a buyer is furious that she's made five offers and still has not landed a successful contract, she might be revving up to blame you, those stupid listing agents, or all the greedy sellers. In her mind, there's a concrete-to-abstract gradient of factors she can blame. In this example, you are the most concrete factor, and the greedy sellers fall at the abstract end of the spectrum. With proper disruptive diffusion, when she begins to direct her anger at you, you can throw it to the ether, far away from any of the sources that could fuel the ire.

You might say, "This is market fuckery foreplay. We have seen it before, and we'll see it again. We all know that stimulation without closure can be frustrating. You'll appreciate it for what it is only when the pent-up and fantastic frustration explodes with the climax of the ultimate christening of your new home." Warning: It is best to tailor the diffusion to the audience while remembering the distraction of abstraction.

SECRETSforClients

If your property is listed for sale and does not sell promptly, obtaining feedback on the showings that don't elicit an offer is critical. Ask your agent how she elicits feedback. Ask what she might say to move an agent with a potentially interested buyer closer to the offering stage. For example, many times I have said that if a co-operating broker brings me an offer, I will make her wildest dreams come true. This can be adjusted up or down the sexual gradient by the simple removal of the word *wildest*, but *I* usually don't.

ADVANCE READING COPY. NOT FOR SALE.

Another successful way to use disruption is to distract your clients when somebody else is being an asshole. Once in a while, you will encounter this a-hole in the form of another agent. Pointing out that she is being unreasonable can satisfy your need for immediate gratification, but it won't help your clients. And if it doesn't help your clients, it won't make you money. Even if your buyers or sellers come to a similar conclusion about the snippy agent, it is best not to reveal your true opinion. Instead, use a hook to pique your clients' curiosity and then draw it away from the asshole agent. For example, "Do you know why that agent seems so stubborn? Why she wouldn't 'lend a hand' when we were touring her listing?" When your clients shake their heads, explain, "It's because she's a proud alumna of the Fighting Lepers of CU, Calcutta University." Okay, that's not appropriate—but you have to admit it is distracting.

True**STORIES**

A very grouchy agent called me bitching about my buyers' repair request. Rather than refute every point, I just said, "Oh, Jim, do you know why you hate me so much right now? You're jealous of the fact that I look better in pumps than you do."

It's true that I did know Jim, and he was normally very fun outside of real estate—and very gay in and out of real estate—so this was disruptive but not totally inappropriate. When he's negotiating for his clients, however, he tends to take things a little more personally than the recommended dosage of taking things personally. My complete non sequitur acted as a form of disruption that actually refocused the conversation and got the negotiation back on track. He was able to displace his anger about the repair request with his anger at the fact that he knew damn well that he looked way better in pumps than I did and I was simply refusing to acknowledge it.

Using humorous non sequiturs can be a helpful and fun tool. Be judicious in using these with people with ADD, as you might have a tough time getting them refocused. But when the focus is

ADVANCE READING COPY. NOT FOR SALE.

going in a direction that is not to your liking, this method might be a risk worth taking. Certainly be careful in using sexual undertones with nuns, priests, and other allegedly celibate clients.

If you don't grab people's attention, they just won't listen to you. And if they won't listen to you, they won't do shit for you. They also won't stop doing shit *to* you.

ADVANCE READING COPY. NOT FOR SALE.

CHAPTER 29

GOOD GAL, BAD GAL

Once upon a time are the words that precede life's greatest lessons. Storytelling informs everything—how we relate, how we remember, how we justify, how we're pissed off, and how we're turned on. The essential conflict of stories is out there lurking in the real estate world, and the role you're cast in is determined by the story you tell.

True**STORIES**

A real-life client once called me at 3:00 a.m. to tell me that there were ninjas trying to use the lockbox to break into her house. I had not realized that ninjas targeted lockboxes—one thing that's great about real estate is all the unusual factoids you learn. She said she was working with me because I am Jewish, and she knew I would have some great spy contacts in the Israeli military. I was surprised to learn about an anti-Ninja branch of the Israeli military, but I thought that perhaps the lapse in my knowledge was due to my lack of sleep due to her constant interrupting. I didn't want to let on that we Jewish folks aren't all in the ninja loop, but she figured it out. When she found out I was not on speed dial with the Israeli Mossad, she fired me. For real.

No matter how much you read, re-read, memorize, and buy this book for all your friends and family, you will have some fucked-up experiences. Okay, maybe you won't if you buy enough copies. Wa-wa-wa. Life isn't fair, and rarely is it unfair in the right way. How does that happen? Can it be the conspiracies working against us? The ninjas? Your membership card to the Illuminati got lost in the mail? Sometimes shit happens.

Betrayal

You have done everything right for your clients. You have explained how you work, the commitment or lack of commitment that you require from your clients, and the commitment or lack of commitment that you are giving in return. You are working hard at the relationship and providing rock star representation. Then it happens. Someone tells someone who tells you that your clients have put in an offer on a property…without you.

Depending on the size of the transaction and the thinness of your wallet, you might swear or you might cry. Should you do this? I don't give a shit.

You might call the clients and nicely—or firmly—point out that they have done you wrong. Should you do this? No.

People will justify their decisions. When people stray from a relationship/lose their moral compass/touch another in the morning and then just walk away, the last thing they want to do is call themselves a douchebag. They will claim that they were stuck with their rocky relationship for so long that they are justified in finally allowing themselves the happiness they deserve. When clients break a commitment with you, they will justify that decision too.

They even have a grab bag of client excuses. It's true! Check these ones out:

- I tried to call you, but you didn't answer, and I knew the house I wanted to buy would sell quickly.
- I sent you an email about this.
- I told my wife to call you.
- The seller didn't want to work with any agents.
- The listing agent said there were many offers and I had to act right away…with her.
- You didn't find the house anyway.
- You didn't show me this house (even though it's twice what I told you I would ever spend).
- I knew that you wouldn't like this house.
- My friend at work told me that I needed to deal with the seller directly.
- I knew that I couldn't afford it if you had to get your commission.

ADVANCE READING COPY. NOT FOR SALE.

- I've been thinking of calling you for weeks... This just isn't working out.
- After you wrote five offers for me, I realize that I needed to go in a different direction.

Don't be surprised if they follow any of these up with, "Oops, I didn't get the house. Can you show me seventeen more houses this weekend?"

SECRETSforClients

Be honest with your real estate professional. Finding the perfect property is no longer the big event for the best agents. Ask your agent what inspections he would have on his own house. Ask him what inspections he thinks he will be recommending in five years. Ask him the scariest thing he's found on a title report, his philosophy on agent-appraiser relationships, his experience with undisclosed life estates, easements, unrecorded boundary disputes, overlays... I assure you that the list of valuable things excellent agents do will blow your mind. Less valuable agents will have no idea of the services they fail to provide. They, too, might think that finding the perfect property proves perfect service.

Many agents are now using buyer contracts that legally bind a buyer and a buyers' agent. Some states require these types of contracts. Even if you don't have a contract with a buyers' agent, if you have committed to an agent, don't be a cowardly dick and go behind her back. If you have to justify your behavior, it's not the right behavior. If you already did it, be willing to admit that you were a cowardly dick and make it right. This free advice transcends real estate.

When clients break a promise to you, they will justify their decision. It speaks to their internal reputation meter and psychological equilibrium. In their mind, it's better that they cast you as a shithead in their life story than admit that they're the douchebag villain. If you point out their missing moral compass, you will be cast as the antagonist in the story of their life. You will lose.

ADVANCE READING COPY. NOT FOR SALE.

Reactions

You don't *have* to react to everything. I used to get into so much trouble in my youth because I was unable to control my reactions to anything funny. I tried to hold in my laughter as my teacher ranted at me to stop disrupting the class, but it didn't work. If he would have only zipped up his fly while he yelled that I go directly to the principal's office, I think I could have stifled long enough to rush into the corridor before exploding with laughter. The white of his underwear was literally poking through the open zipper of his brown corduroys, for god's sake.

When it comes to laughter, I have matured a wee bit since then. I'm guessing you have always been better than I have about this, as I don't remember anyone getting into as much trouble as I did. But laughter isn't the only reaction that could stand to be stifled once in a while. Pointing out the absurdity of an argument, winning the last word, and indicating when you're not being treated fairly are also areas that don't always require immediate reactions.

In the scenario of your clients' betrayal, you likely want to rant and rave about the unfairness of the douchebaggery. There's a more effective way to instill guilt and still salvage the relationship when you suspect unfaithfulness, though. Try these nine easy steps:

1. Wait a half a day to see if they call to confess.
2. Make sure you did not drop the ball. (In this example, this could be if you missed introducing your clients to the perfect property.)
3. Call your clients and tell them you are digging around for property and just wanted to check in with them.
4. Shut up for at least fifteen seconds.
5. If they confess that they have strayed from the relationship, listen quietly for just a few seconds beyond what is comfortable.
6. Ask if they love the other house.
7. Ask questions to find out if the betrayal warrants a breakup.
8. Make comments like, "Wow, that does sound intriguing."
9. Throw in a funny line like, "I suppose the seller's ugly ex-wife was a Realtor and that's why they want nothing to do with me helping you with this transaction."

ADVANCE READING COPY. NOT FOR SALE.

See the difference between that line and coming right out with, "Why didn't you call me? The seller might have been willing to pay a commission for me to represent you!" That difference is what determines the future relationship between you and your client. *Note: At your buyer consultation, you will have already gone through the scenario of sellers not wanting to work with buyers with agents. They know what they should have done. This will, therefore, be a reiteration of what was already discussed.*

SORTAFacts™

Justification Station is a place where 100% of us go from time to time. 78% of all power comes from having every justification…and not using it.

—Courtesy of Sortafact

Their Move

Upon being confronted with their less-than-stellar behavior, clients can react in many ways. If they are mad about being confronted, they might dig back in the grab bag of excuses. Because you were smart enough not to accuse, their angry reaction means they feel guilty.

As much as their guilt seems appropriate, calm these turbulent waters before they create a tsunami. Bring in humor here. Tell them that you so hope that their transaction goes smoothly and, if it gets bumpy and they want out, you will be there to discuss picking up where you left off.

If you no longer trust them because you had to pry the truth out of them like a pesky eyebrow hair between waxes, this is a good time to wish them well and point out how much fun you had working with them. If this conversation takes place over the phone, you have lots of room for you to flip them off with a smile in your voice. But do not leave it at that.

If you're really nice to them and they do not deserve it, they will know this deep down. They will continue to feel guilty, and your graciousness will fuel that guilty fire. Because people do not like feeling guilty (even Jews and Catholics, who are experienced

ADVANCE READING COPY. NOT FOR SALE.

guiltfessionals), they will be left in that yucky disequilibrium…and you will be seen as the cause. You will be cast as the antagonist in the story of their life. *Hey, that's not fair!* you might think. Get over it; I got fired for my lack of ninja-catching skills.

Here's the juicy part! Assuming you have been totally gracious and their guilt has peaked, you must give them a chance to be a hero. You say, "Now you owe me something big, and that's on top of the top-shelf margarita that I'm thirsting for. If you have any friends or relatives who are as enjoyable as you, the second they mention the words *real* and *estate*, you must send them to me. I would be so grateful for any referrals." By using this opportunity to get referrals, you have offered them a chance to reduce their guilt and restore their equilibrium. Then, instead of spending their energy justifying their mistreatment of you, they will feel a call to absolve their cheating selves of their guilt. You can even ask for a specific number of referrals: "Okay, you had better refer me eight nice people within the next twelve months or I'm posting your Mensa exam results on Facebook." Don't use this with your smart clients, though, as they will intentionally avoid referrals to get that posting and bragging rights.

We live for stories. The roles we play cast us in the story of our lives. Since the sane among us have an innate psychological need to be cast in the good-witch role, we surround ourselves with the best supporting characters. For a happy real estate career, it's better to be a Munchkin to Glinda the Good Witch than it is to die under the house. When you pull back the curtain on this truth, you'll find that understanding stories and the best roles to play is the only way to real estate Oz.

ADVANCE READING COPY. NOT FOR SALE.

CHAPTER 30

It's Not Me—It's You

What's love got to do with it? You don't have to love it to sell it. You don't have to love them to sell it to them. They don't have to love you for you to sell it to them. They don't have to love it for it to be the thing they should buy. Selling is persuasive communication and, like Tina Turner, the best at this art know that love is just a secondhand emotion.

Think about all the things you could sell. My mind jumps immediately to shoes and cringes far away from microprocessors. That is because we tend to sell what we like. It's tied to that "follow your passion" mantra that stokes the passionless fire of my soul. Many people go into real estate because they love houses or buildings or land. In times o' real estate plenty, this interest alone is often enough to put food on your table. In normal markets and especially in struggling ones, though, this passion for pretty houses has very little to do with creating a successful real estate career. It also has very little to do with helping people.

Love Hurts

Love can taint the truth. So can like…and hate. This is one reason that great salespeople do not have to love or like the products they're selling. People don't always buy things they love or like. People buy a property they don't love because it is in close proximity to something they need to access frequently, it will impress their friends, it's a wise investment, they can use it as a stepping stone to something they desire, or they are convinced that they need to.

The best salespeople are like the best online dating search engines. They dig deep to understand needs, desires, history, and motivations in order to draw conclusions about what these things might mean for people today. Their passion lies with the hunt of understanding long before they try to apply it as a solution. Owning real estate is not for everyone always. A great real estate professional cares first about finding out what is right for the clients, long before (and sometimes in lieu of) finding the right match. If a real estate salesperson is to love anything, it should be the love of this hunt for understanding.

TrueSTORIES

Before attending an auction where I knew the urologist who had generously donated his services in a Snip-and-Suds package, I helped my husband picture teaching his youngest child to ride a bike while he was pushing his own walker. He did not like that image at all. Since he had made his true desires clear, he should have not looked so terrified when I competitively and successfully bid on the auction item that would mark the end of his procreating life. When the auctioneer shouted, "Sold! The Snip-and-Suds goes to bidder number...101," my husband publicly grabbed his crotch in a protective manner.

The next day he gulped down the first beer in the case by his side as he made the vasectomy appointment. He didn't love the gift, nor did he love me for buying it, but I knew it would be the best way to accomplish his goal and it was, therefore, a perfect gift.

SECRETSforClients

Ask your prospective real estate agent why he went into real estate. If he says he loves houses, ask him if he loves all houses. Ask him how he sells houses he doesn't love. If he says he loves people, ask him if he loves all people. Ask him how he makes love to people whom he doesn't love. Be sure to embrace your inner Stephen Covey and begin with the end in mind. See how much his answer can truly benefit you.

ADVANCE READING COPY. NOT FOR SALE.

Love Yourself

Now you are convinced that loving real estate has very little to do with being a great real estate professional. There is something, however, that you should probably sort of dig before you expect anyone to dig you: yourself. Before clients ever buy or sell property with your help, they have made an initial purchase: you.

This is a very personal profession, and if people choose not to invest in us, our feelings get hurt from time to time. We feel so judged! But remember, if people don't want to work with you because of your personality, that's really okay. Blame your parents. Or better yet, blame their parents.

There are precisely nine attitudes people have about other people:

- Love them
- Want them
- Like them
- Want to be them
- Don't like them
- Dislike them
- Cannot stand them
- Hate them
- Want to learn from them

You probably move among all these attitudes when it comes to different people in your life. Maybe there are even some people who fall into all the categories in the same time. The more you interact with some people, the more categories they traverse. Often the more you know someone, the less you *want* them but the more you like or dislike them.

She's Just Not That into You

Remember, too, that you fall into some of these categories for other people. We are so chock-full of biases and prejudices that we generally believe everyone must love us. When a relationship goes sour, it's hard to honestly assess if we are the cause. I'm

ADVANCE READING COPY. NOT FOR SALE.

going to break it to you. There will be people who don't want to work with you, and there are a few reasons why it will be almost totally your fault.

If you are guilty of any of these scenarios, you're to blame when a client relationship doesn't work:

- Clients don't think you are knowledgeable enough to get the job done.
- They don't think your personal brand is a good reflection on their property or themselves.
- They don't really like you.
- They think working with you will adversely affect your relationship.
- They think you're an idiot.
- They don't like your company.
- Your drunk confession of undying and unreciprocated love still stands as an awkward presence in the room whenever you're together.
- They want their rejection to adversely affect your relationship.

More to Love

Early in your career, when your skills are not fully developed, it is fair for you to be rejected by buyers or sellers. What if you're new and you just don't know how much you don't know? Figure out what prospective clients might object to about your knowledge or lack thereof, and work out ways to overcome those objections. Maybe you have incredible contacts, but you don't know anything regarding contracts beyond what you learned in real estate school. Maybe you have an incredible knowledge of contracts but are new to town. Perhaps you're a history buff about architecture and neighborhood details, but you're clueless about pretty much everything else.

If your knowledge gaps have turned into stumbling blocks that trip up prospective clients, ask a few successful, generous agents to help fill in those gaps. When asking for advice is not enough to overcome those objections, you can ask a more experienced agent to share by co-marketing a home that you are working to list or to partner with you to work with a buyer. There might be

ADVANCE READING COPY. NOT FOR SALE.

a successful agent with a strong business in the condominium market. You have some good contacts for prospective buyers or sellers in the condo market, but they feel that your experience outside of suburban ranches is too skinny to take a chance on working with you. This could be a good opportunity to co-brand a listing with the agent who has a strong condo presence. Now your client can have confidence in the experience representing the job, your career can be anchored to a successful condominium experience and agent, and you add a stream of income for the agent helping you out.

Every perceived gap that gets in the way of a client feeling confident in you can be filled without delay. This is true whether you're successfully established in the business and are looking to change or expand your focus or if you're brand-new to the business. Sure, you can learn this stuff over time, but those buyers and sellers don't want to wait years for you to get good—even when you're so cute and charming that they simply cannot envision working with anyone else.

You Decide

Although you *can* remove many of these relationship roadblocks, you must assess whether or not they *should* be removed. Just like you might not be the right person for some buyers or sellers to select as their agent, some buyers and sellers might not be right for you.

The initial consultation should be as much about your potential clients giving you an indication as to whether they're right for you as it is about you selling yourself. Okay, maybe not *quite* as much, but it's definitely important. Reserve the option to reject them. If they are looking to buy or sell outside of your area of expertise—or outside of your desired area of expertise when you are yet to have any expertise—it's not an ideal match. It's hard to reject them if you have personalities that probably will work well together, but it must be done for the sake of your business.

Spend some time deciding what you want your business to stand for or you will develop the all-too-common Reactionary Real Estate Syndrome. I should know, because I suffered from this syndrome for many years.

ADVANCE READING COPY. NOT FOR SALE.

After a lifetime of experiencing and studying the best and worst communication and sales strategies, I entered the real estate business with the proper archaeological desires. I knew how to mine the mind of clients to find out what was best for them. I did not, however, strategically think about how I wanted my real estate career to develop. I worked with whoever would have me. Because of this, I failed to witness a very well studied and obvious factor that any businessperson with a half a brain would recognize: opportunity cost.

I would spend weeks schlepping clients around without a thought about the percentage of time that I should have been identifying, targeting, and cultivating the business I wanted to develop. I lied to myself and patted myself on the back for being so busy so early in my career. I forgot that a smart work ethic is far more positively correlated with true success than is a strong work ethic. I was a busy dolt. The truth is that I have always suffered a wee bit from Reactionary Real Estate Syndrome.

A nice, cute, appreciative prospective client can be very enticing and can make you susceptible to the syndrome. These clients can trick you into forgetting all about your business plans and opportunity costs. After all, it's so nice to spend time with nice people who like you. If you're establishing your business around working with nice, cute, appreciative clients, you might be poor and happy—and there is nothing wrong with that. It can help you forget all the other aspects of business that may be less desirable. Heck, being okay with being poor can even eliminate the need to have a business plan.

Just be aware of whether you are making this choice or the choice is being made for you. You might think you have a strong work ethic because you work a lot, but you are being a bit lazy if you haven't proactively targeted what you want your busy you to ultimately accomplish. If you're savvy enough to understand opportunity costs and what your business stands for, you have to stick to your business plan. Kindly refer these clients to an agent who will better represent them, and ask both the clients and the agent for referrals in return.

ADVANCE READING COPY. NOT FOR SALE.

Scoring a thoughtful referral will be a bigger boost to your business than will taking every client with a pulse. People will not feel rejected if you decline them in a way that they know is in their best interests...not just yours. This takes finesse and tact—skills that are not as difficult as they might sound. Follow these steps:

1. Explain that where the clients live or where they want to live is an excellent place.
2. Confess that the area of their home or desired home is outside of your area of expertise.
3. Sell them on what an expert you are in the area of *your* expertise or desired area of expertise.
4. Ask them to refer to you all of their friends and family looking to buy or sell in your area.
5. Tell them to really make an effort to refer friends and family who are just like them.
6. Explain that you want to make sure they get a great level of service and expertise and that in order to do that, you will hand-pick someone who can provide them with the knowledge and service you know they deserve.

Practice this in advance—if for no other reason than to do this in a less cheesy way than I have described.

Just Say No

If you have been good and strategic about your business and some prospective clients fit the profile of your target business, that's a good start. But if you can't stand the clients, don't work with them. Note that I did not say, "If you don't like the clients, you should reject them," as not liking is less severe.

There may be people who you don't like, but you should consider working with them anyway because that is in the best interest of your business. Chances are, if you can't stand them, they will ultimately vibe this out and feel the same way about you. Be assured that if they can't stand your personality, they won't work with you, so you are just nipping things in the bud by choosing not

ADVANCE READING COPY. NOT FOR SALE.

to work with them. If either of you proceed with the relationship with the red flags waving, you will end up with a bitter breakup or a bad chain o' references.

If you reject them, explain that you want them to have a great and successful real estate buying/selling experience, so you want to make sure that they have the right partner. Then help them find another agent with an equally crappy personality and a willingness to pay a referral fee. Hook them up with one another, and it's a win-win.

SORTAFacts™

93% of people are stingier with their love stories than with their hate stories. 84% of story listeners prefer to say, "Oh my god, that fucking sucks," to "Awww, isn't that wonderful?"
— *Courtesy of Sortafact*

Sometimes you screw up and start to work with someone you shouldn't have. It's best to extract yourself from the relationship before your sour feelings spread to other clients. If you don't, they will be dissatisfied and complain to other potential clients, sending you to the bar to get away from all their bitching. And you should not jeopardize your sobriety.

I always thought that my sassy fifteen-year-old self said it fairly well when I told the asshole customer at Burger King, "Listen, lady, I make my $3.35 an hour whether you eat here or not." However, that paled in comparison to one of the most liberating lines I have ever heard. It came from David Sedaris in *The SantaLand Diaries*, in which he describes a manager who tells a customer, "Don't tell the store president that I called you a bitch. Tell him I called you a fucking bitch because that's exactly what you are. Now get out of my sight before I do something we both regret." Firing clients can be so fulfilling. Unless you like having a part-time job in addition to real estate, do so sparingly.

True**STORIES**

I once had a client who, from the initial meeting, I really didn't like. Because that is rare but not the rarest of events, I did

ADVANCE READING COPY. NOT FOR SALE.

not refer this client to another broker right away. I thought I could stand her but just didn't like her and, as I've said, that is fair game for hanging on to a client. Plus, I was out of firing practice. I forgot to remember how this kind of referral can be a good tool to take care of a new, annoying client and get paid without having to waste any gas.

This client went from being just annoying to constantly asking to be shown only extremely prestigious areas. She even went so far as to ask to live where the "fancy people live." I find that extremely pathetic, but if I had been on my game, I could have easily found an equally striving agent from whom to extract a referral fee.

Instead, I explained that my agency covered many wonderful areas and it was best to tell me a little about what she liked and didn't like about where she lived before. She said she hadn't been able to afford to live in the type of desirable neighborhood that she can now afford, but she knew that she wanted to be around other people like her…people who look like her…people with a similar complexion.

Now, I have many bruises that have accumulated over the years from kicking myself when I didn't think of the perfect thing to say until two or more hours after the time I should have said it. This time, though, I was bruise free.

I told her that it was extremely important that I never have unsatisfied clients. She nodded appreciatively. I told her there were two major ways that I made sure to never have unsatisfied clients. She anxiously awaited my sage words of saleswomanship. "One is to satisfy my client," I said. "The other is to make the person not my client. In your case," I told her, "I am going to choose the latter." It was all I could do not to fist pump the air as I picked her jaw up off the dashboard of my car.

While I found firing this client extremely satisfying, it was not lucrative. The story should have ended here, but now this woman found me even more prestigious because I was deemed successful enough to fire clients. When I bumped into her later, she was very solicitous and friendly and even a little desperate for us to work together again. My satisfaction was so complete that I didn't even bother to make a referral.

ADVANCE READING COPY. NOT FOR SALE.

Love is not a necessary emotion for a successful real estate experience. Hate, however, is certainly not an optimal substitute. Sweet success often lies in a deeper, harder-to-find spot. When the search for that spot is too elusive, though, it is best to give up and move on.

ADVANCE READING COPY. NOT FOR SALE.

CHAPTER 31

MARKET FLACCIDITY AND THE VIAGRA YOU NEED

Delicious good times and nasty bad times sandwich the love wedge of normal times. Markets fluctuate—normal is rare, and even then we know shifts are out there, leering at us. However, unlike the nuclear fission or pharmaceutical industries, where most of us know we don't have a damn clue, real estate is an industry familiar to most people. This gives us false confidence in spotting those lurking shifts. Since we're addicted to prediction, we grab our handheld mirrors and predict real estate market trends with confident vigor. The truth, though, is that market shifts are best seen from a rearview mirror, and beside every outcome lies the one-night stand of another useless prediction. Rely on the fact that the only thing reliable is the existence of market shifts. Prepare accordingly.

SECRETSforClients

Asking how many sex partners your date has had will not help determine whether they're good in the sack. Relying too heavily on the quantity of homes sold by your real estate professional to accurately judge the quality of service might give you a similar disappointing result. Sure, experience matters, but only if it is the right kind of experience—coupled with just the right kind of service. A booming market is like a straight guy at a Mary Kay convention. In a booming market, a less-than-stellar agent can sell a shit-ton of property, but that does not necessarily mean he is a good choice for you. The numbers game can be misleading. There are better tests of what will help you achieve sell-sational results.

Quality Does Not Equal Quantity

During the years when making money in real estate sales was like getting laid at a Dungeons and Dragons convention, there were many agents who made a lot of money but behaved horrifically. They weren't the slightest bit curious about why moneymaking was so easy for them at the time. They would often try to school experienced agents, saying their unorthodox and suck-assed business approaches had incredible success, so they knew best. As the market shifted, many of those same agents were forced to explore their career options in the wonderful world of fast foods.

This pisses me off because my teenage sons could not find the grease-filled work necessary to teach them that special orders will, in fact, upset them and it's important to excel in school. As bad as those agents were, they were still more likely to get the job than pimple-fighting teenagers who suck at filling orders of burgers, fries, and Diet Coke.

Thinking of the boom before that crash, I find it's sweet to recall when people referred to real estate as an assured appreciating asset. I get nostalgic reading the sales techniques prescribed during the go-go years. If we had a chance to do it all again, tell me, would we, could we? Thanks, Barbra Streisand. The answer is: yes, we would. Are you freakin' kidding me? We would so go back to working until eleven every night to catch real estate transactions and closings like teeth in a boxing ring. People talk about achieving balance in their lives, but balance is always there when the market returns to normal. Who needs sleep?

The key is to know that markets do return to normal...and then they can suck again...and later we find a new definition of *crazy* in the really good. Remind yourself of this fact. Share this reality with your clients. Admit to them that jubilant go-go years provide opportunities to be exploited judiciously. If you are only there for the sexy days of real estate, it is not fair to your clients. They need you to help them gyrate with the market properly, with the understanding that it's not possible to predict with certainty when the beat will change. Let them know that you will be there through hard times and they will stick with you for life.

ADVANCE READING COPY. NOT FOR SALE.

SORTAꞘacts™

One of the most important quotes to come out of 2004 is, "It's better to be a surfer in a tsunami than a weatherman on the beach." 91% of the world's smartest people can figure out how this quote applies to shifting markets.

—Courtesy of Sortafact

SECRETSꞘorClients

Be careful to avoid hiring a real estate professional who is attempting to exploit only the most bountiful seasons and then sneak out of the business. In the best-case scenario, hiring the wrong real estate professional can cost you a ton of money and you will never know it. In the worst-case scenario, it will be glaringly apparent.

First vs. First Best

If you long to help people, you need to find *and* cultivate the people you plan to help; this involves the often-dreaded client, or lead, generation process. Even if you're the first to identify the lead and you have the requisite script firmly in your grip, without the yearning in your loins to provide desirable value, you will not nail that lead. One of the biggest shifts in the sales industry has come about because of a shift in access to information. It is no longer enough to be the first to provide information because so little data is limited to industry insiders anymore. Back in the day, all it took to elevate the neighborhood gossip status of Ethyl's home price was an empty flyer box. That was back when data dissemination alone was a sales strategy.

Providing information is no longer enough to entice clients. Prospective clients want value…and they want it for free. They want an interpretation that is real and matches the market. When you provide free data to prospective clients in a way that clearly benefits only you as the agent, the stink of bullshit will be obvious. Prospective clients will determine the value of the information

ADVANCE READING COPY. NOT FOR SALE.

by how relevant it is to them. The lead aspect won't matter. You won't need to be the first to reach them as prospective clients — you will need to be the first to provide relevant value that is beyond what they can easily access for free.

Don't tell them, but the information won't really be free. What you should aim to get in return is contact information. Prospects should be intrigued with what you flash them and yearn for more of your value-producing action. Obtain their contact information so you can follow up and actually fulfill the promise to get back to them with even more worthwhile, relevant information. If they love what you gave for free the first time, and you enticed them with a peek at your valuables the second time, keep fanning the fire of their desires and you will have turned those prospective clients into paying clients.

TrueSTORIES

I was out of town to attend a costume-themed birthday party for a good friend. Most people at the party did not know me nor did they know that I was in real estate. Even if they did know me, they would not have recognized me in my embarrassingly heinous costume. There were several other real estate agents in attendance, and they all seemed to be trying to make sense of a huge market shift.

It was great eavesdropping as they whispered in panic among their costumed selves. It was clear that only one of the agents had experience in markets that were anything less than insanely appreciating, but several were not afraid to pontificate anyway. They dispersed themselves among the other partiers, and I was anxious to listen to how they fielded the real estate questions from prospective clients.

Real estate was on everyone's mind. Prospective clients were ripe for the cultivating. The cocktails were flowing, and it was clear that most of the people had been spending their spare time on a lot of real estate porn — some of the partiers were way more informed than several of the agents.

ADVANCE READING COPY. NOT FOR SALE.

One tall, cross-dressing Madonna (theme appropriate) had clearly done his/her homework in preparation for his/her move across the country. He/she was also well versed in short sales, having been a lucky winner in a bidding war at the moment the market had peaked. He/she approached one of the agents to inquire about the market. All I heard from this agent was, *"It's a great time!!!"* Not only could I see this was a totally disingenuous representation of how this agent felt, Madonna knew it was bull-shit too. It had very little relevance to the fact that he/she needed (not wanted) to sell to move out of town. I saw the agent whip out his card and hand it to the victim.

A few minutes later, I saw this very same Madonna approach a second real estate agent to inquire about the market. Clearly there was more to this inquiry than bored curiosity. This time, however, the agent started the conversation with a question, seeking to understand what aspect of the market insight would be important for Madonna. When it became apparent that the situation was neither happy nor hopeful, the agent skillfully shared just one free and valuable strategy that she had used to successfully help a client in a similar situation. When Madonna asked for her num-ber, she apologized for not stuffing cards into her costume but grabbed a pen and small piece of paper to jot down Madonna's name and number. She knew that making bra space for *getting* contact information was more important than making space for *giving* contact information.

Later that night, I found the business card of the first agent on the ground by the outdoor fire pit. A month later the host of the party told me about the second agent's name swinging from Madonna's for-sale sign.

The good thing about shifting markets is that they tend to push real estate to an elite topic of interest. In severe shifts even celebrity gossip and sports can be forgotten stepchildren at parties and events. This means that you had better be at those parties and events (*see:* "Party People in the House"). In downtrending markets you may have fewer dollars to spend on more passive marketing

ADVANCE READING COPY. NOT FOR SALE.

materials, but your voice, company, and intellect are free. Party more in shifting markets and you will reap more benefits than you would wallowing in your pajamas or bitching with your fellow agents at your office. Just be sure to bring your prospecting party hat and to leave plenty of room in your undergarments for jotted-down contact information.

Prediction

Be curious. Pay attention to what is happening in your day-to-day life. If you pay attention and don't rely too heavily on what outside experts write about the real estate market, you have a huge advantage. Don't worry; you won't be totally in the dark. You should know that the market has adjusted by truly minding your own business and watching the business of other agents. Ask people about their immediate experiences and you can find out what the data will show a few months later. It takes time to compile the data. It takes longer to analyze the data. You're living the data in real time—take note. You can benefit your clients if you can help them see a shift a wee bit before it is reported. This does not require skills in prediction; it requires opening your fucking eyes.

SORTAFacts™

Data lags behind experience nearly 99% of the time. Over 82% of experts analyze data without the hands-on and intimate experience of working day-to-day in the industry they analyze.

—*Courtesy of Sortafact*

Reaction to Change

The psychological reaction to change is generally out of whack with what is warranted. Sellers may be more fearful of declining prices than is warranted by the ultimate bottom of the market. Buyers generally obtain the best prices when this fear is in full swing. If there are a lot of indicators that the market still has a good chunk of downward momentum, that might be a good time to point out to buyers that the sellers' fear of the market floor is below where

ADVANCE READING COPY. NOT FOR SALE.

the actual market might be headed. It could be a better time for buyers to pounce than when the market is in its truly flaccid state.

Once at the true bottom, guess what direction the market always goes? See? Viagra! It's the new Eureka! That may be a good time for sellers to sell. Really. Although most real estate training focuses on how to get sellers "realistic" about pricing (read: willing to take lower than they want), it is equally important to temper fear when you experience early rumblings of a positive schwing in the market.

There are transactions to orchestrate in every market. There are opportunities to exploit. The opportunities are not equal for everyone. No matter how much agents want to earn a commission, long-term success will be determined by an understanding of and honesty about this fact. Some opportunities might be hidden from clients. The real estate professional's job is to expose those opportunities and help clients put their fears into proper perspective. Use the key to release the chains of fear. Let the lessons in the previous chapters be the guide.

Some of the opportunities will be cock-blocked by economic factors that have nothing to do with what can be done about the psychology of fear: no money, bad credit, big debt, looming jail time, title entanglements. Creativity can help overcome some of these pesky problems. Time can help overcome others. When these factors send patrons into a fear-filled frenzy, let them know the answer to their request is rarely *no*, but it is sometimes *soon*.

Seasons

Shifts in market happen seasonally as well. There are generally not huge swings in these seasonal changes from year to year, but there are often small shifts. When you're new to the business, it's easy to obtain historical information on these seasonal changes, and it is not totally stupid to use this history as a template for what you might expect.

Distressed Sales

People's lives have shifts that will determine how to plan and react to market shifts. In the first decade of my real estate career,

ADVANCE READING COPY. NOT FOR SALE.

distressed properties were a rare specimen, and I rarely thought about this foreign concept. Later many salespeople jumped on the distressed-sale bandwagon because it was such a growing and very enticing segment of the market. For those who simply refuse to acknowledge that distressed sales could possibly be of relevance, as I did for a time, to them I say, "Oops."

Emerging market trends are always relevant for assessment. Jump on these opportunities with a keen eyeball fixed on your greater brand. When enticing opportunities emerge, it is critical to evaluate how much time and energy should be pulled into those markets and whether that will be the right thing for business over time. Real estate professionals who continue to cultivate core business while judiciously reacting to new opportunities are able to maintain the erection of a robust and consistent brand.

True**STORIES**

At an office meeting an agent, Courtney, was bragging about how she adeptly handled potential sellers who were fearful about an increase in bank-owned homes hitting the market and adversely affecting prices. She told her in-city clients that foreclosed-upon properties would not affect them because distressed properties were only in the suburbs. This was mostly true, at the time.

At a meeting a few weeks later, Courtney was lamenting that she did not get a listing for which she suggested a much higher asking price than the other agents did. A foreclosed property had just been listed next door to her in-city prospect. By telling the in-city prospects that foreclosures were not a threat in their area, she had boxed herself into an absolute, nullifying her credibility.

It would have been totally accurate and okay to suggest that current trends in foreclosures seemed to indicate a concentration in the suburbs, but these trends tend to leave no area untouched. It's best to *partner* with clients, acknowledging their fears and agreeing to stay on top of the ever-changing market so neither of you get caught with your pants down.

ADVANCE READING COPY. NOT FOR SALE.

Same Clients, Different Market

Phone calls with clients who are selling the same home they purchased at a much higher price, with your help, can be uncomfortable. Discussing all the possible scenarios when you help them buy the home can lessen the discomfort if they call you to sell during future market flaccidity. Divorce, layoffs, illness, in vitro–induced litters of children, or permanent housemate mothers-in-law can add to the shift. Keep in touch with your clients and be a voyeur on social media to see if you can see those life shifts coming. You will be better equipped to help navigate market switcheroos.

Breaking Bad

When real estate agents constantly contradict bad economic news, they look suspiciously commission hungry. Admitting to bad news affords more credibility than does trying to create an eternal-sunshine view. People will look for the silver lining if you at least admit that there are clouds.

Look for good news and bad. It's wise to know what's discussed in the industry, but realize the media's obvious limitations when you read five articles that provide so many contradicting statistical analyses that you want to scream. Stick with Sortafacts, or better yet, just skim those analyses while you squint your eyes *just* so. That way, you can see your own revelations. Sort of like those 3-D posters…and certain tearful religious idols.

Skyward-soaring markets don't totally suck. Happy news can put a smile on your face like sunshine and housebroken puppies. Enjoying good times is obvious. It's an easy lay. We see all our successes as a result of our excellence, strong work ethic, sacrifice, intellect, and good grooming. In strong markets our reputations soar with glory.

SORTAFacts™

Research has shown that the one trait that 91% of the world's most successful people all share is most evident during challenging times. That trait is a strong sense of curiosity.

—*Courtesy of Sortafact*

ADVANCE READING COPY. NOT FOR SALE.

The real estate market, like so many things, experiences ups and downs. It's what makes it so sexciting to try to predict. While it's sometimes tempting to rest on your knees, always remain on your toes and ready for the shift. The time to get busy is when things are hard. You know this.

ADVANCE READING COPY. NOT FOR SALE.

CHAPTER 32

THE END

This orgy of patrons and professionals is a first. I hope you laughed, sneered, learned, related, rolled your eyes, and fell asleep after the really arousing parts. For salespeople (say it loud, say it proud), it can be revealing to get under the sheets with clients. For clients, the pressure to perform can leave you feeling suspicious or complacent in ways that rob you of achieving a real estate climax. With the pillow talk in this book, you have the chance to leave that fear behind and get to know each other in a real estate Kama Sutra sort of way.

I'd love to hear your inciting insights of arousing the buy curious. Get turned on or turn me on at www.ArousingTheBuyCurious. com. After sitting on my ass and writing this book for so long, I could use a little fire.

I hate to sound romantic, but I actually hope that this is just foreplay for all of us. In my wildest dreams, this book will launch your inquiry into biases and prejudices, what turns us off, and what turns us on. I know that this is asking a lot for an arousing little book, but one can—and should—fantasize.

ACKNOWLEDGMENTS

This real estate romp is the outcome of a great collaboration among many family members, friends, professionals and clients who have shared their lives and stories—knowingly and unknowingly. None should worry as the names have all been changed, but all should know that I'm extremely grateful.

In addition to my hilarious, Jennifer Felberg, thanks to Lucille Ball, Gilda Radner, John Bulushi, Chris Farley, Amy Sedaris, David Sedaris, Stephen Colbert, Tina Fey, Amy Poehler, Chelsea Handler, Samantha Bee, and John Stewart.

Thank you to all of these most excellent people: Ali McCart, Vinnie Kinsella, Kristin Thiel, Jessica Glenn, Tina Granzo, Laura Domela, and Jim Parker.

I'm eternally grateful to Stephen, Barkley and Dane. It's hard being told to leave me alone and then three minutes later being beckoned to provide feedback. It's your fault for continuing to leave me alone and then providing incredible feedback and ideas upon my requests.

I dig you all.

CPSIA information can be obtained at www.ICGtesting.com
Printed in the USA
BVOW010945020413

317072BV00002B/15/P

9 780989 093507